PUTO

PUTO

Plays

Ricardo A. Bracho

Edited and with an introduction by Jennifer S. Ponce de León,
Richard T. Rodríguez, and Randall Williams

With a foreword by Cherríe Moraga

and an afterword by Juana María Rodríguez

Duke University Press   *Durham and London*   2026

Project Editor: Liz Smith
Designed by Dave Rainey
Typeset in Garamond Premier Pro and Peridot Devanagari
by Copperline Book Services

Library of Congress Cataloging-in-Publication Data
Names: Bracho, Ricardo A., [date] author | Ponce de León, Jennifer,
[date] editor | Rodríguez, Richard T., [date] editor | Williams, Randall,
[date] editor | Moraga, Cherríe writer of foreword | Rodríguez, Juana
María writer of afterword
Title: Puto : plays / Ricardo A. Bracho ; edited by Jennifer S. Ponce de
León, Richard T. Rodríguez, Randall Williams ; foreword by Cherríe
Moraga ; afterword by Juana María Rodríguez.
Other titles: Plays
Description: Durham : Duke University Press, 2026. | Includes
bibliographical references.
Identifiers: LCCN 2025022034 (print)
LCCN 2025022035 (ebook)
ISBN 9781478032908 paperback
ISBN 9781478029496 hardcover
ISBN 9781478061670 ebook
Classification: LCC PS3602.R326 P886 2026 (print) |
LCC PS3602.R326 (ebook) | DDC 812/.608—dc23/eng/20251118
LC record available at https://lccn.loc.gov/2025022034
LC ebook record available at https://lccn.loc.gov/2025022035

Cover art: rafa esparza, *paños puñales. you can see it in their faces. uno
(faggot handkerchiefs . . . one)* (detail), 2011. Blue ball point pen, blood,
urine, saliva, black ink on white waist boxer. Courtesy of the artist.

This, all of this is for
Horacio N. Roque Ramírez
How could you leave us?
With so much love,
Bracho

Patrick "Pato" Hebert, from *Yo Soy Lo Prohibido Series*, 1996.

US-SEER

Come home come home don't stay out too late. Bleached Bones Man may get you n take you far uh cross thuh waves, then baby, what will I do for love?

—Suzan-Lori Parks,
Imperceptible Mutabilities in the Third Kingdom

CONTENTS

FOREWORD

Cherríe Moraga

He Who Gave Voice to Sycorax
The Four Directions

UNO

Perhaps I was invited to write the foreword to *Puto: Plays* because I knew the puto-playwright before he was a playwright (I can't speak to the puto part). Ricardo Bracho—just a boy of nineteen, hair down to his ass, and a considerable beauty in his own right (write).

He slaps a thin leaf of poems onto my UC Berkeley lecturer's desk. I scan the work, his eyes watching me, and in minutes I wonder of the sort sitting in front of me. He, so young. A tactile queer lust in his language and an entitled rebellion in his voice. No shame.

Years later, we would reminisce about that moment, he admitting he thought me just a bit "crazy" when I had expressed awe at the plain courage of the work. He was freer than I; that much I knew for sure.

We would go on together as queer camaradas. After Berkeley, he came to work with me in my recently formed Drama Divas—a queer youth of color Writing for Performance group at Brava Theater in San Francisco. We collaborated in this project (and many others) throughout the 1990s, including the premiere production of *The Sweetest Hangover (and Other STDs)*, which I midwifed, and the birth of my son (which he did not).

Everybody got history. You live long enough, you got more history. Ricardo and I have history.

At the time of this writing, he's looking at fifty-five and I, seventy-two. Hard to believe on both counts. I knew Ricardo best as an emergent writer-thinker who came of age in the age of AIDS. We were familia, yes, he and I and all of us queer and "colored" folk of the period. There was something particularly special about these young gay men who had found feminism, something my generation of brothers knew little about because they didn't have to, not yet, until they started dying in droves.

From birth, Ricardo was fiercely framed by a communist "overeducation," as he describes his parentage. His queerness was evident from his earliest childhood "Sissy" years, followed by a critical feminism garnered through women of color classmates and teachers at UC Berkeley (Barbara Christian, Myrtha Chabrán, and Norma Alarcón, to name a few). These influences may not be "intersectional," which Bracho critiques, but they did inform sites of identity and the name-calling thrown at us that have coalesced and collided at the multiple junctures in Bracho's own thirty-five years of thinking and writing.

One singular example comes to mind. Sycorax is a character in Bracho's 1999 play *Fed Up: A Cannibal's Own Story*, in which Bracho gives embodied voice to this unseen and much-maligned figure—the "witch" mother of Caliban—in Shakespeare's *The Tempest*. The speech Ricardo ascribes to her is one of the strongest women of color monologues written by a man that I had ever heard. Although not included in this volume, it is emblematic of the feminist anticolonial promise that has always marked Bracho's work.

Like the artist Martín Ramírez of Bracho's *The Mexican Psychotic*, Ricardo is a brilliant outlier who may one day unwittingly find himself similarly "exoticized" by his own self-naming. But for many of us, Ricardo is just our queer Chicano intellectual. A "whore" perhaps, and a Marxist yes, but not capitalized, not to us; his política, more lowercased, residing among la plebe, where the word *subaltern* is never uttered.

First and foremost, Bracho is a writer. He is less interested in form and more interested in critique. Much of his works are, in fact, dramatized essays composed by one of the best-read people on the planet (in English). Through those works we glean a worldview that refuses any easy place to settle. Here language may even obfuscate truths. Here queer desire is ravenous even when being well fed, while daily it battles a bought-off world and the writer's own pitiful devils that are never to be mentioned.

Emotion may not be Bracho's forte—his gift of gab twists and averts the personal into a tight knot of crossed-armed "Yo-sé-todo. ¿Y qué?" Still, the best of Ricardo's work resides in his deep love for those "amorous men"—the "Adonis and Adán(s)" of the world making out behind the curtain of the Drama.

His is a deeply compassionate heart for "colored boys," their losses and findings in the midst of a remembered revolutionary communist father and dying queer compas. In this sense, Bracho is the queer's queer ("old-school gay," as he puts it). Perhaps that's why his people love him. He is unbeatable in this regard. *And who's gonna fight Bracho with words, anyway?*

CUATRO

The oeuvre of Ricardo Bracho's work is being published for the first time—a visionary project on the part of the coeditors, given that many of his plays have seldom been fully produced on a main stage. There are reasons for this: It is not safe work; it is not commercial and it is also Chicano. His work resides in that dearth of radical transgressive writing outside the restrictions of academia and the "American Theater." It thrives on the intracultural, the unspoken, and the underrepresented that neither Black nor White criticism has really considered. His texts depict the broken taboos that shape many lives. And there is much to learn from the portraiture.

Perhaps over the years I have come to understand Ricardo as an installation artist of sorts (something I've learned through my partner, artist Celia Herrera Rodriguez); that you can't fully know what a "Work" is until you are there in the room with it, whether a gallery, a museum, or a storefront church, putting together the puzzle of the final pieces, the afterthoughts, the re-visions. To that end, as a playwright, I would like to see more of Bracho's work re-vis(ion)ed, embodied on stage, better known. This is not a bourgeois aspiration but a playwright's requirement.

Perhaps this collection will help get him there.

AUTHOR'S ACKNOWLEDGMENTS

I am a Bracho of the Westside Brachos, so I must first thank my late father and mother, Humberto Bracho and Martha Abreu, for a singular, beautiful childhood, which I hope to never outgrow; and for their disciplined tutelage, which my unruly ass still resists.

My sister, Claudia, and her children, Bianca, Fiona, and Diego, for their strong fashion and (un)common sense; my brothers Francisco for his constancy and Beto for being smarter and funnier than my writing could ever be. We miss our brother, Gus, his wife, Martha, and their eldest, Carlos.

Also, the late Natalie Smith Parra, who became family to us all, and many of the books mentioned within these plays came off her shelf.

I had the honor of having Connie Barrett, Barbara Christian, and Myrtha Chabrán, all gone now, as teachers. I teach and write within the memory of their lessons.

Cherríe Moraga and Celia Herrera Rodriguez for their visionary leadership in my life, art made to liberate, and for every discussion across their kitchen table in Oakland. Also, to the entire Moraga-Herrera clan: Rafa, Camie, and on for being ancient and innocent, tradition and mystery.

Willy Chavarría and Persephone Gonzalez are friends who have become family and their imprint is in me and in these words as well.

Nicole Fleetwood is my water-sign cousin, generous friend, a strong and true light in my life. I thank her for her shine.

Juana María Rodríguez is my femme kaleidoscope mirror. Thank you for your words within here and for dancing across clubs and discourses with me.

Joelle Estelle Mendoza, for her wild ways, for making the music and the instrument, puppets and gardens. You're up next, Gold Star!

I met Augie Robles thirty-five years ago. We were both working on our writing. Last night, we once again communed over words and images. I thank him for his bravery and perversity, for all that he knows and shows of our brown-eyed desires.

Keith M. Harris, Luis Orozco, Javier Hurtado, Rafa Esparza, Joe Jiménez, Brian Bauman, Dino Dinco, Ubaldo Boido, Manuel Gonzalez, Kieran Scarlett, and Loras Ojeda are brothers to me and these wor(l)ds.

Lisa Thompson is my day one sis.

Rafael Melendez es mi luchador.

Edwin Ramoran and Ivan Monforte son mis comadres.

Gary Gerard Robinson and Juan Carlos Cuadrado are my gay fathers.

Cauleen Smith, her work and on-point ethics, laugh, and perception, have been a beacon for me from the first day we met. I will soldier for you all day, any day, Smith.

I cherish each meal and museum outing with Dahlia Elsayed and Andrew Demirjian. They are the best artists, educators, and friends. Sushi, soon.

I don't see Deb Vargas and Erica Edwards nearly enough. But when I do, I am always home.

In the Bay: Rosi Reyes, Rana Halpern, Vero Majano, Prado Gomez and Mariya Sparks, Deborah Cullinan, Sean San José, Saun-Toy Latifa Trotter, Angela and Carmen Reginato, Norman Antonio Zelaya, and Miss Kelly Fox are love. Gina Paoli is my big sis.

Reggie MacDonald is a friend of my mind and I await the next time his hand is in mine.

In LA: Elisa Bocanegra, Xavi Moreno, Armando Molina and Evangeline Ordaz, the late Diane Rodríguez, Cristina Frias, Fabi Torres, Laurie Woolery, Lee Sherman, Sigrid Gilmer, Tina Sanchez, Kila Kitu, Ephraim Lopez, David Leonardo Padilla, Rose Portillo, and Richard Azurdía made art making fiercely fun. Ofelia Ortiz Cuevas and Tisa Bryant, head and heart strong sisters, were wonderful to write and eat with. Hushidar and Hakhamanesh Mortezaie are Persi brilliance. I thank Gerard Gonzales for dim sum mornings and hot spring desert nights, Drain Juarez for dog walks and girl talk. Sofia Gasparian and her beautiful fam, especially my Byzantine Queen, MGM, for keeping the memory of the queers of yesteryear and guerrilla art alive. Old Chola and Ghetto Girl, ¡por vida!

In Chicago: Jaqueline Lazu, Phyllis Griffin, Helen Jun, Marc Pinate, Milta Ortiz, and Ruben David Adorno held me down and lifted me up.

In New York: Joe Mejia, Fernando Mancuello, Seth Abrames, Ela Troyano, Alina Troyano, Andrea Thome, Samiya Bashir, Gabriel Morales, Gabriel Stover, Janelle Rodriguez, David Kazanjian and Josie Saldaña, and Rachelle Mendez made the struggle to make epic work from scraps worth it.

Here in Philly, I thank Christopher Cirillo, man of books, for his third eye. At Penn, Juliet Dempsey, Ava Haitz, Sof Sears, Adrianna Brusie, Nicholas Plante, Emily Dunlop, Andrés González Bonillas, Gigi Varlotta, Mars Berger, Ivanna Berrios, Malkia Okech, Oludare Marcelle, Wenxi Chen, Robert Slovikowsky, Grace Bridy, Deborah Thomas and the Center for Experimental Ethnography crew, the GSWS Gang (Kathy, Melissa, Gwendolyn, and especially Luz, Roz, Maria, and Arielle), Armie Chardiet, and Emma the Great kept me on my pedagogical-artistic toes and taught me, as Gwen McCrae sings, to "keep the fires burning / keep them burning hot."

I miss Michele Serros, Luis Saguar, Assotto Saint, Chris Turnbull, Donald Woods, Roger Romero, David "Cousin Danny" Banerje, Darien Kincaid, Sean Sasser, Tede Matthews, Aaron Olivares, Josh Chambers, dear sweet James Gubera, Nacho Nava, and so many more, each and every day.

This book was Ricky Rodríguez's idea. I love all our conversations across the years/states/escapades and will never forget all he has done for me. We got the green light many years ago, but losses and accomplishments on both sides stalled the book. My longtime comrades Randall Williams and Jennifer Ponce de León would not let the project go, even when another round of deaths took me under. I thank them for their Leninist persistence and caring for my work when I did not. I thank Stephen Wu and Andrews Little for always showing up for me and my shows.

Adela Vázquez, girl, I thought when the day came that I had a book of my work, I would head to your place in SF with it. You would skim through it, pat the cover, and say, "Good for you, girl." And then we would discuss what really mattered: her garden, our barbed-wire hearts, the meal she would be making us, men who are foolish if fine. I can't believe you're gone, but the world should know how much you taught me, inspired me, made some of the characters in these plays and all our lives possible.

Patrick "Pato" Hebert, from *Yo Soy Lo Prohibido Series*, 1996.

EDITORS' ACKNOWLEDGMENTS

The editors are grateful to Armie Chardiet for editorial assistance. Ivanna Berrios assisted in the transcription of talks and interviews by Bracho. Andrews Little's insights improved this book's introduction, and his encouragement and support buoyed this project over many years. We are also grateful to the anonymous reviewers for helping make this book stronger. Finally, thanks to Courtney Berger at Duke University Press for her unfaltering commitment.

INTRODUCTION

Jennifer S. Ponce de León, Richard T. Rodríguez,
and Randall Williams

A Raucous Debut

The Sweetest Hangover was Ricardo A. Bracho's first full-length theatrical production. It premiered at Brava Theatre Center in San Francisco's Mission District in
June 1997. The play is set in the early 1990s at the fictional Club Aztlantis, part of
the Bay Area's booming underground club scene.[1] Outside this ephemeral space of
nocturnal liberation, the AIDS pandemic is raging, with San Francisco as an epi-
center. Inside this house, djdj lays down hard-driving beats and pulsating rhythms
"dedicated to the sonic liberation of the legendary children of life." The collectivity that gathers here every weekend and makes up the "family of Aztlantis" is
a multi-everything motley crew that "is *not* based on the superficial real of your
color, crotch or couture, but in the treble and bass of your soul, sex and shade."
What unites this queer assembly and keeps the dedicated denizens coming back
is a shared commitment to dancing all weekend long, taking copious amounts of
drugs, having lots of furtive, illicit sex, and enjoying the fuck out of life (while
they can) in this House of Libidinal Pleasures created by and for the displaced
youth of all diasporas.

By all accounts, Bracho's *Sweetest Hangover* had quite a raucous theatrical debut. According to one San Francisco theater critic, the opening night was "like
attending a community celebration—perhaps crossed with the peak hour at a

popular gay nightclub." In other words, the crowd was decidedly *not* your typical bourgeois theatergoing audience; attendees were overwhelmingly young, loud, queer people of color. The critic continued, "The crowd, or a substantial portion of it, greeted the world premiere of Ricardo A. Bracho's 'The Sweetest Hangover' as if it were a celebration of a community that rarely gets to see itself depicted in any genre."[2] Indeed, night after night for the duration of its debut run, *The Sweetest Hangover* succeeded in capturing the theater for a different audience.[3] It was *as if* Club Aztlantis had suddenly reopened, on stage at the Brava Theatre . . . and it had.

Ricardo Bracho was raised in Los Angeles, California, in a Marxist-Leninist household (not unlike the semifictional family in his play *Sissy*). After attending college at the University of California, Berkeley, Bracho lived between the San Francisco Bay Area and New York City until the early 2000s. In addition to writing and partying, Bracho worked in the arts and public health, focusing on theater and creative writing for queer/trans youth of color and Latino gay men, and harm reduction and health/arts education for Latino high-risk populations and incarcerated men. Following *The Sweetest Hangover,* Bracho had his first New York City production, *A to B*, at INTAR in 2002. Through a residency with the experimental theater company Mabou Mines, he began to develop his most formally experimental work, *Mexican Psychotic,* a silent play about the Mexican outsider artist Martín Ramírez. Bracho continued developing *Mexican Psychotic* while working as a Scholar/Artist in Residence at the Center for Chicano Studies at the University of California, Santa Barbara—a position that brought him back to Los Angeles. LA provides the inspiration and setting for two full-length plays included in this volume: *Sissy*, a semi-autobiographical picaresque set in the 1970s, and *Puto,* a dystopian science fiction set in the near future. *Sissy* was produced by Company of Angels in Los Angeles in 2008, and *Puto* received a 2011 workshop production at the Theater School at DePaul, anticipating Bracho's move to Chicago the following year. While working as Visiting Multicultural Faculty at DePaul's Theater School, Bracho wrote *El Santo Joto: Juan Rodríguez Day*, one of the short plays collected in this volume.

In 2019, Bracho moved to Philadelphia to become the inaugural Abrams Artist-in-Residence in the Gender, Sexuality, and Women's Studies Program and the Center for Research in Feminist, Queer, and Transgender Studies at the University of Pennsylvania. While holding this position, he produced and directed a workshop production of *Opus Siniestrus,* a feminist play by surrealist painter Leonora Carrington; a video version of his play *Mexican Psychotic*; and "A History of Hands," a multimedia spectacle on the history of queer and trans Philadelphia. In keeping with Bracho's biogeography, the plays collected in this volume have been assembled in terms of place and time. There are two plays set in California in the early 1990s: *El Santo Joto* and *Sweetest Hangover*. There are three "Mexico plays"—*Ni Madre, Mexican Psychotic*, and *Appetites I Have Inherited*—and three "LA plays": *Sissy, Puto*, and *A Black and A Brown*.

The worlds Bracho composes are principally peopled by Black and Brown proletarians of varied nationalities and genders. Most are queer and many are immigrants, with phrases in Spanish and Spanglish shaping their dialogue. Equally striking about Bracho's work is what does not appear in it: Bracho's plays are largely unconcerned with representing White US identities or "Whiteness." Also notably absent are heterosexist bourgeois social norms. Queer social practices are not represented vis-à-vis their difference from these but are instead simply coherent within the multiethnic, multilingual, and multiclass lifeworlds Bracho writes. There is nothing in any of this that should be confused with identitarian ideologies or intersectional politics. As Bracho himself has said, "Rather than the intersectional, I am far more intrigued by how various discourses disrupt one another. I would like to form a praxis that could incorporate, in dialectical friction, antihumanism and whoring; a heart that belongs to Fanon, Marx, Luxembourg, and Genet, as well as a fanboy's interest in the Bolivarian Revolution, FARC, the Intifada, and the mythmaking of conceptual prog-rockers, the Boricua and Chicano LA Tejanos, the Mars Volta."[4] Along with the international geopolitics, sexual practices, and select revolutionary writers and artists that fuel Bracho's words, his biogeography has played a major role in helping to contour the gorgeously complex figures who make up his dramatic productions. In this introduction to his work, we will provide a short description of each of the ten plays collected in this volume organized by setting, followed by a brief account of Bracho's ideological engagements and unique form of dialectical theater.

The San Francisco Plays: "Ephemera Is Our Institution"

Bracho's plays *El Santo Joto del SIDA* and *The Sweetest Hangover* are set in the San Francisco Bay Area of the 1990s. Places like the fictitious Club Aztlantis provided a critical, even if brief, respite from the ongoing and systemic "state-sanctioned production and exploitation of group-differentiated premature death."[5] In these works the illicit, furtive desires of young, queer men of color take center stage. Indeed, throughout his oeuvre Bracho insists on the centrality of characters never before seen as central. He counts the uncounted and romanticizes (without sensationalism) the quotidian lives of those who prefer the ephemera of experience and sensation (drugs, sex, dancing, etc.) to durable forms of community organizing and institution-building. Of these ephemera and phenomena—the after-hours club, house party, the broken-into warehouse that becomes the site for this weekend's rave, and so on—Bracho says, "These are really interesting anti-state formations that don't always . . . have an articulated state critique. [Rather,] they are the politics of resentment and a good, unstructured time. . . . Particularly for urban gay men of color, ephemera is our institution." There is something unique about the jotos and putas and the motley collectivities that receive beatification in Bracho's plays, and *El Santo Joto* and *The Sweetest Hangover* provide us with some of the most exquisite of exemplary figures.

The Sweetest Hangover

The Sweetest Hangover is set in the early 1990s Bay Area inside Club Aztlantis, a fictional club whose name combines two mythical places: the island of Atlantis; and Aztlán, the homeland of the Mexica people. The club serves as a space of provisional freedom where an array of displaced peoples have come together to form a house:[6] Octavio Deseo, a Chicano club promoter; djdj, a Salvadorean DJ; Plum, a Black female college student who performs at the club along with Black drag queen Natasha Kinky; and club regulars Miss Thing 1 and Miss Thing 2, two young gay men, a Black Puerto Rican and a Filipino, who read and shade (in rhyme at times) all the play's goings-on. And finally, Octavio's love interest, Samson, is a Filipino/Chicano tattoo artist by day and by night works security at Aztlantis. In his analysis of *Sweetest Hangover*, the Cuban American performance studies scholar José Esteban Muñoz argues that "Bracho's multiethnic ensemble signals a new moment in minoritarian performance and cultural work in which the strict confines of identitarian politics are superseded by other logics of group identification."[7] Indeed, what Muñoz identifies in this early play is true for the entirety of Bracho's corpus to date: The social relations, affiliations, and commitments represented in them are not structured by ethno-nationalist ideologies or identitarianism. However, *pace* Muñoz, affect does not perform the trick of constituting a Brown community, and there is no affective racial difference or so-called Brown feeling in *Sweetest Hangover* that miraculously creates a cultural map of a Latino/a/x lifeworld. The ephemeral material space depicted in *Sweetest Hangover* simply does not have an identitarian structure of feeling. Moreover, as we will argue in "Negations and Alignments," such culturalism is anathema to Bracho's aesthetics.

El Santo Joto

Three distinct altars. Three different chairs. Two jotos y una jota. In Bracho's *El Santo Joto* (Saint Faggot), an unholy trinity of Latinx queers have returned to grieve for a generation lost and to expropriate a day of remembrance for their very own: December 12. Traditionally, this is the historic day that La Virgen de Guadalupe was said to have made her second appearance to a young Indigenous Mexican man, Juan Diego, and provided proof of her appearance in the form of roses growing in the middle of winter. In *El Santo Joto*, however, no virgins appear, and December 12 becomes "Juan Rodríguez Day," marking the day Juan Rodríguez died. Rodríguez, Bracho's friend and colleague, was a leader in gay men of color AIDS work who created the first national HIV media prevention campaign for Latino gay men. *El Santo* memorializes Rodríguez along with a litany of other artists and writers of color lost to AIDS: Essex Hemphill, Reza Abdoh, Sylvester, Marlon Riggs, and Assotto Saint. Their naming signals Bracho's refusal, in his capacity as documentarian, of a disremembered status, and exalts their defiance of all that the state and the church deem unseemly and unholy, if not also immoral and illegal.

The Mexico Plays: Servants of the World Unite!

In his seminal account of mythology, French literary theorist Roland Barthes describes how myth works as follows: "In passing from history to nature, myth acts economically: it abolishes the complexity of human acts, it gives them the simplicity of essences, it does away with all dialectics, with any going back beyond what is immediately visible, it organizes a world without contradictions because it is without depth, a world wide open and wallowing in the evident, it establishes a blissful clarity: things appear to mean something by themselves."[8] In Bracho's Mexico plays, the mythic figures of La Malinche (the traitor), Martín Ramírez (the insane), and the exoticized Mexicanos (the maraca boys) in *Night of the Iguana* are recast in a decidedly antimythical mode, replete with complexity, contradiction, and dialectics. Each hitherto mythologized character is imbued with historical materiality and the erasures that attend to their becoming other / becoming myth. This rearticulation from below serves as a counterpoint and antidote to the workings of traditional mythology, which hollows out history and smooths over contradictions as it ushers in timeless essences and moral tales. Works like *Mexican Psychotic* and *Ni Madre* confront romantic pseudo-history and nationalist ideologies with the actual, messy histories of class struggles they obscure. In each of these plays, the folklorish aestheticization of cultural difference and concomitant flattening of history is not only absent; it is also mocked and itself historicized.

In 2003 producer/director Diane Rodriguez of LA's Center Theatre Group commissioned a national group of Latino/a/x playwrights to do an anthology show
based on *Amor Eterno*, a book by Patricia Preciado Martin. Out of this project
came Bracho's short play *Ni Madre*. Like every play in the series, *Ni Madre* is set
in the lobby of the Biltmore Hotel in downtown Los Angeles. It revolves around
La Malinche (Malintzin) in her post-Cortés days. The historical Malinche was the
daughter of a Mexica cacique (local ruler) and was enslaved and made to act as an
interpreter for Hernán Cortés, the Spaniard who led the conquest of the Mexicas
(or Aztec Empire). Within the postrevolutionary Mexican nationalist ideology
of mestizaje, which celebrates the supposedly "racial" intermixing of European
peoples and Indigenous Americans, the figure of Malinche is made to embody
the history of colonialism, such that, as the "mother" of the Mexican people, she
is simultaneously a traitor and a despoiled victim.[9]

The play's title is a variation of the Mexican slang expression *ni madre*. It is an
expression of categorical refusal akin to the English phrase "No way in hell!" Thus,
the title can be read as a refusal of nationalist mythifications of history that mo-
bilize the figure of the mother as a naturalizing metaphor for a nation, imagined
as a biological unit. As Bracho says, "I wanted to be sacrilegious with Malinche."
Contra Octavio Paz, Bracho's Malinxe is neither castigated as La Traidora (The
Traitor) nor La Chingada (The Fucked One), nor is she revered as La Madre del
Mestizaje. Rather, the Malinche of *Ni Madre* is much more complex: a highborn
Nahua woman who over the course of her life came to traverse class and caste
divides via enslavement and concubinage, marriage and motherhood, and who
now orders servants around. She is accompanied by her Indigenous servant, Girl,
as they are checked into the hotel by another indentured Indian servant, Nana.
The result is a unique sci-fi chamber play examining the servant/served dyad, and
showing us that servitude connects the past of world conquest and enslavement
to the present of global capitalism and superexploitation.

Mexican Psychotic

Written in 2004 and adapted to video two decades later, *Mexican Psychotic* centers on the life of Martín Ramírez, a Mexican worker, immigrant, and self-taught
visual artist. It is the most formally experimental play in this collection, and its
form carries much of its meaning. Its staging mimics a silent film, with omni-
scient third-person narration and dialogue appearing as text projected onto a
screen behind the actors. Naturalism is eschewed. Scenes that recount the history of Ramírez's life are interspersed with surreal, allegorical episodes and his-

torical anecdotes whose protagonists include Mexican revolutionaries and wild animals that populate Ramírez's drawings. Halfway through the play, its narration reverses and begins anew. These formal features each echo aspects of Ramírez's biography that are featured in the play's narrative: his silence while interned, his exposure to Hollywood films, and the mythologization of his biography by professionals who commercialized and promoted his art. The alienation effects they produce underscore the play's thematic concern with the misrepresentation and marginalization of proletarian histories within dominant historical (including art historical) narratives. It is decidedly Brechtian, insofar as it formally produces a sense of alienation that spurs cognitive reflection, including on the apparatus of representation itself.

While paying homage to the disturbing beauty and historical significance of Ramírez's art, *Mexican Psychotic* is principally concerned with the alienating and exploitative social relations Ramírez experienced during his lifetime. It recounts key elements of his biography: from growing up in poverty in Mexico to working on the railroads in California, to his arrest and long internment in a California psychiatric hospital; his dedication to drawing, and the eventual "discovery" of his art by a psychiatrist who introduces it to the art world. The play's most striking formal feature—wherein its narrative is suddenly stopped, rewound, and revised—reiterates the play's critique of the petit bourgeois professionals who marketed Ramírez's art and a mythicized figure of him for their own profit. By exposing them as unreliable narrators, the play also exposes to scrutiny its own claims to authority vis-à-vis the artist's biography. While *Mexican Psychotic* corrects popularized misrepresentations of Ramírez biography, it does not attempt to offer authentic, unmediated access to his past. It also refuses any desire for a biographical interpretation of Ramírez's art. Instead, it foregrounds the transnational history that shaped Ramírez's life and informed his art, while also acknowledging that many of the details of his biography are lost to history—a fact that itself reflects Ramírez's social position as an immigrant and worker. At the same time, the play's form also reminds us that Ramírez's drawings are indeed a manifestation of history (not some mystical notion of genius or madness, often cultivated by bourgeois art history), and that this is indeed what makes them so marvelous.

Appetites I Have Inherited

In *Appetites I Have Inherited* we are privy to a pointed and revealing conversation between two Mexican actors, Adonis and Adán, who discuss the utility and attendant disposability of them, and of Mexico, to the Hollywood film industry. They are on a break from performing silent roles in *The Night of the Iguana* (1964), a John Huston–directed Hollywood film that was shot on the Mexican isle of Mismaloya. In the film, the two Mexican actors represent exoticized sexual objects. Speaking no lines, they inexplicably dance around in tiny shorts while playing the maracas, respond to an undifferentiated "Pepe," and essentially serve as adornments to the sexual fantasies of the film's White protagonists. This is represented most memorably perhaps when they go night swimming with their boss, a lusty resort owner played by Hollywood star Ava Gardner.

Appetites I Have Inherited imagines the artists consigned to sexy silence in Huston's film having much to say about their skills and the industry in which they work. Cognizant of the minor yet essential roles delegated to those made to represent sexual and racial otherness by the US culture industry, Adonis and Adán are well aware of their talent despite being cast in lesser roles. Reading the film's scene as not only superficial but vacuous for how all Mexican men are rendered "Pepe" ("Todos somos Pepe," notes Adán), the two exchange information about which Hollywood could care less and channel this deep knowledge to charge their ascribed one-dimensional roles. Parsing out an all-encompassing "Pepe" to additionally account for "Pedro," these two create not a docile or conniving duo that one might expect from a characteristic Hollywood treatment, but instead a pair of amorous men whose shared kiss tops the signifying force of the film's clichéd screen kiss with Gardner.

The Los Angeles Plays: "Have You Been to LA?"

In 2020, when Bracho was asked if he intentionally wrote his play *Puto* without White characters, Bracho quipped, "Have you been to LA? . . . There are White people, but who knows where they are. They're like behind a gate somewhere, in the Palisades, in Malibu. They don't matter in the day-to-day of life, so they don't matter here." He later added, "That's always intentional: I write about Black and Brown people not only 'cause it's what I know, but that's what I'm advancing."[10] In his reply, as in his work, Bracho provincializes White identities with a historical fidelity attuned to the historically multinational, multilingual composition of the working classes of the United States and Mexico. This reality is rarely reflected in representations produced by the United States' capitalist culture industries, including and especially those sited in the very Brown City of Angels itself. Calls to rectify these industries' historically racist representations are too often met with the production of tokenistic, folklorish pablum defanged of social critique, or liberal-reactionary historical revisionism with a multicultural cast (of the Lin-Manuel Miranda variety). Against this backdrop, Bracho's representations of nationality, race, and language are intentional engagements in ideological struggle within the realm of culture.

According to Bracho, his representation of non-White multilingual communities reflects a social reality he has always known, having been raised by Mexican communists in the multiethnic, multilingual metropolis of Los Angeles. As he noted in the 2015 interview included in this volume, "I was raised in internationalism. I was a child of overeducated people whose neighbors were also Mexican immigrants, but also, they were gardeners and maids. And Belgian miners and Black project organizers and various South American intellectuals, and political folks were always coming through my door."[11] The internationalism Bracho describes, as a form of proletarian ideology as well as daily social practice, is foundational to the two plays included in this volume that are set in Los Angeles: *Sissy* and *Puto*. Both are peopled by Mexican, Central American, and Chicanx proletarians and feature communist protagonists. The latter are portrayed without romanticization but, rather, with a comedic sympathy for their struggles with their own and society's contradictions.

Sissy

Bracho began writing *Sissy* in 1996, while *Sweetest Hangover* was in rehearsals, and it became his first full production in his hometown of LA in June 2008. *Sissy* is a day-in-the-life tale set in Westside Los Angeles in July 1979. While in *Ni Madre* Bracho confronts and transforms an ur-myth of Mexican nationalism, Malinche, his play *Sissy* does something similar in its representation of the Mexican American family and its heterosexist mythologization in Chicano nationalism. The protagonist, Sissy, is a clever-tongued Chicano kid raised in a Marxist-Leninist household (like Bracho himself) who is turning twelve years old on this day. Much to Sissy's chagrin, his birthday party is overshadowed by the world-historic significance of the day, the overthrow of Nicaraguan dictator Anastasio Somoza Debayle and the momentous success of the Sandinista Revolution. While the Sandinista Party takes over in Managua, Sissy leaves the birthday party his family has organized for him and takes flight to be protogay in a quixotic quest across Los Angeles (from Culver City to Boy's Town). In this coming-of-age picaresque tale of the post-'68 generation, Sissy encounters a merry band of multilingual misfits and underrepresented characters of impossible to identify genders, races, and sexualities, who lovingly guide him along his way.

In *Sissy* Bracho has given us a "Chicano family" far more expansive and inclusive than hitherto acknowledged, just as the Sandinistas themselves were busy redefining what constituted a "family" as any group of people living under the same roof who were dependent on one another for economic survival and well-being.[12] Fuck gay marriage; revolutionary remakings of families reject the exclusivity of the marriage form in favor of expanding our recognition of the myriad ways in which people actually live and survive and love and fight together.

While addressing the nuclear family as a key site of ideological reproduction, *Sissy* also offers a rare portrait of a nuclear family as a site of communist ideological formation. Historical icons of global communism and Latin American anti-imperialism are part of Sissy's family's quotidian lexicon, as are theories like historical materialism and democratic centralism. Recognizing theatergoers' likely lack of familiarity with this lexicon, Bracho and his comrades produced a *Sissy* glossary, with brief descriptions of all the historical events and personages referenced in the play.

Puto

Puto is a dystopian comedy set in a militarized and segregated Los Angeles of the near future. Its plot follows the activities of its eponymous protagonist over the course of twenty-four hours. Puto is a commercial and fine art photographer, but he also has an underground life as a counterfeiter and fellow traveler of the communist cell CREW (Communist Revolution Every Weekend). Puto's artistic work is not of use to CREW, but his dual US/Mexican citizenship and access to dollars are. In this dystopia, the US-Mexico border has been closed, and immigrants and felons are barred from access to US citizenship and dollars. Los Angeles is carved up by internal borders, where Homeland Security agents police mobility, sort citizens from noncitizens, and ensure the latter's containment in ethnic catchment areas.

As Puto's passport allows him unusual mobility across apartheid LA, he delivers messages and contraband for CREW. His motivations for traversing the city are not only political; they are also always libidinal for this play's namesake. As Puto travels across Los Angeles, he meets up with other artists, his comadre and her child, various ex- and potential lovers, and members of CREW. The distance between CREW's concerns and the posh lifestyle of artists and intellectuals (the "check-writer bumper-sticker crowd") is made plain. The play's narrative arc leads Puto to resolve this contradiction, and ultimately he decides to commit class suicide and become a cadre of CREW. This transformative decision is a synthesis of his creative, political, and libidinal desires, which are themselves thereby transformed. The play closes looking toward a future with armed struggle against the US state on the horizon. As Bracho has said, "I think of *Puto* as a dystopia that becomes utopic at the end, 'cause we're going to win this thing."[13] Its utopianism manifests itself in its affirmation that the decolonization and socialist transformation of society is possible, but that it can be achieved only through organized armed struggle.

The "abysmal point of inspiration" for *Puto* was the police's repression of an immigrants' rights march held in Los Angeles on May Day in 2007. As Bracho has explained, he wanted *Puto* to uncover the systemic violence that was on display that day, in an effort to "make the unseen seen in terms of the state and its imperial machinations."[14] It does this through allegory, estrangement, and a Marxist dystopian realism that grounds itself in history.

Through its dystopian realism, *Puto* addresses how US elites' class warfare has historically relied on racist forms of social control, stratification, and repression that are regularly exercised through state and parastate violence. The play not only shows how such dynamics have and could potentially operate within the United States; through its critical interrogation of citizenship and borders, it also calls attention to the mechanisms of control and repression imperialist capitalism exercises on an international scale. It thereby "reveals the interrelated uses of citizenship, borders, criminalization, incarceration, and racism to control and divide the global proletariat and thereby intensify its exploitation."[15] By simultaneously depicting a plausible dystopian future sited in LA, while also metaphorically representing history at an international scale, *Puto* "demonstrates that what may appear from one perspective as a potential fascist future" is already history for persons "rendered hyper-exploitable or expendable" by (neo)colonial class relations.[16] Bracho has described *Puto* as the most overt and literal in its politics among his plays: "Every single word: I wanted to mean it.... It's a hammer to the head. It's a hammer and sickle to your head, rather."[17]

A Black and A Brown

Bracho has repeatedly remarked on the formal challenge of representing the machinations of the US state: "How do you expose the state, because its operations are everywhere and nowhere, ... but not have it Bread and Puppets style, like Uncle Sam with a big dollar sign on him (which I'm not above—though I don't like to, 'cause then you have to make an actor play that part and it's kind of a bummer after a while)?"[18] Bracho grappled with this question when police repression of the immigrant rights movement inspired his penning of *Puto*. In 2020, he returned to this same challenge: exposing the violence of the bourgeois state to enable the analysis of it. This time, however, Bracho was writing from Philadelphia—a city that was occupied by the National Guard and put under a 6 p.m. curfew because its denizens protested against racist police killings. Yet the racist policing evinced in his writing is not exceptional but, rather, institutionalized across the entire US territory. Its scope was made plain by the 2020 protests and riots that rocked the entire country, repudiating the police's killing of George Floyd and so many others.

A Black and A Brown is an excavation, through dialogue and memory, of the powerful role of state violence in racialization and subject formation. It involves a Zoom session between A Black and A Brown. The gay couple are filling out an online Marxist questionnaire on interpellation and state-mandated death. The solidarity between the two characters in Bracho's play is dialectical rather than intersectional; that is, solidarity is predicated on negotiation rather than facile concurrency. It is sexual and political rather than some surface-level genuflection before the altar of well-worn clichés of collectivity. It also returns us to the site of the nocturnal, that generative temporal moment that brings Bracho's men in close proximity to those populating the pages of Jean Genet, John Rechy, and Samuel Delany. After all, as A Brown quotes the first surrealists, "the revolution begins at night."

As it was at the time of Bracho's first play, *The Sweetest Hangover*, a plague is spreading, cops are still beating and killing poor Blacks and Browns with impunity, the youth have taken to the street, and our characters are horny, one slightly more than the other. All is still as it shouldn't be. Within Bracho's Marxist worldview, our formation as subjects emerges from the material practice of our lives. Just as we are subjects in and of history, shaped by it, we also act to shape history.

Negations and Alignments

The plays included in this volume, which do not exhaust Bracho's oeuvre, are evidence of his commitment to formal experimentation (no two plays have the same form) and to the representation of history from below. Few other US playwrights have so successfully combined these formal-ideological aims. Yet despite his unique contributions to American theater, many of Bracho's works have yet to be produced. Though this may seem paradoxical, Bracho's work teaches us otherwise. That is, it pushes us to recognize the class politics of the bourgeois cultural apparatus and concomitant conditions of artistic labor: a condition Che Guevara described as an "invisible cage," where "those who play by the rules of the game are showered with honors—such honors as a monkey might get for performing pirouettes. The condition is that one does not try to escape from the invisible cage."[19] Bracho has not played by the rules of the game. In his plays and other work, he has been an outspoken critic of US empire and its cultural apparatus, including liberal identitarian discourses that predominate in institutions where he works.

On Queer of Color Critique and Sexual Liberation

At the 2014 annual meeting of the American Studies Association, Bracho delivered a manifesto with the fittingly dialectical title "A Proclamation on, of, and by Negation." In it, he distinguished his own politics regarding sex and gender from discourses prevalent in contemporary academic theorizing: "I'm not queer, though I do use the term to describe the grouping of perverse us. . . . I am old gay, languaged in the Black and Brown gay club, dive bar, drug den, rave and underground house scene, which meant then butches and femmes and switches of varying hue and genitalia and trans before the term was in use."[20] Yet, more than a generational difference, what impels Bracho to mark his distance from much of contemporary queer culture is its incorporation into the institutions and ideologies of US imperialist liberalism in what Michael Warner refers to as its "retreat from its history of radicalism into a new form of postliberationist privatization."[21] Bracho has said of this historic shift, "One of the reasons I call myself gay is because it used to stand as adjective to the noun *liberation*, though this is well before the North American gay's rightward drift, what Keith Harris terms the heterosexualization of homosexuality and what I call the constitution of the gay and lesbian neoliberal norm."[22] On numerous occasions Bracho has endeavored to mark the difference between his own political alignments and those imputed to his work by academics. Metaphorically describing himself as being "on the sale rack at the Queer of Color Boutique," Bracho critiqued this intersectionalist school of thought:

> The other overdetermining way me and mine get talked about or are given the permission to narrate, to use [Edward] Said's term, is via the rubric of "queer of color." My fundamental problem with this "queer of color" formation is political. Because as far as I can tell, it isn't or, if it is, it participates in the liberalized discourses of the academic circuit and politely accepts these limits in order for a seat at the table. . . . Both academically acceptable Chicano cultural nationalism and queer of color critique are unacceptable for the art I want to make and the artists and politics with which I seek alignment.[23]

While critiquing culturalist discourses that have been promoted by the US academy, Bracho instead seeks ideological alignment with cultural traditions of revolutionary Marxism, anarchism, and anticolonialism. In this regard, the history of gay liberation serves as a key historical referent for the sexual politics in Bracho's life and work. Born in the cycle of antisystemic struggles of the 1960s, and catalyzed by the Stonewall Rebellion in 1969, the Western metropolitan gay liberation movement theorized the struggle for sexual liberation as inextricable from the struggle to end imperialist capitalism and militarism, sexism, and racism. When speaking about theorists and artists associated with this movement who have most influenced his life and work, Bracho has frequently cited Mario Miele, Gayle Rubin, Guy Hocquenghem, Monique Wittig, Jean Genet, and Rainer Werner Fassbinder, as well as Richard Dyer, Cherríe Moraga, Amber Hollibaugh, Jan Zita Grover, Cindy Patton, and Jeffrey Escoffier, among others.

On the political front, Bracho's preferred historical reference for gay liberation has long been Third World Gay Revolution, an organization of largely Black, Asian, and Puerto Rican gay men and drag queens whose 1970 manifesto includes demands for

- the right of self-determination for all Third World and gay people, as well as control of the destinies of our communities;
- the right of self-determination over the use of our bodies;
- liberation for all women;
- full protection of the law and social sanction for all human sexual self-expression and pleasure between consenting persons; and
- a revolutionary socialist society where the needs of the people come first.[24]

This sexual liberationist ethos is evidenced in Bracho's unabashed celebration of sexual practice and desire in his plays, as well as their representation of myriad forms of social bonds that are forged not through the logics of property or bourgeois law but through eroticism, care, communication, solidarity, and shared political commitments.

Puto most clearly demarcates the liberationist sexual ethos Bracho embraces from liberal queer politics. The play celebrates the eroticism entwined in political organizing, and it "casts the pursuit of sexual freedom and self-determination as integral to the communist struggle for human emancipation."[25] The play also includes a biting critique of queer assimilation to US militarism and imperialist liberalism in the figure of Carlos Moreno, a gay police officer. Through its critique of Carlos, as well as of careerist artists and academics, *Puto* insists that the individualist pursuit of fulfillment (whether sexual or professional) has nothing to do with the practice of liberation, as it could just as easily be operating against the liberation of others.[26]

On Cultural Politics and Decolonization

Decolonization is a noun. It is the colonized seizing the state, usually violently. Bringing your abuela's tablecloth to your college campus does not mean that you have decolonized that space. I know this makes me statist, but I don't care.
—Ricardo A. Bracho, "A Proclamation on, of, and by Negation"

Bracho's representations of racial and ethnic difference defy the cultural essentialist and identitarian logics that suffuse many products of US culture industries. His plays pointedly refuse the identitarian precept that individuals' political alignments follow from their ascriptive identities and that political constituencies are formed around such identities. For instance, in *Puto* the one character who is clearly on the other side of the proverbial barricade (or, in this case, border checkpoint) from that of the communist protagonists is a gay Chicano cop who is simply seeking personal gain in a system that pays him to betray his fellow racialized workers.

Nonetheless, according to Bracho, identitarianism and culturalism have been wrongly attributed to his work by US academics. In "It Is the Libido," a lecture delivered at Stanford University in 2008, he stated,

As an extra-academic intellectual I am often perturbed at how me and my work get talked about when I and they circulate in the US university.... Besides getting called an activist, something I have never been, I am often spoken of as a cultural nationalist. Even in my college MEChA [Movimiento Estudiantil Chicano de Aztlán] era, I have not spent one day of my life as such. I have an abiding interest in the political nationalism of colonized peoples, formed mainly by my reading of Fanon and Cabral. However, even in his acute analysis of and advocacy for the violent seizure of the state by the colonized, *The Wretched of the Earth*, Fanon includes a chapter [titled] "On the Pitfalls of National Consciousness." Cabral's far more logistical readings of revolutionary violence and national sovereignty collected in *Return to the Source* were also a product of his position within internationalist Third World Marxism.

In this talk, Bracho emphasized the difference between Chicano cultural nationalism, which accommodates US racial liberalism and hegemonic identitarian ideologies, and revolutionary Marxists' understanding of national liberation struggles—that is, as class struggles waged against the forces of colonialism and neocolonialism within the context of a global struggle for human emancipation from imperialist capitalism. He also explained his critique of cultural nationalism with reference to Aijaz Ahmad's argument that "the ideology of cultural nationalism is based explicitly [on a] tendency towards national and civilizational singularization that lends itself much too easily to parochialism, inverse racism and indigenist obscurantism, not to speak of the petty bourgeoisie's penchant for representing its own cultural practices and aspirations, virtually by embodying them as so many emblems of a unified culture."[27] Bracho acknowledged the importance of other Chicana/o/x writers' interrogation into what he terms "the Chicano question" (Marxist shorthand for the national question as applied to Mexicans within the United States). After noting that he was particularly influenced, in this regard, by the writers and visual artists Lorna Dee Cervantes, Helena María Viramontes, Cherríe Moraga, Rudy Acuña, José Montoya, and Celia Herrera Rodriguez, he concluded, "I don't think the answer to the 'Chicano question' in their work or mine is 'yes.'"

Bracho's understanding of the national question is influenced by Marxist analyses developed around the world since the early twentieth century. Indeed, the "Chicano question," as Bracho calls it, has been analyzed in light of communist theories of nationhood and revolutionary strategy by multiple Marxist organizations.[28] Yet, just as Marxist epistemologies have been actively repressed within US politics and culture in the context of counterrevolutionary revanchism, Marxist organizing and theorizing have been marginalized in Chicano politics, as well as in scholarly accounts of its history. Despite the presence of Marxist cadre within the Chicano movement, Chicano studies was often dominated by "ideologically flexible" "capitalist friendly forms of cultural nationalism," as Ben V. Olguín and Edward Giardello write. After subsequent years of capitalist and imperialist revanchism, "the liberal reformist as well as blatantly free-market-oriented trajectories of el movimiento inevitably metastasized into contemporary proto-right-wing ideological nodal points in Chicana/o/x and Latina/o/x departments, programs, and centers throughout the nation," they argue.[29] This history helps to explain why Bracho described himself in a 2012 manifesto as an "LA Mexican who is tired of Chicano grammars of struggle."[30]

Bracho's clarification about not being an activist is consonant with his insistence on distinguishing art practice from political organizing, and his refusal to romantically inflate the political consequence of the former. He made this point clear in his 2014 talk "Anger and Love," which he delivered at Human Resources in Los Angeles: "We need to let go and ease up and kick the fuck back on some of our rhetoric, including and especially the sloppy and basic use of *decolonizing* and *decolonized*. Decolonization is done with guns. And, in instances when it is not, the insurgent colonized have been met with the hegemon's firepower: Grenada, Venezuela, Bolivia, Honduras. One's tears or poems or drawings do not decolonize anything, even if you are the ascendant class well-educated descendant of colonized subjects, as many of us Brown and Black artist-intellectual types are."[31] This is, at once, a withering appraisal of contemporary forms of idealist theorizing in which the concept of decolonization is not only disconnected from actual political struggles against imperialism but also, in practical terms, emptied of meaning. It is also a critique of the tendency among "artist-intellectual types" to romantically inflate the political consequence of the individual works or ideas of professional intellectuals like themselves. While this characteristic has been attributed to the petit bourgeoisie (or professional managerial class) in general, it has also been specifically historicized by Adolph Reed Jr. as a symptom of US professional intellectuals' increasing isolation from concrete political movements since the 1960s, as well as the weakness of the organized left in the United States, in general.[32] Reed's critique of US intellectuals' embrace of "cultural politics" (i.e., resistive cultural practices) and concomitant disinterest in self-conscious, organized political activity (particularly if it hopes to exercise state power) is rooted in his class analysis of the social position intellectuals occupy. He writes, "Cultural politics and identity politics are class politics. They are manifestations within the political economy of academic life and the left-liberal public sphere—journals and magazines, philanthropic foundations, the world of 'public intellectuals'—of the petit bourgeois brokerage politics of interest-group pluralism."[33] This Marxist critique of US identity politics and cultural politics, which overlap and mutually reinforce each other, sheds light on Bracho's avid public rejection of these ideologies, as well as his critical representation of their entwinement in his public talks and plays.

An interrogation of the class position of US artists and intellectuals of color, which Bracho has offered in public talks, is a central theme of *Puto*. As Bracho has said of the play, "I always tend to have characters in a play who are an artist and they're always . . . it's a fraught position. . . . I wanted to always be self-critical about how I make my money."[34] *Puto*'s plotline and dialogue repeatedly demarcate the labor of political organizing from the activities of professional intellectuals and artists, who are referred to as "the check-writer bumper-sticker crowd." The play situates US "artist-intellectual types" (including women and racialized persons) within the labor aristocracy (a class stratum that enjoys more wealth and protections than the rest of the global proletariat), and it shows how this poses material disincentives to their making practicable contributions to revolutionary praxis.

On Dialectical Theater and Marxism

After attending Anton Chekhov's play *Uncle Vanya* (1898), the renowned Russian novelist Leo Tolstoy was said to have exclaimed, "Where is the drama? What does it consist of? It doesn't go anywhere!" The demand that dramatic theater must *do something* and must *go somewhere* has a rather long history (and bourgeois class fix) that continues to linger on in various contemporary guises. The historic durability of this idea of the "well-made play" derives from the fact that, whatever are its specific contents or privileged forms, at any particular conjuncture, it is always and necessarily *antidialectical*. In other words, for a play to be "well made," dialectics must be subsumed by plot (structure/causality) and contradiction superseded by resolution (coherence/unity).

Beginning in the 1920s, the great German playwright and theorist Bertolt Brecht took aim at the antidialectical imperatives of bourgeois theater and began to develop a counter-theory, which he initially called "epic theater." Toward the later years of his life (mid-1940s to early 1950s), Brecht reworked this conception of theater under the new heading "dialectical theater," presented as a series of dialogues called *The Messingkauf Dialogues*, or "theory in dialogue form" (*Viel Theorie in Dialogform die Messingkauf*).[35] For us, Bracho's plays have their genealogical origins here, in these scattered, unfinished, never-to-be-completed fragments, scenes, notes, and plans that comprised Brecht's postwar effort to rethink the political and ideological capacities of theatrical production and produce a new theory of dialectical theater. From *Sweetest Hangover* to *Puto*, Bracho's form of aesthetic praxis is insistently dialectical. The drama, or dramatic effect, is generated by dialectics, both as form (dialogue) and method (materialism). À la Brecht, Bracho turns dialectics into "a source of enjoyment," eliciting pleasure "from the unexpectedness of zigzag development, the instability of every circumstance, [and] the joke of contradictions."[36] So, *what happens* in a Bracho play? Dialogue happens. Conversation turns lyrical. Theory battles. Contradictions motor. Dialectics direct. Ideology takes center stage.

A good example of Bracho's artistic praxis can be gleaned from his method of constructing characters. As he has explained in talks and interviews, despite not being a Hegelian, Bracho does utilize a Hegelian model of subjectivity, or identity formation, to craft characters in his plays: "I do use Hegel in his tripartite identity formation because it's a really great makeup of character. A subject in itself, a subject for itself, and a subject for others, that's basically a character on the stage. It's a very easy formula, and I learned it from Norma Alarcón in a lecture she was giving. I was like, 'Oh! That's how you make a character in a play.'"[37] As Bracho suggests here, using a dialectical conception of subjectivity to write his characters is quite convenient, and it is so in two critical ways. First, it installs a defamiliarizing, dialectical dynamic element at the level of the character that mitigates against the types of closure that typically attends the capitalist-modernist ideology of the individual. And second, it is convenient because it resonates directly with, and critically on, the contemporary subject of identity politics. In other words, the *subject* of identity politics and the *character* in traditional theater are complementary ideological analogues that underwrite the cultural foundations for US imperialist capitalism. Both are conceived as self-contained, whole, non-contradictory, unified unto themselves, and essential, and both serve as forms of ideological capture and political containment. Identitarianism is marked by a corralling and marshaling of struggles and possibilities for liberation into the grammar of liberal pluralism, while the protagonist or character of the well-made play imposes a structure of containment (the grammar of the free individual) that serves to coordinate and enclose habits of thought and sense-making within those of the dominant culture and repel those that are irreconcilable. It is, then, in and through this method of character writing, working out how that subject might be a subject for others—others on the stage, others in the audience, readers of the play, and so on—that Bracho's politics can be understood to permeate and constitute his plays, while at the same time being dispersed and diffused along the various lines of dramatic, dialectical flight.

Bracho's plays can be understood as experiments in theorizing in dialogue form. The theatricalization of theory has been something of a consistent feature since his first full-length play back in 1997. As he said in "It Is the Libido," "The tweakers of my first play *The Sweetest Hangover*, these beautiful criminalized gay men of color and their sisters, came to me through puns. I wanted to question two questions, Gayatri Chakravorty Spivak's 'Can the Subaltern Speak?' and Leo Bersani's 'Is the Rectum a Grave?', only in my versions they became 'Can the sub-altern fuck?' and 'Is the rectum a rave?'"[38] Indeed, this has been the case throughout his entire body of work. As he says of a more recent unfinished work, "It is less of a play than a staged essay, or form, involving characters, dialogue, movement, singing, and reading." Bracho's staged experiments are not, however, simply exercises in style, or the stylization of theory. Rather, his provocations serve a sharply different purpose by being directly inscribed within the circumstances of class conflict, the history-making movement of decolonization, and the struggle between global capitalism and international communism. It is this situated alignment that provides a link between provocative experimentation and the struggle for a radical transformation of society, and it is these linkages that confer on Bracho's work a peculiar type of pleasure and relevance. As Bracho says of his de-sire(d) praxis: "I want to be a Marxist critic of empire and neoliberalism even as I am a race man with a serious jones for dick. I want this criticism to exceed my practice as a playwright and in the beginning and end of my every day, I do want my political alignments to matter more than my chosen craft. I have been a Marx-ist and a cocksucker for far longer than I have been a theater artist."[39]

As even a cursory survey of the plays collected in this volume reveals, each of Bracho's plays differs markedly from every other in terms of their formal and generic qualities. The playwright has never sought to repeat or refine a particular style or format. He has never worked within the same genre twice. Rather, with each successive play, Bracho adopts a different set of formal mechanisms and dramatic techniques with which to experiment. The intent is not to perfect the formal conventions and produce the well-made play—which matters only if your intent is to reproduce the dominant ideology—but, rather, to rework those conventions and forms in ways that *counter* the dominant, or better, as Brecht says, "take a hammer to it." It is through his various attempts to rework (or hollow out) traditional theatrical forms and scripts—such as the protagonist, the plot, the arc, causality, the one-act play—that Bracho attempts to leverage the ideological field and advance an internationalist politics of culture.

NOTES

1. The portmanteau "Aztlantis" references two mythical places that have a powerful allegorical function: the island of Atlantis and Aztlán, the homeland of the Mexica people.

2. Robert Hurwitt, "Celebrating 'Hangover,'" *San Francisco Examiner*, April 14, 1997.

3. As Bertolt Brecht once wrote, the capturing of the theater for a different audience is a goal: "This generation doesn't want to capture the theater, audience and all and perform good or merely contemporary plays with the same theater and to the same audience; nor has it any chance of doing so; it has a duty and a chance to capture the theater for a different audience. [. . .] They are not going to satisfy the old aesthetics; they are going to destroy it." Brecht, "Letter to Mr. X, 2 June 1927," 23.

4. Ricardo A. Bracho, interview with Jennifer Ponce de León, December 4, 2015, in this volume.

5. Gilmore, *Golden Gulag*, 247.

6. This is inspired by Ruth Wilson Gilmore's description of abolition geography as concerning "how and to what end people make freedom provisionally, imperatively, as they imagine *home* against the disintegrating grind of partition and repartition through which racial capitalism perpetuates the means of its own valorization." Gilmore, *Abolition Geography*, 491.

7. Muñoz, "Feeling Brown," 75.

8. Barthes, *Mythologies*, 143.

9. The concept of mestizaje has been critiqued for entailing anti-Indigenous and anti-Black racism and for celebrating what Mexican anthropologist Guillermo Bonfil Batalla refers to as the "de-indianization" of Indigenous Mexicans that has resulted from European colonization, i.e., the separation of Indigenous people from their cultural patrimony and the destruction of their forms of social organization that causes their renouncing of a distinctive identity. See Bonfil Batalla, *Mexico Profundo*, xvi. On mestizaje, see also Saldaña-Portillo, *The Revolutionary Imagination in the Age of Development*, 212.

10. Ricardo A. Bracho, talk at the University of Pennsylvania, Fisher-Bennett Hall, February 18, 2020.

11. Bracho, interview with Ponce de León, December 4, 2015.

12. For a critique of normative Chicano family arrangements, see Rodríguez, *Next of Kin*.

13. Bracho, interview with Ponce de León, December 4, 2015.

14. Bracho, interview with Ponce de León, December 4, 2015.

15. Ponce de León, "After the Border Is Closed," 746.

16. Ponce de León, "After the Border Is Closed," 746.

17. Bracho, talk at the University of Pennsylvania, February 18, 2020.

18. Bracho, talk at the University of Pennsylvania, February 18, 2020.

19. Guevara, "Socialism and Man in Cuba."

20. Bracho, "A Proclamation on, of, and by Negation."

21. Quoted in Liu, *Queer Marxism in Two Chinas*, 1. See also Duggan, *The Twilight of Equality?*; Puar, *Terrorist Assemblages*; Reddy, *Freedom with Violence*; Spade, "Under the Cover of Gay Rights"; and Nair, "American Gay."

22. Bracho, "It Is the Libido."

23. Bracho, "It Is the Libido."

24. Third World Gay Revolution, "What We Want, What We Believe," 364–67.

25. Ponce de León, "After the Border Is Closed," 762.

26. Ponce de León, "After the Border Is Closed," 759–60.

27. Ahmad, *In Theory*, 8.

28. See, for example, Tenayuca and Brooks, "The Mexican Question in the Southwest"; August 29th Movement, *Fan the Flames*; League of Revolutionary Struggle, "The Struggle for Chicano Liberation"; Mariscal, *Brown Eyed Children of the Sun*; and Gómez, *The Revolutionary Imaginations of Greater Mexico*.

29. Olguín and Giardello, "The Forgotten Foundations of Chicana/o/x and Latina/o/x Studies," 214–15.

30. Bracho, "A Proclamation on, of, and by Negation."

31. Bracho, "Anger and Love."

32. Reed, *Class Notes*, vii–x.

33. Reed, *Class Notes*, xxii.

34. Bracho, talk at the University of Pennsylvania, February 18, 2020.

35. Brecht, *The Messingkauf Dialogues*.

36. Brecht, *Brecht on Theater*, 277.

37. Bracho, talk at the University of Pennsylvania, February 18, 2020.

38. He goes on: "I knew I wouldn't be writing about actual subalterns but rather the metropolitan minoritarians who are sometimes their stand-ins, to use Gloria Anzaldúa's term, which Ruth Wilson Gilmore quotes in her trenchant essay 'Terror Austerity Race Gender Excess Theater,' which I saw her give in 1990-never-you-mind and remains central to my playwriting praxis." Bracho, "It Is the Libido." See Gilmore, *Abolition Geography*, 154–75.

39. Bracho, "It Is the Libido."

Augie Robles, *THE END UP NEW YEAR'S DAY*, 1994.

THE SWEETEST HANGOVER

My heart's not clean. Your heart's not clean. But we can be washed again.
—Mary J. Blige as interviewed by Veronica Webb, *Vibe Magazine*

For The House Nation

The Sweetest Hangover was first performed in April 1997 at Brava Theater Center in San Francisco, California. It was directed by Roberto Gutiérrez Varea with dramaturgy by Cherríe Moraga. The cast and crew were as follows:

Octavio:	Vidal M. Perez/Sean San José
Samson:	Art Desuyo
Plum:	Saun-toy Latifa Trotter
Natasha:	Berwick Haynes / B. Chico Purdiman
djdj:	Al Lujan
Miss Thing 1:	Gabriel Morales
Miss Thing 2:	Alan S. Quismorio
Sons of Sonics:	Jason Jones and Mario Zapp
Line Producer:	Amy Mueller
Executive Producer:	Ellen Gavin

The version of the play contained in this collection was used in a May 2008 Stanford University production at Pigott Theater, which was directed by Nia Witherspoon with Cherríe Moraga as dramaturg.

CAST OF CHARACTERS

Octavio:	Chicano club promoter, a fine and brilliant mess
djdj:	Salvadorean DJ, he has taken a vow of silence/sonics
Plum:	Black woman, college student, bougie and fierce
Natasha:	Black drag queen, on the threshold of transitioning
Miss Thing 1:	Black Puerto Rican, gayboy clubkid, prophet of shade
Miss Thing 2:	Filipino, gayboy clubkid, reads and tweaks
Samson:	Chicano Filipino, tattoo artist and club security, doubly brown n beautiful

Prologue—Welcome to Aztlantis

(On a mic, Octavio opens the night.)

Octavio: djdj, give me a sweet sweet beat. *(djdj does.)* My name is Octavio Deseo and welcome to my house. Aztlantis, two lost cities, lost in music—dedicated to the sonic liberation of the legendary children of the life. Deseo. *d* to the *e* to the *s* to the *e* to the motherfuckin' o-vah. Deseo. djdj give my girl something to walk to. In category 1, Bangy Feminist Realness. Plum take the runway! Our doordiva, go-go sistergirl here, my ace boon coon comadre, gives flawless face, sickening body, and ill theory. All in beauty, black black very black. She'd like the sisters out there to know the category is open—all homegirls welcomed. *(Plum freezes.)* Thank you, Plum. In category 2, we have Natasha Kinky, fairy freak sister of the House of Deseo. *(Natasha takes stage.)* Natasha Kinky de Deseo will work this stage with Miss Plum every Friday, unless one of her other identities takes over. The Cats are out of the Hat! Meet Miss Thing 2 and 1 *(lights up on Things, perched at their seats)*, the Filipino–Puerto Rican alliteration alliance. They rhyme, they read, they sit and have been known to give an eclipse worth of shade. The newest member of our family, direct to you from Manila y Mexico, the master tattooist of the Mission, Samson—he of myth and muscle mass. *(Samson does not take stage, can be seen working in audience.)* He's shy but gives you ethnicity twice and masculinity thrice. djdj is the rootworker of this house and my partner in fighting five hundred years of crime. He'll be sending us on our subterranean, transnational, galactic house groove voyage. My name is Octavio Deseo and thank you for joining the family of Aztlantis. Aztlán/Atlantis. Two lost cities, a broken landmass, and many displaced peoples, coming together to form a house, based not on a superficial read of your color, crotch, or couture. But in the treble and bass of your soul, sex, and shade. In the house of your desire.

Scene 1—The Gray Girls

(Dance floor. Miss Thing 1 has a camcorder and is very intent on filming. He is wearing "explorer gear": khakis, pith helmet, ascot, etc. Thing 2 nudges him.)

Miss Thing 2: Whatever are you doing?

Miss Thing 1: Shh. Be bewy, bewy, bewy quiet. We're hunting honkies.

Miss Thing 2: You're after one of those gray girls?

Miss Thing 1: *(Taking camera away from his eye, exasperated.)* I'm documenting their ancient rubber-chicken-with-its-head-cut-off dance ritual. *(He simulates dance.)* It's for my film, *Paris Is Gagging—A Study in Whiteness and Other Forms of Madness.*

Miss Thing 2: Sounds ovah. I didn't know you were into filmmaking.

Miss Thing 1: My therapist suggested that I try a project around my *(whispers)* "problem."

Miss Thing 2: Lolita Cabrón, you have a problem I don't know about!

Miss Thing 1: Well, if you must know, Ms. Imelda Mecos, I have a slight case of colonial regression.

Miss Thing 2: Is it curable?

Miss Thing 1: No but it need not be terminal, contrary to current HIV infection rates and prison pop stats. My shrink thinks that the primal scene for a whole lot of colored people is the colonial encounter—when we first saw white people and experienced "The Lack."

Miss Thing 2: What's "The Lack"?

Miss Thing 1: Girl, I'm not too sure but it sounds positively dreadful, don't it? It has to do with my inability to see white people. To me they're just thieves of the land, stealers of spirits.

Miss Thing 2: Come again, Kunta Crackhead?

Miss Thing 1: They're ghosts. Tricks with mirrors and murder.

Miss Thing 2: It's Friday night, could we find a more up-tempo topic. I came out to get dank and drank and maybe catch a booty or some digits. Enough with the crackers. You know what you need to do, girl?

Miss Thing 1: What?

Miss Thing 2: Blink.

Miss Thing 1: Say what?

Miss Thing 2: You're suffering from overexposure to whiteness. Next time just remember to blink . . . and you'll be returned to darkness.

Miss Thing 1: . . . Damn, bitch, that's deep.

Scene 2—Laying On of Eyes

(Dance floor. Octavio circulates, hugs and kisses Things. Samson cruises the perimeter, trying to look busy while he is really busy looking at Octavio. Octavio catches him and begins to play back. djdj catches all of it, lays down "Don't Lose the Magic" or "My Heart Beats like a Drum.")

Octavio: *(Referring to djdj.)* This is my song!

(djdj catches Octavio's eye, waves. Octavio does that thing colored boys do when they like a song.)

Samson: So, what's up with the DJ?

Octavio: Whatever do you mean?

Samson: Well, I been knowing 1 from the neighborhood my whole life and 2 for a minute. You and the girls been cool enough but I have been here three weeks and your DJ ain't said shit to me, he straight mad-dogs me every weekend.

Octavio: It's nothing personal, but he's not going to talk to you. He hasn't spoken to anyone since he took his vow of sonics.

Samson: Sonics? What kinda shit is that?

Octavio: djdj's commitment to pure sound. If you don't understand him through his music then he's got nothing to say. Shit. He even broke up with me with a song.

Samson: You and he?

Octavio: Used to be.

Samson: So, you ain't you got no man now?

Octavio: Well, no, 'cept for my candyman. Let's go do a bump.

    (Octavio and Samson approach dressing room.)

Plum: OK, paper scissors rock for final number.

Octavio: *(Bursting into dressing room with Samson.)* You got company girls.

Natasha: Women. Is there a problem?

Octavio: No, why?

Natasha: Cuz you got security in tow. Thought there might be some illegal eye lining going on.

Samson: It's all good.

Natasha: I'm sure you are. *(Plum socks Natasha.)* I mean it is.

Plum: Leave the brother be, we got five minutes to get into character.

Octavio: *(To Nat.)* You want a bump?

Natasha: Hells ya. *(To Samson.)* You get into this baby?

Samson: Nah, I'm working, man.

Natasha: I already explained we're women.

Octavio: *(To Samson.)* Don't mind this bitch, her tuck is too tight and all the blood is rushing to her fangs. And don't trip, we're champagne socialists, labor never interrupts pleasure here at Aztlantis. Toma. *(Gives Samson a bump.)*

Plum: Once you're done doing that madness could you do something useful, like getting me a drink?

Octavio: Will that be a Beautiful or a Midori Sour, Miss Ross? *(To Samson, indicating his nostrils.)* Am I clean?

Natasha: Leave me some. *(Octavio tosses Natasha a bag.)*

Octavio: Ima go carry before I have to introduce y'all.

Samson: ¿Quieres bailar conmigo?

Octavio: Sure. *(To girls.)* See yous after the show.

(Octavio and Samson leave dressing room for dance floor.)

Natasha: *(Imitating Octavio.)* "See yous after the show."

Plum: "Quieres bailar conmigo."

Together: Lucky bitch.

Scene 3—Disco Theology

(Natasha goes downstage. djdj plays side 3 of Donna Summer's Live and More *album. Natasha lip-syncs to opening monologue [Or can do it herself, whichever's clever]. We then enter djdj's mind. Natasha becomes Donna Summer.)*

Natasha: "Alright. Alright. It's a very, very special day today, uh or night tonite. Venus is out, you're out. I'm here. Anything can happen. It's a magical, mystical night. I also want you to know that you're on a live recording. And I want you to try me cuz I know we can make it. Whew!" *(Natasha freezes.)*

djdj: At eight, disco became my religion. My virgin was a whore named Donna Summer.

Natasha: *Try me try me try me / just one time / oh try me try me just one time / try me for love / now baby don't you think you should.*

djdj: When she sang in silver lashes and powder-blue eye shadow close-up

Natasha: *Oh, I need you by me, / beside me, to guide me, / to hold me and to scold me / cuz when I'm bad / I'm so so bad*

djdj: after seeing thank God it's Friday thirteen times, I started my very own exclusive one-member fan club and got a maroon and gold scrapbook to keep photos, articles, and the announcement of her Oscar win in. Then disco died, she married that Italian dude she sang

Natasha: *Heaven knows it's not the way it should be and heaven knows it's not the way it could be and heaven knows*

djdj: with and found God. Then Donna did worse with her born-again self,

Natasha: *I believe in Jesus I know him oh so well and I'm going to heaven by and by cuz I've already been through hell*

djdj: said us fags deserved AIDS—their

Natasha: God-mandated deaths.

djdj: so miss donnagirl, do you think your career deserved to die, too? Like me . . . your number one fan, your God's unchosen one. *(He puts on "Love to Love You Baby.")*

Scene 4—Tattoo Parlor

(Samson is in his tattoo parlor, cleaning and closing up. Octavio walks through door.)

Samson: *(Hears bell go off.)* We're closed. *(Looks up.)* Oh, what's up?

Octavio: Not much. *(Looking around.)* I was supposed to meet the Things n Plum here.

Samson: They were here earlier. They're over at my mom's having pancit.

Octavio: I thought your mom was the Mexican one, not the Filipino.

Samson: My dad's Tita and my Lola taught her how to cook.

Octavio: How's business?

Samson: Good enough. What's up?

Octavio: I want to get some work done.

Samson: *(Stops mopping.)* You want a tat? *(Puts mop in bucket, approaches O, circles, and inspects him at an exhale's distance.)* You don't even have your ears pierced. *(Touches lobes, then grabs and outstretches O's arm.)* And look at those virgin arms. *(Runs his index finger along the inner side of O's forearm.)* I bet you don't have one herida on that lil hairless body of yours. *(Drops O's arm.)* Besides, whose name would you get? Booty Call? *(Laughs.)*

Octavio: I want wings. Cotton-white wings on sun-orange fire. Angel's wings burning.

Samson: I don't do none of that Satanic shit—go get one of those punks in the Haight for that.

Octavio: No. I don't want the wings of the fallen angel Lucifer. I want the wings of Icarus.

Samson: Ica-who?

Octavio: Icarus. He's the dude who tried to fly up to the sol with paper wings, but he got too close, and they burned from the heat.

Samson: That's stupid.

Octavio: This from a man who's got half of the Old Testament on his back.

Samson: That's different, man. My pops, que descanse en paz *(crosses himself)*, didn't name me Samson for nothing. *(Samson admires his tattoo through a full-length mirror. It is the biblical Samson amid his crumbling columns. He admires it over his own shoulder through a full-length mirror.)* This is arte, man, not pinche paper wings.

Octavio: *(Moving behind him and into the mirror's frame, touches columns and debris.)* It's nice.

Samson: I know.

Octavio: Who did it?

Samson: This old biker dude named Nando. He's got the Last Supper on his forearm that he did himself.

Octavio: Maybe he'll do mine.

Samson: He's a Christian now—no more false icons. Now he does cover-up and removal work for Victory Outreach.

Octavio: *(Grabs his hands.)* Give me my wings.

Samson: *(Breaks away, grabs appointment ledger.)* I can get you at three on Friday.

Octavio: No, now.

Samson: Man, I'm tired. I did a bunch of anklet rosaries for this one gang of girls and then I had to shave this huerco's back to do a fucking fireball. How 'bout first thing mañana?

Octavio: I want to get it after-hours, at night.

Samson: Damn, you a particular bitch. How'z your man put up with it?

Octavio: I already told you the other night, I ain't doin' nobody. I ain't that big of a hooch—you must have me confused with someone else, perhaps yourself.

Samson: Man, you're fucked up, coming in here askin' for favors . . .

Octavio: I can pay for it.

Samson: That ain't the point—estoy cansado, man, and all I want is a 40 and some 420.

Octavio: I'll buy you a 40. I'll even throw in an eighth.

Samson: Is it green?

Octavio: As money.

Samson: You got a deal, cumpare. So where do you want your wings?

Octavio: . . . on my ass.

Samson: Which cacheta?

Octavio: Neither. I want them coming out the crack of my ass.

Samson: You're a bakla loca, c'mon.

(They move to the back. Samson sets up his case of needles and ink. Octavio takes off his jacket and he's face down on the table.)

Samson: Take your belt off—push your pants down a bit.

Octavio: Alright.

Samson: I'm gonna draw it on first and see how you like it. Umm. Could you raise your ass a bit?

Octavio: Yeah.

(Samson pulls Octavio's pants further down, exposing more of Octavio's ass.)

Octavio: Oh—that pen's cold.

Samson: The needle will warm you up. Why'd you want it here? Why not at your neck or back or something?

Octavio: Cuz I want y'all to see it—you know while we're in the mix.

Samson: *(Interrupting and ignoring Octavio.)* Oh, this is gonna look bad—I'm making the wings silver—they'll reflect nice off light. Don't you want to be able to see it?

Octavio: Oh, I already do—every time I open my legs, I see those wings flying to the sun. It's a warning.

Samson: How you mean?

Octavio: Motherfuckers think all a culo is is a dark hole that goes nowhere. I want them to know that what they're really approaching is the sun, flying out of orbit with melted wings. I don't want them to burn up like Icarus . . . and die.

Samson: Shit, you think you the sun. Nobody's shit that good.

Octavio: What have you heard? *(Turning around.)*

Samson: Lie still, ho.

Octavio: Don't be calling me no ho . . .

Samson: Yeah, yeah. Can we talk about something else?

Octavio: You getting shy on me?

Samson: No . . . hard. And I ain't about to . . .

Octavio: To what?

Samson: Get busy with my new boss.

Octavio: We're in your place of business.

Samson: Stand up—let's go to the mirror.

(They cross to mirror.)

Samson: Well, what do you think?

Octavio: The silver's cool. The tips need a bit more red. What do you think?

Samson: You have a nice fucking ass.

Octavio: I know.

(*Samson grabs Octavio.*)

Octavio: Samson.

Samson: Delilah, you ready for takeoff?

Octavio: Yeah, (*Octavio hands Samson a condom*) but here's a parachute.

Scene 5—The Goddess Have Mercy Seat

(*At club, during off-hours, Plum is being interviewed by White Woman Reporter, to be played by another actor with back to audience, wearing an absurd blond wig.*)

Plum: Race? You want to know what I think about race. Shit, I'm a black woman. With this much fashion sense and arrogance, what else would I be? But I can see how I might confuse ya. I am a Pisces.

White girls either find me too prim for their conception of a with-it, right-on, dynomite groovy gal—à la Wylona or worse Penny on *Good Times* or too race-based to be their multicultural headwrapping bangle-wearing sister—you know, the Whoopi-Audre-earthy-gumbo-goddess. Black men think well of the bigness of my behind but not of my mouth. Momma says she didn't spend good dead presidents on prep school, horseback riding, and a Chanel suit for law school interviews to have me sliding down poles with my ass out.

The Poles? It's part of WADDUP's new dance piece—The Polar Bear Pas de Diaspora. We got actual bars on the proscenium which we slide down stripper style in our polar bear bodies—I'm making them with white and black faux fur on mesh frames. Then we strip down to reveal lily pond G-strings and Botticelli Venus clam bras. We do a Rockettes can-can to that hip-hop version of "Sometimes I Feel like a Motherless Child."

What's WADDUP? I called us the transnational niggasista alliance, but Mylena said we'd never get grants with that name. So now we're Women of African Descent Dancing Under Pressure. WADDUP!

What was the question?

Oh yes, I've considered myself a black feminist since I was seventeen. And I don't mind once that my father was absent. Which is the wrong thing to admit, especially if you want to get dick. Don't print that.

Scene 6—Things Waiting on a Cab

(Thing 1's apartment, waiting for a cab. Miss Thing 1 files and buffs her nails while Miss Thing 2 tweaks.)

Miss Thing 2: How long ago did you call that cab? I hope you didn't call Yellow. I hate their cabs. Always worry about getting piojos in one *(scratches his head)*. . . . DeSoto, they got the best stereos and the most comfortable seats. *(Motioning toward 1.)* Do you have one of those cuticle-pusher-backer things? *(Without waiting for an answer.)* Did you call de Soto like I said? What time is it? Maybe we should go flag one down. If we walk to Valencia where the white people are we can get one.

Miss Thing 1: How long has it been since you've slept?

Miss Thing 2: What's today?

Miss Thing 1: Friday.

Miss Thing 2: A nap on Tuesday.

Miss Thing 1: And when was the last time you ate?

Miss Thing 2: *(A beat while he thinks.)* Does the ice in my cocktails count?

Miss Thing 1: You too high to talk to.

Miss Thing 2: You did just as much as I did, besides the fact that you spilled some. We didn't even do the whole bag yet. Should we do some more before we go—or wait 'til we get there. Should we take the pipe? You taking your backpack? I'm not, could you . . .

Miss Thing 1: Cállate, sangana come mierda.

Miss Thing 2: Are you trying to fuck with my high?

Miss Thing 1: Nothing's wrong with me. I'm beat and my 'fit is on hit.

Miss Thing 2: Should we go sit and wait on the stoop?

Miss Thing 1: You crazy. In these outfits?

Miss Thing 2: You right. You sure you called a cab?

Miss Thing 1: Uh-huh.

Miss Thing 2: Could you reload the pipe?

Miss Thing 1: Uh-huh.

Miss Thing 2: Should I change?

Miss Thing 1: Mmm-hmm.

(Cab honk from offstage. Things gather up bags and coats to leave.)

Scene 7—Bones, Bochinche, n Bogart

(In club, Octavio, Plum, Natasha, and Samson play dominos.)

Octavio: That's fifteen points for the brown side! *(Gives Samson dap.)*

Natasha: Mmm, lemme see. Sweet Jesus. Twenty-five points for New Afrika. *(Gives Plum dap. To Octavio.)* Payback is a bitch. And I am that bitch.

(Things burst in.)

Miss Thing 2: Hey, hi, hello. What's up everybody? It was hell getting here. Can I get a drink already? What are you all looking at? We look fierce, right?

Natasha & Octavio: Day 5.

Samson: *(Passing blunt.)* Want a hit off this dos?

Miss Thing 2: No, but I'll take a light. *(Pulls out glass pipe.)*

Natasha: *(Shady.)* How ever did such a nice little thing like you get so gutbucket?

Miss Thing 1: *(To Plum.)* What be the t, sugar?

Plum: Trying to play some bones but these faggots talk too much. Throw something down, Samson!

Samson: *(Watching djdj.)* Take over for me, 2, I gotta get to work.

Octavio: *(Watching Samson watch djdj.)* Play for me, 1. We're playing black against brown.

(Octavio and Samson give their seats to Things.)

Miss Thing 1: Black against brown?! Why Puerto Ricans always got to be forced to choose?

Plum: *(Lighting joint.)* OK, then it's Islands against the Motherland. Wash them dishes, I.

Natasha: Now, quiet as it's kept, you know that Octavio used to be with the DJ?

Miss Thing 1: Uh-huh.

Natasha: And now he's with Samson.

Miss Thing 1: Nah-uh.

Natasha: These Latin children are killing me. *(To Plum.)* Let me get a hit off that. *(Plum doesn't pass the blunt.)*

Miss Thing 1: Hold up. I'm having pains in my gagular vein. I've known Samson since I was six and it took Octavio less than a month to grab that piece?

Plum & Natasha: Uh-huh.

Things: Where were we?

Plum: At Samson's moms.

Miss Thing 1: I told you we should have gotten our tatuajes that day. But no, you had to have some of your national food products.

Miss Thing 2: Don't take this out on me. Your people like pork just as much as mine.

Plum: Like I said, y'all faggots talk too much.

Natasha: And you're bogarting the weed.

Miss Thing 2: Talk too much. Well, I'm offended.

Miss Thing 1: And I'm having another series of gagulations. Let's go check out the crowd.

Plum: Do you still want to play?

Natasha: No, but I would like some of that smoke.

Scene 8—Marry Me, Suck Me

(Octavio in his office counting money, separating ones, fives, tens, twenties into piles. Samson watches, smokes a bowl.)

Samson: Don't you ever get tired of this shit? *(Pause.)* This ain't what you're supposed to be doing with all that education.

Octavio: Hold up, Ima lose count.

Samson: You got the schedule of a vampire. When was the last time you went to bed before midnight? Who else you know whose weekend start on Thursday and end Tuesday morning?

Octavio: *(Octavio places down the last bill.)* There. *(Turns to Samson.)* Wha'happen?

Samson: Give it all up—'specially the crystal.

Octavio: I don't see you passing up bumps.

Samson: It's not my life. Marry me.

Octavio: E'cu'me?

Samson: You can't live your whole life waiting for your dealer to recop. Live it wit me. Elope with me right now.

Octavio: Baby, that's sweet, but we haven't been together that long, I don't have my dowry in order. If the club keeps going this well, you can tell your moms I'm worth two wild boars and a goat. But no dog! *(Ha.)*

Samson: Fuck it, then. If you won't do it now, I take back my proposal.

Octavio: Just throw a papa sack over my head and throw me into your hooptie.

Samson: Huh. Why didn't I think of that?

Octavio: Samsie,

Samson: Don't be calling me that.

Octavio: Nobody's around Samson. I didn't see no ring attached with that proposal and elopement or not—you gonna have to invest in this shit. How about we go straight to the luna de miel?

Samson: How about we go to my car? *(Samson tosses Trojan to Octavio.)*

Octavio: You high? *(Octavio places Trojan on desk.)* We work here.

Samson: You right. See you do love this club more than me?

Octavio: And you love that damn car more than you do me—and I ain't about a tres lados tonite.

Samson: A three-way?

Octavio: Yeah—you, me, and the Impala. I know. *(Octavio spreads piles of bills across desk.)* Let's give a new definition to the word *greenback*.

Samson: You is a trip.

Octavio: You gonna ride or not?

Samson: I'm still waiting. For you to, you know.

Octavio: It's not gonna happen.

Samson: ¿Y porque no?

Octavio: Would you really like for me to tell you I love you cuz you asked to hear it? ¿Me vas a creer?

Samson: I know you do. You just won't say so.

Octavio: I don't use that particular three-word phrase. I like polysyllables and compound sentences.

    (Samson bites Octavio's neck. Octavio moans.)

Samson: No hables más. Ima get your body to say it.

    (Samson kisses Octavio.)

Octavio: Suck it.

    (Samson unbuttons Octavio's shirt, starts to suck Octavio's nipple.)

Octavio: Not that.

Samson: What you say, chulo. *(Samson goes back to sucking.)*

Octavio: My dick.

Samson: What?

Octavio: Suck my dick.

Samson: Mmm. What are you talking about? Don't this feel good?

Octavio: *(Pulls Samson's head from his chest.)* I'm talking about you sucking my dick. C'mon, man, pélamela.

Samson: It's weird when you ask for it like that.

Octavio: What? It's wrong for me to ask my man to do me?

Samson: No. I don't know. It's just strange, is all.

Octavio: You like the way I do it.

Samson: Baby, you know I do. Eres el mejor chupero en Califas.

Octavio: Thanks, I'll enter the state fair.

Samson: That's not how I meant it.

Octavio: All I'm asking is for you to return the favor more often.

Samson: I can do you so many ways—make you cum without touching it.

Octavio: Touch it, taste it, lick it, fill your throat with it.

Samson: Stop talking like that.

Octavio: Who's the one with the scan'less mouth—"whose shit is this?"

Samson: Don't even play like you don't like that talk. *(Pause.)* You like it.

Octavio: I do. It scares me how much you like it, get into it. You forget it's just talk. I want my dick sucked. I shouldn't have to point that out to my homosexual male lover.

Samson: Oh, this is gonna be one of those damn lessons about my internalized que sé yo. Leave the books out of this man. This is about us.

Octavio: This is not about us. This is about me. I like being your baby, your chulo. I love calling you my papi, mi esposo. We're both men . . . I wish you'd remember that when we're fucking. *(Pause.)* Ima go do the payouts.

Samson: Just like that, Octavio, huh? Amazing how you can go from wanting to get busy to all business. Does anything or anyone really matter to you? You pop off with all this shit about wanting to be sucked. Well, Octavio, you do suck, homes. I'm gonna go play some pool somewhere, just bring my check home with you.

(Samson picks condom off of the desk throws it at Octavio's back. Samson exits. Octavio stops, picks up condom.)

Octavio: Thanks. My brand.

Scene 9—Le Papillon Noir

(Plum dances to Labelle's Chameleon album, side B, "Gypsy Moths." Plum cannot find a style to cling to—ballet, Haitian, Fagan, Graham. Cuts music and continues to dance. Nat enters and watches. Plum catches the spirit and her dance becomes brilliant—merging battle with ballet. She crumbles to the floor.)

Natasha: What was that?

Plum: The 60 million or more niggas who live in death at the bottom of the Atlantic and who have only now come up for air.

Natasha: That's a awfully long title.

Plum: Just a subtitle, it's from the Chrysallis section of my Le Papillon Noir piece.

Natasha: It's dope, girl—but how you expect to put your body through that for a three-week run.

Plum: That's not me and my body—it's all those dead Africans, who were denied the opportunity to become slaves, spooks, toms, baps, niggas.

Natasha: You awfully stuck on that word today, girl.

Plum: *(Irritated and doing floor stretches.)* No, I am stuck on trying to find a language where dark and female, sin and sex are not collapsible terms. Since there ain't one known to MANkind, I'm hoping these-here niggas I got hold up inside me will teach my body to speak. Break me out of my coon cocoon.

Natasha: That's a title I could get behind. *(He stretches out his hand, helps her up.)* Who else gonna be in it from WADDUP?

Plum: Just 60 million and 1 niggas is all.

Natasha: You giving yourself a solo? That's not very collectively correct of you, Plum.

Plum: *(Breaking away.)* Nat, I need your, help not your sass.

Natasha: With what—you all over that dance—although how you going to remember when to weep and when to make your body do that fluttering moaning stuff is beyond me.

Plum: I'm gonna let it pour through me, just the way a caterpillar know to go and spin its cocoon, unaware that it will emerge as a black-and-gold-speckled butterfly.

Natasha: I do not think, and I'm sure the orishas and the Surgeon General are with me on this one, that the stage is the proper place to lose your goddamn mind.

Plum: Well, my dear sweet-like-cyanide sista, where would you have me lose it?

Natasha: That's not the point, what . . .

Plum: No, that is the point—I do want to lose my mind. Go Plum crazy, Ma Rainey mad, Tituba hysterical, ape-shit Assata insane.

Natasha: In public?

Plum: If I don't do this dance, Ima do some damage in this world. Better I dance it here than in San Bruno County Jail.

Natasha: And who you plan on hurting with that three-hundred-year hurt you got up in you?

Plum: I'll start with that faggot ofay who writes for the *Dance Review*, then move on to that cracker witch from that performance magazine.

(Silence.)

Natasha: The reviews for the Polar Bear show were that bad?

Natasha: Ahh, don't cry baby girl, you got me and 60 million other black nigga African motherfuckers who need you strong and moving.

Plum: *(Trying to repress tears, wipe them away, they keep pouring.)* They ain't tears.

Natasha: They ain't?

Plum: Nah, just saltwater from deep in the Atlantic of my body.

Natasha: Let's go get ready for tonite's performance. I didn't really get Tavi's script, did you? So, who's missing, anyway?

(They exit.)

Scene 10—Missing Histories

(Octavio plays Seeker, Nat is the Clerk, Plum dances; or Thing 1 is the Seeker, Thing 2 is the Clerk, Plum dances.)

Seeker: Hello.

Clerk: Good morning. How can I help you?

Seeker: I'd like to fill out a Missing Histories Report.

Clerk: We don't have those forms—this is a Missing Persons Bureau.

Seeker: Fine. Then I'd like to fill out a Missing People's Report.

Clerk: OK. Well, you need to fill out the blue, then this pink form and then this green slip. Here's a pen. *(Long pause.)* Do you need some help filling out these forms?

Seeker: Yes.

Clerk: Well, it's really not in my job description, but you do seem like you have a special case. Here, hand me back those forms. OK, name of missing person.

Seeker: Los Taínos, the members of the Middle Passage, Tituba, Geronimo, Malinche...

Clerk: Wait, I need first and last name and middle initial.

Seeker: ... Tupac Amaru, Vincente Menchú, four girls in a Birmingham church, Oscar Zeta Acosta.

Clerk: Hold on. It's beginning to sound like you lost everyone you know. Was there a mass kidnapping?

Seeker: Yes. The nations of Aztlán, Hawai'i, Puerto Rico.

Clerk: Look, you're confusing me. Did that queen over in shipping and receiving send you over here?

Seeker: No.

Clerk: OK. So, this is for real. Damn, this is gonna take a mess of forms. So, you're saying that Mr. Taynose and all his buddies were taken to all these places.

Seeker: No, the places were taken by...

Clerk: Burglary is down the hall. I just need to know who not what's been taken.

Seeker: The Baader-Meinhof, the street children of Brazil, drag queens in Chiapas, hustlers in the Polk, hookers in San Diego.

Clerk: Vice is two stories up, and we don't do international business here. For kidnapping I need to know if there were any ransoms or threats.

Seeker: Yes. The Bay of Pigs, Panama, Grenada, Desert Storm, the MOVE bombing, the massacre at Hebron.

Clerk: Look, you keep on talking, but you haven't told me a thing about this missing person. I don't have all day, my lunch break is in fifteen minutes. Have any of the ransoms been paid?

Seeker: Not exactly, but we are in negotiations in Palestine, South Africa, and South Central.

Clerk: For the return of . . .

Seeker: For the return of our lives, ma'am. *(Pause after she has given him a look.)* Miss.

Clerk: I don't think you understand this process. I need a name, a photo, Social Security number. A real live somebody who's actually missing from some goddamn where.

Seeker: Well, that would be me.

Clerk: You?

Seeker: Yes. I am a somebody, a sum of small bones and sufficient melanin and several strands of ancianos crossing circuits, and I am missing from history. From anywhere vaguely to be named a home. Mostly I am missing from myself and I have been lost in the loss of men who were never fully mine.

Clerk: Well, can you give me their names?

Seeker: Joe Beam, Rodrigo Reyes, Sergio Anguiano, Donald Woods, David Frechette, Craig Harris, Tede Mathews, Assotto Saint, Douglas Yaranon, the Reverend Bill Smith, Aaron O, Ronnie Salazar, Juan Rodríguez, Luiz Goñi.

Clerk: And since when have they been missing?

Seeker: Since they died.

Clerk: Homicide?

Seeker: No, homocide.

Clerk: Could you stick to one story. So, who is it?—and now I want one name, one address and one short, very short, say three sentences describing this missing person.

Seeker: Well, it's like I said. I'm missing. And I am missing from history. In fact, I am that point of negation where history meets the scribe's eraser.

Clerk: Sir, I'm sorry, but if you are in fact missing, you'll have to find someone else to report it. Preferably a spouse, relative, or employer.

Scene 11—Domestic Bliss

(Samson's bedroom. Samson watches Cheech and Chong's "Up in Smoke," Octavio talks on the phone.)

Octavio: *(In bed, on the phone.)* Look, Miss Cosa, I already told you we're staying in. *(Pause.)* Yeah, it was his idea. *(Pause.)* Staying home and watching a movie is not selling out the community. Say hi to everybody for me. Take some flyers and passes with you. *(Pause.)* Alright. I'll call you before Friday. *(Octavio hangs up phone, picks up Roland Barthes's* A Lover's Discourse.*)*

Samson: *(Gets into bed.)* ¿Quién era?

Octavio: Thing 1. They're all going out tonite.

Samson: You sure you don't want to hook up with them?

Octavio: No. This is where I want to be.

Samson: You mean that?

Octavio: I said it, didn't I?

Samson: I'm real proud of you, baby.

Octavio: What's that supposed to mean?

Samson: It means you're gonna make some changes in your life.

Octavio: For now.

Samson: Now? What you mean now?

Octavio: Is there an echo in here? Samson, I agreed to take a break, but that does not mean I'm going to permanently reside in this domestic bliss.

Samson: Why not? Is it so awful here with me?

Octavio: Promotion for Aztlantis is going well without me, but that may not always be the case. I'll be back out there, believe that.

Samson: Then what are you doing here with me tonight? Cracking off?

Octavio: No, but we could get some drugs, crack on, and then have something to come off of. But none of that would change your conventional, Cro-Magnon ways of thinking.

Samson: I'm not the one stuck on repeat, same bars, same drugs, every weekend. Don't you want more?

Octavio: Sure I do. Look man, if they invent some new drugs, I'll try those too.

Samson: Asshole.

Octavio: Who isn't giving up any ass tonite. Go to bed.

Samson: Go to hell.

(Samson turns his back to Octavio and goes to sleep. Octavio reads Roland Barthes's *A Lover's Discourse*.)

Octavio: *(Octavio opens book, reads.)* "In the loving calm of your arms: The gesture of the amorous embrace seems to fulfill, for a time, the subject's dream of total union with the loved being." Yeah, right. *(Octavio closes book, hits light.)*

Scene 12—Dreaming in Disco(urse)

(Octavio and Samson sleep. Plum and Natasha enter and go to Octavio. They pull him from the bed, speak lines from Roland Barthes's A Lover's Discourse. *Or this can be done on video and projected and no one enters.)*

Plum: *"Besides intercourse,*

Natasha: *When the Image-repertoire goes to the devil,*

Plum: *there is that other embrace, which is a motionless cradling*

Natasha: *we are enchanted, bewitched*

Plum: *We are in the realm of sleep, without sleeping*

Natasha: *This is the moment for telling stories*

Plum: *This is the return to the mother*

Natasha: *In the loving calm of your arms*

(Things 2 & 1 enter [or appear on video].)

Miss Thing 2: *In this companionable incest,*

Miss Thing 1: *everything is suspended. Time, law,*

Miss Thing 2: *prohibition*

Together: *Nothing is exhausted, nothing is wanted*

Plum: *All desires are abolished*

Natasha: *For they seem definitively fulfilled"*

(Samson rises, djdj appears on video or onstage.)

("Love Hangover" by Diana Ross comes on. Samson offers his hand to Octavio.)

Samson: Dance with me.

Octavio: Me siento raro.

Samson: Baile conmigo.

Octavio: Eres bien guapo. Eso sí me gusta.

Samson: Hold here and here.

Octavio: I've met you before.

Samson: Yes. We dreamed the same dream.

Octavio: We did?

Samson: Bésame.

Octavio: It would be bad luck.

Samson: Who told you that?

Octavio: They forbid it.

Samson: Who?

Octavio: The dead. The dream-weavers.

Samson: I want to kiss, you want me to kiss—it is part of our dream.

Octavio: It is a curse.

Samson: A kiss.

(They kiss and dance. They kiss again and Samson pulls away, begins to exit.)

Octavio: *(To Samson's back.)* Te quiero, querido.

(Samson stops, turns, faces Octavio.)

Octavio: I love you.

(Samson exits.)

Things: *"Jealousies, anxieties, possessions, discourses, appetites,*

Natasha: *Once again*

Plum: *amorous desire was burning*

Natasha: *everywhere.*

Octavio: *I was trying to embrace one last time.*
I was performing.
A denial of separation."

THE B SIDE (AKA ACT 2)

Scene 1—djdj Exposes

(At the club, djdj sets up for the night. Puts on Exposé's "Point of No Return.")

djdj: I met a man last night, and kissing him was hearing Exposé for the first time.

Things: *Taking me to the point of no return*

djdj: Not the words

Things: *uh-oh-oh*

djdj: or the tempo

Things: *uh-oh-oh*

djdj: just that time of my life: high school keggers, after-parties hanging with the popular girls and all the doggish jocks and

Things: *lookout weekend cuz here I come*
because weekends were made for fun

djdj: this is the late '80s high nrg cha-cha

Things: *and six minutes, six minutes, six minutes*
doug e fresh you're on
uh-uh-on

djdj: time. Yeah

Things: *it's like a jungle sometime getting*

djdj: wasted

Things: *and I think I'm going under*

djdj: this numb feeling of ludes and Michelob as I dance with Michelle to Shannon's

Things: *Let the Music Play*

djdj: or is it Lisa Lisa

Things: *Oh Baby I'm Lost in Emotion*

djdj: Kissing him was a party in some football player's backyard where the cops would come, Eddie would start a fight with Lisa, Anita would leave to the back-seat of a car, Daisy would fall in love with somebody else's boyfriend for the second time that weekend. Straight mating rituals done to

Things: *the roof the roof the roof is on fire*
don't need no water
let the motherfucker burn
burn motherfucker burn

djdj: Kissing him was like that, we could have been in his car outside a party in the Mission, coming back from a beer run, Stacey Q singing "We Connect" and we do. But this is Collingwood Park, 3 a.m. and I don't know what song is on his radio. I'm kissing him and I feel the jets in my pulse.

(The Jets' "Crush on You" comes on.)

Scene 2—Things Sniff It Out

(At the club, djdj brings in equipment for evening. Things enter, Thing 1 sniffs at djdj's trail, Thing 2 follows suit.)

Miss Thing 1: That's it.

Miss Thing 2: What?

Miss Thing 1: The smell.

Miss Thing 2: What smell?

Miss Thing 1: Oh dear,
oh damn,
oh well.
I hate to tell.

Miss Thing 2: If you smell the smell
I suggest you share,
I mean it would only be fair.

Miss Thing 1: I can tell
from my olfactory wells
that death is singing
and a ringing its bells.

Miss Thing 2: Now now please explain,
how is it that your nasal orifices
are so ordained?

Miss Thing 1: Since I was a child
a wee little niglet
I have been able to perceive
the presence of death
in the air I breathe.

Miss Thing 2: That would be an awful way to sniff,
not knowing if the next breath
carried death's whiff.

Miss Thing 1: Yes, 'tis a burden,
'tis a bundle
but my grams taught me
to never groan and grumble

at my faculty
for foretelling mortality.

Miss Thing 2: I wonder, ponder, and fear
why death should draw near us here.

Miss Thing 1: I question that too.
For though I have been able to tell this smell
from where it comes I have never known, boo.
So like Cassandra,
though I know when the ship comes in
it don't matter
since I'm
the only one
listenin'.

Miss Thing 2: Cassandra?
Now who would she be,
or why haven't you told me
that you are a he-she.

Miss Thing 1: Oh Cass!
She was a Greek girl with sass
and the ability to predict
then the misfortune
to be killt over dick.
Though she always knew
what was to transpire
everyone treated her
as a tart and a liar.

Miss Thing 2: Thanks for the story,
even if it was a tad gory.
I hope you are quite done
I believe we should move on, hon.
Let us take our perch
begin our search.
Acid and ecstasy
for you and for me.
Actually
there's enough for 3.

I have a mind to live tonight
barring any more scented blight.

Miss Thing 1: Oh by all means
let us make light
of this night
for who knows
what the day brings.

Miss Thing 2: Girl that didn't rhyme. You fucked it up.

Miss Thing 1: I'm sorry,
I do apologize
but I got to thinking
that this power to prophesize
may be of little relief
once we enter
the stench of grief.

Miss Thing 2: You did retrieve the rhyme
but now you have troubled my mind.
How's about we . . .

Miss Thing 1: Give up this rhyming game
and get lit?

Miss Thing 2: You got it,
that's it.

Scene 3—O's Gotta Go

(On the dance floor.)

Octavio: Girl, I gotta go. Watch the club for me.

Natasha: Bitch, this ain't no baby. This club is a couple hundred full-grown adults who are not my responsibility.

Octavio: I know that. I'll be back quick. Tell Samson . . .

Natasha: Tell him yourself. He's right behind you.

Octavio: Fuck.

Samson: What?

Natasha: Octavio's got something to tell you.

Samson: Yeah?

Natasha: Go on ahead, Tavi, tell him. Tell him how you just got to go, how you can't be here tonite and how you was gonna leave without saying shit to him.

Octavio: Natasha, I think you better go to the dressing room and add another layer of foundation. Your brick is beginning to show.

Natasha: Samson tell that stupid bitch of yours to review her own hookey and drug policies. Ima go plan my show. Later for you, Miss Crack Attack. *(Nat exits, Plum enters.)*

Samson: What's up?

Octavio: I gotta go.

Samson: Where?

Octavio: To . . . I just gotta . . . I left something at home.

Samson: Send somebody else. You got work to do.

Octavio: I'll be back in half an hour.

Samson: O, the only thing you can do in less than thirty minutes is a quarter. *(Octavio looks caught.)* See. I knew it. Fuck it. Run your fucking errand up your nose or through a pipe or a fucking vein for all I care. *(Up in Octavio's face.)* You're a fucking punk-ass . . .

Plum: *(To Samson, getting between them.)* What's up, nig?

Samson: *(Backing off.)* Not much. Just quitting this sick-ass place and that fuckin queen.

Octavio: Give us a second Plum. *(Plum moves away but stays within earshot along with Things. djdj watches intently. To Samson.)* Tell them at the door to pay you cash, so you won't ever have to come back for your check.

Samson: Keep your pennies, you might have to roll them for a five-dollar rock.

> *(Samson removes his headset and battery and hands them to Octavio. Samson exits. Plum reapproaches.)*

Octavio: Girl?

Plum: Yeah, girl?

Octavio: Is the moon waxing or waning?

Plum: It's full to bursting.

Octavio: And it's in . . .

Plum: Taurus.

Octavio: Mercury is retrograde?

Plum: You got that right.

Octavio: I gotta go.

Plum: You gonna follow him?

Octavio: Fuck no.

(Octavio turns to leave, djdj puts on "You Better Think Twice.")

Octavio: Oh God, not you too. I'll be right back. . . . te lo juro . . . It's not that big of a deal . . . I know . . . I know . . . I won't miss your entire set. . . . C'mon now, play me something . . . I'm still your good luck, right? *(Octavio exits.)*

Scene 4—A DJ Spins to Death

djdj: *(djdj in booth.)* What do you play for your own death? *(He puts on Alicia Myers's "I Want to Thank You." Cuts it abruptly.)* All I've ever known is body loving—mamilove, motalove girl-n-boy-n-boy after bookstore after park after making them all sweat mack and tweak. But afterwards know what I'd do rather than go home alone? I would never go home. This is the only home I've ever known and this sickness ain't about to stop me Damoso Juan Orozco. I usedta think I was just the conductor, the Muni-man on your mystical magical journey. I flipped the switches, spun the records, broke the beats but the sounds, the song came from somebody else. Now I know I got the speakers to house history beneath my fingertips. On the underside of this palm I got a fuckin symphony. I got Holland-Dozier-Holland in my hands, Phil Spector's wall of sound pours out these pores. *(Pause.)* What happens when they bury a symphony? Do I go to classic house heaven? Where Sylvester is the conductor and Willie Smith and Patrick Kelly design the choir robes? Larry Levan is in charge of promotions and Miss Phyliss Hyman and Minnie Riperton tip in to doo-wop. No, maybe I'm wrong. Maybe it's not a symphony I'm holding in my hands and veins, just a bleeding pulse, this space where we can be free. *(djdj puts on "Follow Me," exits club.)*

Scene 5—Diva Dozens

(Nat, Plum, & Things are all in DJ booth, smoking weed, packing up records. Octavio enters.)

Octavio: Could someone please explain to me how my club got turned into the Land of the Lost?

Miss Thing 2: That's on you, Chaka, you, that's who.

Natasha: Didn't your momma teach you to stay out of grown folk's conversation? *(To Octavio.)* Anyways,

Miss Thing 1: After Samson left,

Plum: And you were audi.

Natasha: dj started to play whack

Miss Thing 2: People started leaving

Natasha: En masse

Miss Thing 1: So, I did the only logical thing.

Octavio: Going into my stash and dosing everyone is not my idea of linear Western rational thought, 1.

Miss Thing 1: But you've never had my famous magic mushroom and grape Kool Aid punch.

Octavio: That's cuz you didn't save me none. *(Pause. Posse begins picking up records.)* Just leave it. I'll come and pack it up tomorrow.

Natasha: You think he's coming back?

Miss Thing 1: Which one? Esposo numero uno.

Miss Thing 2: Or novio number two?

Plum: Y'all are cold-blooded.

Miss Thing 1: Us cold? No that would be she. *(Indicates Octavio.)* The OG Ice Queen of the house scene.

Miss Thing 2: She's cuckoo for Coco Crack!

Plum: Our beloved Count Crackula.

Natasha: Beloved? Don't give that heifer-ho-dawg bitch props. She's the one who chased all the menzezez out of this bi-atch.

Octavio: To answer your question Plum. I hope dj comes back, but if Samson comes back, you're not to let him in. Understood? *(Pause.)* I bid you good day, Ladies and Things.

Miss Thing 1: We'll share a cab with you.

Miss Thing 2: If you'll share your crack.

Octavio: Then come alive, cosas.

(*Octavio leaves, followed by Things.*)

Plum: I'm glad I got law school to fall back on, cuz it don't look like this shit's gonna last.

Natasha: That's the least of my concerns.

Plum: Somethin up? You wanna join me at the End-Up? It's almost six in the morning. We could hit first call.

Natasha: Nah, girl, I need to handle business today.

Plum: On a Sunday?

Natasha: Hormone black market never closes.

Plum: Mones? Girl, we need to talk.

Natasha: Can we hook up later this week for a sistagirl conversation?

Plum: Sure. I'll be home studying for the LSAT.

Natasha: Take care, baby love.

Scene 6—The Blue Blues/Drive-By Fucking

(*Natasha is left alone in the club, with suitcase in hand. Takes the stage, sings Billie Holiday's "Lady Sings the Blues." As she sings Samson listens outside of club.*)

Samson: *(On hood of his own car, with a 40 and a blunt.)* Look at my ride. Blue and well-waxed. An American car from years back far enough so you know it's owned by a Mexican. In my reflection I see it all, maybe it's the smoke. What do Indios think humo holds? Octavio would know. I ain't thinking about him. Shit, good shit. My face come back to me in blue. A rival color but serves me right seeing how I let myself be played, betrayed. This some philosophical shit. What direction am I facing? Octavio, tell me why it matters.

(Samson runs off, lights fade on Natasha. They enter booth.)

(Back at the club, Natasha is by herself. Mica Paris's "If I Love U 2 Nite" plays in background.)

Natasha: I have been in here for at least two past lives and the current one and Ima go off on the next motherfucker who steps on my heel. But I ain't gonna leave, not till they close down the bar, shut down the sound system, make me take my faux fur wrap out of coat check and blast Cheap Trick to send us all packing home. In fact, I ain't leaving the parking lot or alley till I find him. You know he don't you? My future 'usband. Well, if you do, could you please introduce us? I'm looking for the spitting in the streets but always opens the car door for you type of nigga. Rough handed except when it's me he's handling. A mean old lion who snore like a bear and fuck like Tigger bouncing on his tail. Oh my! Somebody who could kick most of the ass in this goddamn bar but is content just to be getting a piece of mine. Naw, forget about the marriage. I'm looking for a drive-by fucking and if I don't find it soon Ima call the cops.

Scene 7—Samson Tattoos Thing 2—Fix Up Samson n Thing 1

(Things 2 & 1, Plum are all at the tattoo shop. Thing 2 holds The Cat in the Hat, *Plum and 1 look through a magazine.)*

Samson: Where's Nat?

Miss Thing 1: We dropped her off at her transgender support group.

Samson: They got groups for lip sync-ers?

Plum: Yeah, and it ain't just about makeup and shows for her no more.

Samson: Oh . . . who's first?

All: *(Fingers indicating Thing 2.)* She is.

Samson: Dos, you're up.

Miss Thing 1: We're going to run down the street n grab some burritos. ¿Quieren algo?

Samson: Beer.

Plum: You are not taking a needle to my skin intoxicated.

Samson: It's for after. It'll numb the pain. *(He laughs. They don't.)*

Miss Thing 2: Hurry back.

Samson: *(Taking book from Miss Thing 2.)* You want both of them or just Thing 2?

Miss Thing 2: *(Sitting down, propping up his leg.)* No, I want the polka dot dress on my ankle and 1 wants the fish in the pot on his shoulder. God, we ain't that literal.

Samson: Look, Octavio . . . *(Catches himself.)* I mean 2.

Miss Thing 2: Don't trip.

Samson: You sounded like him, that's something he'd say.

Miss Thing 2: Miss him?

Samson: I like the married life. Ain't never had a relationship shorter than a year. This shit with Tavi got me fucked up.

Miss Thing 2: How so?

Samson: Never mind, man, I need to get to work on this design. They'll be back soon.

Miss Thing 2: Look strong n silent is a cute look for you—but get over it. Confess your sins.

Samson: I ain't that Catholic.

Miss Thing 2: You're fucking Mexican and flip—that's vergüenza squared.

Samson: Musta just canceled each other out. *(Beat.)* Look, just cuz my jaina's name ends in an O, not an A, don't make me no different from any other blood in this barrio.

Miss Thing 2: What's the problem?

Samson: O. He turns everything into one. He think being a homosexual makes you a part of some special species.

Miss Thing 2: Endangered, right. I've heard that speech.

Samson: We all have. AIDS is a motherfucker, so is gangbanging, crack, ain't never seen no candlelight vigil or quilt for that shit. Fuck—what do people need with blankets they can't sleep under, what do Octavio need with all them ideas in his head. I love the fool. But it's bullshit that we all some extraterrestrial type of people.

Miss Thing 2: Yeah, but Octavio, he's unique.

Samson: He's a fucking freak.

Miss Thing 2: That's another way to phrase it.

Samson: He ain't like no other nigga I've loved. He all contradictory n shit. A bitch of a queen and then a straight-out dick in the way only a male can be. Ghetto n bougie. Sometimes I think he straight-up old school and he take me back to the day when I would take my first boyfriend to the junior high school dance.

Miss Thing 2: And slow dance to "Always and Forever"? You may not have inherited the guilt, Samson, but you have the corny nostalgia gene down. What side do you think it's from?

Samson: C'mon, let's get this puppy going. *(Referencing picture in book.)* You want the hanger, too?

Miss Thing 2: Definitely. *(Beat.)*

Samson: 2, I . . .

Miss Thing 2: Don't trip. I talk shit, but I know how to keep a secret.

Samson: Confessions are strictly confidential, ain't they, Father Thing?

Miss Thing 2: I like that. Or maybe Miss Mother Superior Thing.

(The Posse returns with 40s and burritos.)

Miss Thing 1: ¡Coño, carajo! We were gone forever. You ain't done yet?

Plum: Done, they ain't even drawed it on. We got to go.

Miss Thing 2: And where are you going without me?

Miss Thing 1: To visit djdj in the hospital.

Plum: Could I use your phone to call . . . Octavio.

Samson: *(Nods yes.)* Tell him I said what's up.

Miss Thing 2: I went and saw djdj yesterday and said goodbye. You been yet?

Samson: Wasn't really planning on it, seeing as we share an ex. Not really my place.

Plum: *(On the phone.)* Octavio. Me n 1 are swinging by . . . to take you to see djdj. I don't care if you ain't been in a hospital since you was born, you're coming with us. I ain't got time for it, Octavio, and dj has no time left. *(Everyone looks at her.)* Be ready in fifteen. *(Hangs up phone.)*

Scene 8—The Ice Queen Melteth

(Octavio's apartment. Octavio is a strung-out mess, in front of a large mirror of speed. Knock at the door. Octavio doesn't move, does a line.)

Octavio: It's open. *(Snorts line.)*

(Plum & Miss Thing 1 enter.)

Plum: *(Looking at the altered state of Octavio's apartment.)* Damn. What happened to your place?

Miss Thing 1: Forget about the place. Miss Thing, who carjacked your face? You look a wreck!

Octavio: I know. I don't have any food to offer you guys. Want some water? Want a line?

(Plum starts opening windows.)

Plum: Open up some windows. We're not in mourning yet.

Octavio: Do we have to do this?

Plum & Miss Thing 1: Yes!

Octavio: But I hate hospitals and mortuaries and all that damn baby's breath in all those horrible bouquets of multicolored carnations. I only want gardenias at my funeral.

Plum: Cut the wit.

Miss Thing 1: And stop cutting lines. We got shit to deal with, baboso endrogado.

Octavio: I don't want to deal with any of this—my boyfriend leaving me, my ex-husband dying, my club closing. Sure you don't want a bump, 1?

Plum: For someone who's got the world convinced that they're a mad genius, . . .

Miss Thing 1: . . . you could be such a stupid bitch sometimes. Let's press, Plum, we ain't got time for all this. *(To Octavio.)*

Plum: Call us when you come to your senses, or come down.

Miss Thing 1: Whichever comes first. *(They go to leave.)*

Plum: We'll give Damoso your regards.

Octavio: Damoso? I thought I was the only one who knew his full name. Damoso Juan after Dámaso Pérez Prado—leave it to fuckin truchos to name their son after a Cuban making mambo in Mexico. Only in the Mission. *(Pause.)* Hold up. I'll go. But I need to get dressed.

Miss Thing 1: Yes, you do. Apúrate fea, porque ya me tienes harta.

Plum: And lay off the such until we get through this shit.

Octavio: OK. But I'm doing every known barbiturate until the funeral and either ecstasy or acid the day of.

Miss Thing 1: That's on you. Just hurry the fuck up.

Plum: We got to press.

(They exit.)

Scene 9—Hush Little Baby, Don't Say a Word

(djdj lies in hospital bed, Plum and Thing 1 hug him gingerly and leave a skittish Octavio alone with him. djdj goes to speak, Octavio approaches and shushes him.)

Octavio: Oh, why bother with words? At this point, we get the gist. So, this is what it's come to? Fuck, man, brother, love—you've been all those things to me. So, you think I gave this to you or you gave it to me or we both already had it when we got together? No matter, I suppose. No, I haven't told Samson yet, we're not speaking. I know, I know he's a good man, but he's so, so painfully legible. Like one of his tats, you can see all the details and shading from a distance. Yeah, I do. You must be going crazy without music. I'll bring you a boom box, shit, I'll throw a club up in this piece in a minute. You getting tired? Me too. Can I stay? I'll sleep in the chair. I'll sing you a lullaby. Well, hum.

(Octavio hums, "Hush little baby, don't say a word, Momma's gonna buy you a mockingbird, and if that mockingbird don't sing Momma's gonna buy you a diamond ring.")

Scene 10—Oooh, Ima Tell

(Next morning. Samson & Thing 2 in bed together, after having sex. Janet Jackson's "Any Time, Any Place" plays beneath.)

Miss Thing 2: He'll kill us both.

Samson: No, he'll pick one to die, the other to watch. And he couldn't kill us himself and the only people he know who'd do it for him are my homies. Relax, he ain't finding out, is he?

Miss Thing 2: Not from me. And this is one story not to put into rhyme with Thing 1. But O's gonna take one look at me and know. He know everything.

Samson: Sheeit. All Octavio know is how to spend money on drugs, books, and clothes. Unless you plan on printing twenties with the fact that you got with me, he ain't gonna know. Besides, this ain't gonna be no regular thing.

Miss Thing 2: Oh, like that.

Samson: No, not like that. Ven pa'ca mahal. Let's make some more secrets.

(Phone rings, machine picks up. They ignore it as they kiss. It's Octavio. They stop.)

Octavio: *(Voice-over.)* Hey, it's me. I spent the night with dj. He died early this morning. I've been walking around the city since. It was beautiful, in a way . . . a trip. Beautiful? Huh, I'm tripping. People are beginning to come out. I hate how life just keeps going on. *(Pause.)* I look a wreck, Ima go hide in a bar. But serious, do call me back. If you want to. No, call me even if you don't. Later, pa . . . Samson. Whatever. Bye.

(Miss Thing 2 and Samson sit up in bed stunned, 2 begins to cry. Samson holds him the way one would a wounded child. Lights fade.)

Scene 11—Trans Confessions

(In Plum's apartment, Plum prepares to inject Natasha in the ass.)

Plum: Hold still.

Natasha: I'm nervous. *(Plum injects her.)* Ouch!

Plum: There. One shot against patriarchy. Dag, the boys are gonna trip.

Natasha: Sheeit. I ain't studying those queens. I'm leaving the life of faggotry behind.

Plum: It ain't gonna be that easy. It's not like you can snap your fingers and *bam!*, you a woman.

Natasha: That was just my first shot of perlutal, I'm not about to fly to Thailand tomorrow for the chop. I'm already freaked enough about getting on the Greyhound to tell my momma. I can see myself just showing up on her front porch. Hi Momma, say goodbye to Nathaniel Douglass, hello Natasha Kinky . . . I can't tell my momma I'm kinky!

Plum: Your mother named you Nathaniel Douglass?

Natasha: After Nat Turner and Frederick Douglass. At the height of the movement and her 'fro. Maybe I should just call or write or send a picture.

Plum: Nah, blood, go to her, give her the chance to get to know Natasha. And get yourself used to the loss of that male privilege.

Natasha: I ain't ever been happy to be in this body. Please understand that.

Plum: I do, but I also know waking up and being a sister every day ain't easy. Go home as you are, Nat, think of it as hibernation.

Natasha: Or maybe cocooning?

Plum: Touché.

Natasha: Well, okay. Let's see. *(Nat looks at Greyhound schedule.)* I can make the 4:45 train and still have time to stop by Marshall's and Loehman's and get more daywear.

Plum: You're not gonna stay for dj's services?

Natasha: Nah, funerals ain't my thing. We said our so-longs . . . and he had Octavio give me his Donna Summer scrapbook. *(Pause.)* Could you say toodle-oo to Octavio, the Things, and Samson for me?

Plum: OK, sistergirl, but once you come back you're gonna have to learn to momma yourself. It's just the basics of black womanhood. Have a wonderful journey.

Natasha: Here's my mom's number . . . but just to be on the safe side, ask for Nathaniel.

(They hug and Natasha exits.)

Scene 12—Two Pews

(Samson, Thing 1, and Thing 2 in one pew going through the various gesticulations of a Catholic mass—crossing themselves, standing, sitting, kneeling. Plum and Octavio, in another pew, are lost to the ritual, whisper between each other as they follow the boys, a half step off.)

Plum: What kind of Mexican are you? You don't know any of the right moves.

Octavio: This isn't a dance floor. How you gonna talk? I thought well-raised black girls went to church.

Plum: Episcopalian and Lutheran—I'm from High Church Negroes. Was Damoso religious?

Octavio: Enough that this isn't a betrayal.

(Pause. At the mention of dj's name, the grief hits them both, and they hug. When they break the embrace, they see the boys shaking hands. The service is ending.)

Plum: We have to shake our neighbor's hands now.

Octavio: That move I got covered.

(Octavio and Samson lock eyes, approach, shake hands.)

Epilogue—The People You Love Die

Octavio: We weren't sure where else to have this. But we figured djdj is really buried in Aztlantis, not Colma.

Plum: Those of you who knew Damoso even for a little while knew this is where he truly lived.

Miss Thing 1: He lived to watch the kids living.

Plum: So, we thought we'd just play some music, talk a bit about the silent one

Miss Thing 2: who filled this dance floor with track after beautiful bombastic booty-shaking track.

Octavio: These aren't good times. We're losing this war and many others. Seems we have momentarily forgotten we are indeed warriors. And now we no longer have one of our strongest with us to remind us every weekend. That's what deaths like these do, they take away leadership. The people you love die.

(They all embrace.)

Octavio: We're also closing down Aztlantis, and not because of what you've heard about me. *(He glares at the Things, they smile back.)*

Miss Thing 1: While we twirled to Roger Sanchez, Johnny Dynell, Frankie Feliciano,

Miss Thing 2: Dmitri, Masters at Work, Doc Martin, Tony Largo, Aaron O,

Plum: David Harness, Tim Martinez, Alec Cunningham, and Mauricio Aviles,

Miss Thing 1: djdj was the resident up in here and we close it knowing he and his music will always be presente!

Miss Thing 2: Octavio here is gonna try his hands at another house scene.

Octavio: LA, New York, London, Goa, quien sabe. But it's not true. Like djdj, like all of you, I will always be here. Aztlantis wasn't just a club or a mismatched family or some weird attempt at tribe. It certainly wasn't a business. It was a politic we made every weekend out of synthetic chemicals and fabrics, yes, but also out of the history of our bodies and djdj's sonics. Here in the treble and bass of your soul, sex, and shade. In the house of your desire.

Plum: Thank you for coming, there's food.

Samson: Hey, that was nice, what you said.

Octavio: Thanks. Thank your mom again for cooking so much.

Samson: You could tell her yourself, she's here.

Octavio: She don't hate me?

Samson: No, she doesn't. I don't either. Call me sometime.

Octavio: Well, I am going away, at least for a while, clear my head. But I'm never gonna clean up my act, Samson. I will never be the marrying, law-abiding, clean and sober kind.

Samson: That's fine, just don't be such a dick all the time and come down sometimes, shit. Deal?

Octavio: Deal, except right now I could really use some K or opium or maybe some Klonopin, tengo ansia. Good thing I made sure to invite every dealer to this event.

Samson: Event? It's a memorial.

Octavio: Yes, yes, quite right. Do excuse me, there's a promoter I really need to talk to.

Samson: I love you and your messed-up head.

Octavio: Hey, can I schedule some work?

Samson: The wings can't need a touch-up already.

Octavio: No, I want something on my left hip for Damoso. You know, in homage.

Samson: Of?

Octavio: A record. djdj left me his all his vinyl. This track.

(He puts on "When I Fell in Love.")

El Fin

EL SANTO JOTO

To Juan

For Connie, Jesse, and Loras

Written while the author was Visiting Multicultural Faculty at the Theatre School at DePaul University and presented along with students' work in "An Evening of Plays Not Written by Neil LaBute" organized by Gil Tanner on November 16, 2012; and {YOUR NAME HERE}, A Queer Theater Company, presented the play as part of "Holiday Blips! A Holiday Themed Evening of Short Queer Plays" directed by Gretchen Van Lente at New York's TADA Theater on December 12, 2012.

The DePaul Cast featured Ruben David Adorno as El Joto en Cuero, Cameron Benoit as El Santo Joto, and Lauren Guglielmello as La Jota Bombera.

————————

(Stage is set as three discrete altar spaces.

Stage right is the area for El Joto en Cuero, a Brown faggot in leather. His colors are black and blue. He has a chair and table, perhaps a vanity. His objects include a mirror for looking at himself and doing lines on, a bottle of poppers, and a mini-hourglass, the kind that come with a game like Boggle. A disco ball hangs above him.

Center stage is for El Santo Joto del SIDA, the sainted fag of AIDS, and he sits in a chair posed as El Santo Niño de Atocha, with gourd and fan. His colors are desert sand and sky blue.

Stage left is La Jota Bombera, a Chicana lesbian firefighter. Her color is red, fire-engine/SF 49ers red. She sits in a rocking chair and has a joint and an abalone shell ashtray. A potted tree shades her.)

El Joto en Cuero: When we first met, I found you weak. And I, I was big and loud with undergraduate rage. You were a less than recent grad of the same school. We sat in that Berkeley apartment. Whose? Not Refugio's. Fugie lived in the apartment that had belonged to that South Asian guy who took all those frat kids hostage at Henry's. Not Fugie's but a place like his—'70s Cali bungalow and a person like him—a sucio brown boy cleaning and classing up at the University of California at Berkeley. We sat under fluorescent lighting and the neon condoms went over the bananas and dildo, I want it to be purple cuz I want to complete the tutti-frutti color scheme but it could have been Band-Aid beige or cafeteria milk-chocolate brown.

I got there late, I think. I definitely left early. I wanted to do what I always wanted to do which was talk politics and war and conflict and philosophy and revolution while getting high and then going to the club. I'm pretty sure I ran to the club right after. The White Ho? Or did we head into the city?

Ni modo. You were determined to do your workshop. And were doing it with Martin, who is a stickler for sticking to the script. I wanted to say, and in my head was screaming, this is not useful, this is not how it happens. Fucking, I mean. You don't sit around a room passing around the primary-colored prophylactics and using *Robert's Rules of Order* like we learned in MECHA. Were there chips and salsa? There should have been poppers.

But this was at the peak of CDC funding targeting gay men of color. And I, like you, had long been a Brown boy who hung at Black gay clubs. This wasn't clear to me then. Our connection, I mean. So little was clear to my overly self-important self then.

El Santo Joto: I remember it differently. Not you. You are right. You were an over-the-top obnoxious bourgeois revolutionary brat. But the time.

It was after AZT but before cocktails. Everybody was trying to get into clinical trials like they were in line for that guest-list-only club in SF, Crew. It was like how I imagine walking right after an avalanche feels like. The air hushed, chastened, stilled, and the horrors and tumult of the seconds before already buried deep deep down. We were still burying our brothers at an alarming rate.

El Joto en Cuero: Well, that's inaccurate, we did the loving and the buttwiping and the all-night crying and the ecstasy to get through the funeral. The family or the state usually handled the funeral arrangements. Never open casket, cuz honey, please, who wants to remember someone so fine, I mean all the menzez up at the clubs or at least one every night was his.

El Santo Joto: Who wants to remember him forsaken and formaldehyded like that?

El Joto en Cuero: I do. I want to remember them all. It's been ten, fifteen years since some of them, you, died. I can still hear your voice, defiant and rich.

El Santo Joto: "I don't have HIV, I am HIV."

La Jota Bombera: Wind. Through leaves. Or chimes. And I know it's you. You're not in the constant fog. Or in the regularity of rain and damp that makes San Francisco Frisco. But in the tickling wind that makes strands of seashells sing. There's my Juan. You don't come with pronouncements or lessons or dictates. Just laughter. It's nice. Not to be reminded you're dead. But that you were here.

(The Jackson Sisters' "I Believe in Miracles" comes on.)

El Santo Joto: I believe in God.
I believe La Virgencita watches over us all. Us being raza. I
believe El Santo Ñino de Atocha helped my family make it across
la frontera to this life.
I believe I am sinless.
I believe in sex.

El Joto en Cuero: I believe today, December 12th, should now and forever be known as Juan Rodríguez Day. I think Nuestra Virgencita won't mind, she has already shared this day with Juan Diego por siglos. On Juan Rodríguez Day there is full amnesty without the ridiculous call for compulsory military service, nor is the Dream Act only a dream enacted for young people seeking education. Clean needles are available throughout cities and municipalities, no questions asked, no shade thrown. Condoms, tampons, STI screening, HIV tests, mammograms, pap smears, the pill and the morning-after pill, abortions are all available for free and on demand. Sexual reassignment surgery no longer requires a gender dysmorphia decree and thus being transgender is no longer criminal, a mental illness or imbalance. Childcare, healthcare, prenatal care, heat, running water, electricity are free, safe, and on demand.

Juan Rodríguez (concept development), William Sandoval / Graphic Works (design), and Mark A. Vieira (photography), from the series *¡Siempre con Condón!*, 1988. Courtesy of the University of Minnesota Libraries, Jean-Nickolaus Tretter Collection in Gay, Lesbian, Bisexual and Transgender Studies.

On Juan Rodríguez Day the young have sexual rights, including the right to their sexual sovereignty and autonomy.

On Juan Rodríguez Day, which I proclaim to be forthwith every December 12th dia de las jotas, sex work is not a crime but rather highly skilled union labor.

Textbooks return to classrooms, as does bilingual education.

On Juan Rodríguez Day we are brought to bear witness to our sexual selves and we reclaim the glory holes, the tearooms, the bushes, and the piers. We tell NIMBY and developers to fuck off as we fuck.

La Jota Bombera: I believe in the morning.
In noticing the day change but not the hours click by.
In loving my family, including my family of mujeres, lovers, and friends.
That joints are the best way to smoke weed.
That the government, racists, sexists, homophobes cannot find me if I refuse to be found.

El Joto en Cuero: I just can't believe you are still dead and I am alive and I am now over ten years older than you were when you died. I have, at forty-three, outlived

Sylvester, Reza Abdoh, Essex Hemphill, maybe Marlon and Assotto too. How is this at all possible? Permissible. I don't believe in genius or that we stand on the shoulders of giants—but y'all were my tías and older brothers and while I can't abide the use of the term *elder* except for those who are truly into their crone years, what does it mean when peers become ancestors? How to lead without leadership? I do know, like how Jesse always said of wave 1 and 2 of the homocide, that they took the best of us. The smartest. The most beautiful. The biggest whores. The freest and the truest. We have complacently stayed behind, and whether we care to remember, bother to light a candle, refuse to forget your names, eyes, and cum, we just breathe on while our rage withers away.

La Jota Bombera: The weekend you died, San Diego was pretty as always. The mesas and canyons make even the most city parts of this militarized border place feel like country, rancho. There are more Indian tribes in this part of SoCal than in any other part and not just the Diegeños or Las Viejas. The Indians from then learned these plateaus and valleys. Where to grow things and hide. Stay hid for a century or so until the outlet malls and casinos made 'em a destination again.

The Indians we are, are all packed into one motel room. Me and four stinking snoring men. We have enough money for more rooms. Well, some of us, some of the men do. I don't. Didn't. Then.

But we cram into this space together and smoke weed and laugh and stay silent a lot. Except for the snoring. None of us cry. We are as dry and cool as the December weather outside. There are storms in me. Raging ocean waves of desire and riptides of want. But not that night. The night before your funeral. I am a lake, clear and clean. Drink from me.

El Joto en Cuero: The day I carried your casket into your memorial service, the air smelled like any other San Diego morning. Sea salt, fog, cement, car exhaust, sun, clean Mexicans. We weren't official pallbearers, it's just that your casket arrived and we were there to carry the dead weight of you.

It was after that, after carrying your casketed dead body into your final service after a life of service and struggle cut way too short, that I realized how strong you were. How much fight you had in you. How devastating this disease. How unkind this country. How good this group of Mexicans. How holy this day. December 12th. Juan Rodríguez Day.

NI MADRE

Commissioned by Diane Rodríguez, codirector of the Latino Theater Initiative and associate artistic director at CTG, as part of "Amor Eterno: Six Lessons in Love." Rodríguez directed a staged reading at LA's Ivy Substation in May 2003. Rodríguez produced a staged reading directed by Laurie Woolery with dramaturgy by Cherríe Moraga at Hollywood's Ricardo Montalbán Theater in June 2004. Rodríguez directed a staged reading at El Teatro Campesino in San Juan Bautista, California, in January 2005. It was subsequently enfolded into the first act of Cherríe Moraga's *The Mathematics of Love*, directed by Shayok Misha Chowdhury, which was workshopped at Stanford University May 5–8, 2016, and premiered in San Francisco at Brava Theater Center on August 10, 2017. It was directed by Cherríe Moraga with the following cast:

Girl:	Rose Portillo
Nana:	Carla Pantoja
Malinxe:	Vero Maynez

(The Biltmore Hotel, the Northern Territories of New Spain, circa 1528.)

Scene I

(Nana, an Indian indentured servant, scrubs the floor. A Silvestre Revueltas overture morphs into something from the Kronos Quartet's album Nuevo. *Malinxe enters. She pauses and replaces one pair of black sunglasses with a pair of large red-frame sunglasses and touches up her lipstick. Nana still scrubs.)*

Malinxe: Girl. Girl.

(Girl, Malinxe's servant, an Indian from much farther south whose petulance is in direct proportion-opposition to her social position's required obedience. She pulls a cart with a small pyramid of Louis Vuitton luggage. Malinxe and Girl stand at the front desk, waiting to be served. Malinxe speaks to Girl, who doesn't pay her much mind.)

Malinxe: I, Malinxe, have never been this far north. Don Cortés took me as far south as Honduras, and what an adventure that expedition was. I met all manner of people and spoke at the subjugation of many. Strange, to ride through a battlefield translating Spanish and Nahuatl into Maya telling bloodied limbs and half faces they were now part of the Spanish Crown. I didn't mind except for all the dust. But upon my return, little girl, why poets wrote of me, calling me Mother, quite an honorific, especially when I had yet to give birth.

(Malinxe laughs. Girl rolls her eyes and Nana stands, removes bandanna from her head, folds it neatly into her apron, replacing it with a red cap. When she crosses behind lobby desk, Nana's entire demeanor changes.)

Nana: How may I serve you?

(They exchange looks in silence.)

Malinxe: I have a reservation.

(Nana looks down.)

Nana: Let's see, Malinche Cortés.

Malinxe: That is a prior name and previous relationship. I am Doña Malinche Jaramillo. Or just Malinxe.

Nana: Yes, of course, here you are, please sign here.

(Malinxe signs parchment. Nana looks at it.)

Nana: Malinxe, with an *x*?

Malinxe: I'm traveling incognito.

(Nana rings desk bell and goes into rote performance.)

Nana: Well, here at Mission Spa & Towers we provide the finest in New Spain's care and services. As one of the uppermost outposts in the viceroy's magistrate, we think of ourselves as her crown jewel. But like any jewel, we could all use a good buffing now and then. We offer purgatives and a special Indian package, including a sweat and purification with thistle.

Malinxe: Thistle?

Nana: A thorned plant, specially imported from the Mission down in San Diego. The Indians there use it to beat the impurities out of you.

Malinxe: Me?

(Nana breaks from brochure-speak.)

Nana: One.

Malinxe: I'll just need a large room con vista and a daybed. See to it that my slave, I picked her up en route, and one of yours here at the hotel, carry my luggage upstairs with great care and unpack my things. Then send mine down to accompany me on my walk before we retire for siesta.

(An awkward silence, and then Nana whispers in confidence to Malinxe.)

Nana: We don't allow them to sleep in the rooms. We have daily baptisms and accelerated catechism, and hope to soon have these local rascal nacos under the rule of God and Spain, but we can't allow slaves to sleep in the rooms. *(In a more hushed but clearly audible tone.)* Their feet stain everything and we can never get the smell out of the sheets. You understand? *(Back to full volume.)* We allow them to sleep in the back here for two to four hours nightly depending on your schedule of needs. And for servants of the house, we provide this mat. *(She pulls from behind her desk a rolled straw mat.)* Here.

(Nana holds mat out to Malinxe who doesn't move. Girl goes for it.)

Girl: Just give it here.

Malinxe: *(To Nana.)* Yes, well, thank you. I'd like to sign the girl up for catechism. She has been baptized, but I'd like to have her do her Holy Communion while I rest. *(To Girl.)* We'll get the Indian out of you yet, and who knows, my little slave girl may grow up to become my Christian lady in waiting.

Malinxe: *(To Nana.)* Can you have my luggage delivered to my room?

Nana: I'll have it brought up right away.

(*Malinxe exits. Nana, looking at Girl, scowls.*)

Nana: Well???

(*Girl trudges off with the luggage.*)

Scene II

(*Night floods the lobby with blue-black darkness. Nana enters in sleeping gown, weary from a day, like all of her days, of cooking, chopping, scrubbing, sweating, answering to, wiping some asses and kissing others. Girl enters wearing sleepwear. She is surprised to see Nana rolling out a mat.*)

Nana: What, Girl? *(Girl says nothing.)* Whose feet do you think they made the rule for? *(Nana laughs. Girl remains silent, rolls out her mat, and lies down. After a beat, Girl stirs.)*

Girl: Tell me a story.

Nana: Better yet. I'll tell you a secret. *(Pause.)*

Girl: Is it about mi Doña Malinxe? I know all those.
  After her cacique daddy died, her mother married another cacique and she was either stolen by traveling merchants or sold to them by her step-cacique or her mother and brother. No one knows for sure—and she's not telling. She was sold twice into slavery before being one of nineteen girls "gifted" to Cortés and his men upon their arrival, when she was just about my age.

Nana: She was christened Marina on the spot and given to one of the ship's captains. Her knowledge of Nahua and Maya served useful to the warfaring strangers and she translated as they pummeled and dismantled the Triple Alliance.

Girl: And then she had Cortés's son, el Bastardo.

Nana: That's unkind.

Girl: Yes, but not untrue. Then she married el Don and lives in wealth and luxury in the seat of the Viceroyalty, the Archdiocese of the Catholic Church, the Holy Office of the Inquisition, Mexico City, New Spain.

Nana: Teotihuacán is far too old to be called new, no matter what the visitors say.

Girl: Enough history. What about the secret? I have to wake up soon—before the sun does. I have to bring her food and sponge her in the morning. Help her dress and then clean the room. Then go to catechism.

Nana: *(Interrupting.)* I can time travel.

Girl: *(Not listening.)* Then after that I have to return and see to her needs, which are many. You can what?

Nana: Travel in and through time—mostly backward but some forward. You could do it too, one day, if you concentrate. Why, I can even make time disappear.

Girl: Can you disappear too?

Nana: If I could, I wouldn't be here.

Girl: I don't believe you. I mean, soon it will be time to get up and time to feed her and time to fix her bed and clean up her mess in the room and time to help her dress and time to steal some of her copal perfume and leftover blackberries while she naps. How can you time travel when you can't even tell a good story?

Nana: You are very rude.

Girl: I know, una niña mala.

Nana: Good night, bad girl.

Girl: Good night, worse woman.

(They both go to sleep, smiling.)

Scene III

(The Family Stand's "The Passion" plays throughout scene. Girl enters in passion fruit flower costume.)

Malinxe: *(Laughing.)* What, pray tell, are you, Girl?

Girl: I . . . *(Bowing with much pomp and circumstance.)* I am the passion fruit flower. *(Drops the act.)* Or I was today in our rehearsal.

Malinxe: Rehearsal?

Girl: Yes. We perform tonight to demonstrate our faith and knowledge. I begged to wear the costume to show you and promised to clean the classroom and yard if the nuns let me wear it a bit longer.

Malinxe: But what does that have to do with your study of the scriptures, Girl?

Girl: Study? They aren't teaching us to read. But we are memorizing important lessons. Like that of the passion fruit flower and the suffering of Christ. See my outer green petals? There are twelve; one for each apostle. And the inner ones, all white and purple? They are my favorites. There are five, and they represent Jesus's wounds: one head, two hands, and two feet. And the three fuzzy brown ones are the nails they used to crucify our Savior.

Malinxe: I love parcha.

Girl: Yes, and that shows that you love Christ. *(Quoting the catechism instructor.)* "The Indians' love for the passion fruit shows their hunger to know Christ."

Malinxe: Well, I would enjoy some parcha. *(To Nana.)* Can you see to that?

Nana: Right away, ma'am.

   (Malinxe exits.)

Nana: I hate maracuya. *(She spits.)*

Scene IV

(Girl enters wearing a jacket of ropes, a headdress of heron feathers, and a tumpline [or headstrap] holding a bundle. She has been crying.)

Malinxe: What have you done?

Girl: When I went to return the costume after the show, I got some passion fruit juice on it. It stained.

Malinxe: You thieving witch.

Girl: And the nuns made me wear this, so I would remember what it would be like to be a slave who didn't know God.

Nana: *(Examining the costume.)* My heron feathers disintegrated over time. And this is a good tumpline, I would like one just like it. Take the jacket off, Girl.

Malinxe: She's mine to command, you insolent hag. But yes, do remove the headdress and tumpline and ropes. And you, *(to Nana)* you, take her outside and find a very green branch or some of that thistle you have imported and open up her back with it.

(Girl is stunned and methodically removes headdress, tumpline, and ropes and gingerly folds them. Nana leads her out by the hand. Malinxe goes to the headdress, fingers it, then awkwardly puts it on.)

Malinxe: Let me see if I remember. I must, I was sold at least three times. *(Beat.)* The slave. She who is an axe, a tumpline, the earth, the mud, the the the—oh, what is it—the stones, yes, and then something something, she who has heron feathers and a jacket of ropes, and then I forget, but yes, the ending I remember, she whose dwelling place is the cesspool, the dung heap. *(Happy at first at the prowess of her memory and then dejected by the meaning of it, Malinxe paces the lobby.)* Here I am, with wealth and recognition in the Church, Spain, and all her possessions. Wearing my rightful crown *(she adjusts the headdress)* . . . Queen of the Slaves.

Scene V

(Soft spotlight on Girl, who stands on stage alone in a white Holy Communion veil. She holds white pumps in her hands. The back of her dress is open, and she wears a gauze bandage over her wound.)

Girl: I'm healing now. She didn't use a branch or the thistle, said it cost too much to waste on a slave. Instead, she used bougainvillea, said the thorns would make it look worse than it felt. She told me to stand very still and concentrate. And I did it. I time traveled. As the red petals flew around me and my back bled tears, I traveled through time. Mostly forward. I will return to the far South. Mi Doña will be dead in a year but spoken about throughout time. I will become her daughter's servant. I am the OG criada. When I die, I will have been called Girl for so long that no one, not even me, can remember my name.

(She begins to leave but thinks better of it and stops short, turns to the audience.)

Girl: When Nana was done whipping me, she blew on my back and cooed that she would make me a poultice with medicine she grew. I gave her the tumpline, the nuns will just think I stole it, and I won't be beaten for it twice. And then she turned me toward her and held me soft and told me she loved me.

Girl: *(Stiffly begins to exit, and as she marches out, she declares:)* I will travel this far north again.

(A son jarocho blasts.

Bougainvillea petals rain down.)

End.

MEXICAN PSYCHOTIC

En memoriam: Noah Purifoy, Pedro Pietri, y Martín Ramírez

MEXICAN PSYCHOTIC

Flyer for *Mexican Psychotic* (designed by Fernando Mancuello and Ricardo A. Bracho).

BY RICARDO A. BRACHO

A SILENT PLAY WITH SLIDE TEXT ON THE LIFE AND WORK OF OUTSIDER ARTIST **MARTIN RAMIREZ**

COLLABORATING ARTISTS INCLUDE:
SETH ABRAMES, VARIN AYALA, PATRICK "PATO" HEBERT,
FERNANDO MANCUELLO, RACHELLE MENDEZ,
AOLE T. MILLER, JOSEPH D. SOLIS Y ANDREA THOME

MARCH 22, 23 – 7:00 P.M.
PS 122 BUILDING, 2ND FLOOR
MABOU MINES STUDIO
150 1ST AVENUE AT 9TH STREET

FREE – FOR RESERVATIONS CALL 212.473.0559

Mexican Psychotic was developed in the Mabou Mines Resident Artist Program led by Lee Breuer and Ruth Maleczech. It was first performed in the Mabou Mines Studio in PS 122 in 2004, coproduced by Rachelle Mendez and starring Mendez as Martín Ramírez. The play was completed when Bracho was Artist/ Scholar in Residence for UC Santa Barbara's Center for Chicano Studies, with a culminating performance on campus in June 2005. Bracho has presented the projected text at UC San Diego, Ohio University, Stanford, and UC Riverside. While a Fall 2021 Fellow in the Center for Experimental Ethnography at the University of Pennsylvania, he adapted the play into a video with Nicholas Plante, Emily Dunlop, and Oludare Marcelle. A rough draft screened at the university in December 2021, accompanied by a panel with James Hough, Toorjo Ghose, Jennifer Ponce de León, and Aaron Alarcón, who discussed mental health, art praxis, and incarceration. As part of the Center for Experimental Ethnography's Fifth Anniversary Carnival, programmed by its director, Professor Deborah Thomas, the final version premiered in the Penn Museum on May 1, 2023.

Mabou Mines Ensemble: Rachelle Mendez as Martín Ramírez; and in multiple roles, Aole Miller, Andrea Thome, Seth Abrames, and Varín Ayala. The author built the altar, Cristina Ibarra and Alex Rivera provided tech knowledge for the projected text, and Joseph Solis and Alvin Greathose provided the tamales.

UC Santa Barbara cast: Minerva García as Martín Ramírez; and in multiple roles, Richard Azurdia, Jamie Birkett, Tony Breen, and Cristina Frias. Dahlia Elsayed was the dramaturg, Andrew Demirjian executed the projected text, and Fernando Mancuello designed the play's graphic.

(This play is performed like a silent film. The centered, boldface bits of text are projected intertitles. Other incidental sounds and effects are performed by offstage actors. One actor plays Martín; all others assume various roles.)

(Music plays as people enter, then stops as lights are lowered to black.

The Candy-Striped Girl enters in darkness and crumples a piece of paper with one hand.

Light of the projector is turned on.

She mimes lighting a match while offstage another actor lights a match.

As she burns some of Martín's drawings, music plays and the ffstage sound of horse and train.

Candy-Striped Girl exits.)

"A gasp is better than silence."
Gayatri Chakravorty Spivak

(Four actors take stage and open their mouths wide like hungry baby birds.)

1885
or 1895,
Naces en Jalisco

As beautiful as
sweet white corn
with none to eat

Like you, Mexico was poor and starved

(Three break out of their unison action and fly offstage, one at a time.

Actor playing Martín is left alone on stage, a still-hungry bird.

His opening mouth becomes a cry and then becomes a cough executed by an offstage actor.)

Tuberculosis + hard work as a laundryman + no food = Migration

Martín Ramírez immigrated to the US
sometime between 1900 and 1910
and settled in Los Angeles

(Three actors enter and each takes an LA Mexican pose—one swaggering down block, another selling fruit, one reading off their phone.)

cuz like Tupac say,
LA wouldn't be LA without Mexicans
The Revolution Martín

(Offstage the pop of party favor poppers.)

Here are some scenes from the Revolution you missed
John Reed

(John Reed enters with writing tablet, styles and profiles.)

Socialist New York journalist
Described by Renato Leduc

as "the simpático gringo journalist"
and who would later document
the Russian Revolution
to great acclaim

and be played by Warren Beatty

(Actor walks across stage as Warren Beatty as John Reed.)

first covered the Mexican Revolution
for the *Metropolitan*

These two ensuing scenes
are directly quoted from his account
Insurgent Mexico

The Expulsion of the Spaniards

(Actors enter as General Pancho Villa, British Vice-Consul Scobell, US Consul Letcher. Villa enters.)

Villa: Which is the Spanish consul?

Scobell: I represent the Spaniards.

Villa: All right. Tell them to begin to pack.
Any Spaniard caught within the boundaries of the state
after five days will be escorted to the nearest wall by the firing squad.

(Scobell and Letcher let out gasps of horror, which actors execute offstage. The consuls give a gasp of horror. Villa cuts them short.)

Villa: (*Cutting them short.*) The Spaniards must go.

Letcher: General, I don't question your motives,
but I think you are making a grave political mistake . . .

Villa: Señor Consul, we Mexicans have had
three hundred years of Spaniards.
They have not changed in character
since the Conquistadores.
They disrupted the Indian empire
and enslaved the people.
We did not ask them to mingle their blood with ours.
Twice we drove them out of Mexico.

They returned to steal away our land,
to make the people slaves.
They thrust on us
the greatest superstition
the world has ever known
—the Catholic Church.
They ought to be killed for that alone.

Scobell: Five days is not enough time to reach all the Spaniards with this news.

Villa: Then they have ten.

(Villa exits. Scobell and Letcher are dumbfounded still. Actor hmmms offstage.)

On Women's Suffrage

(Pancho Villa and John Reed sit, awaiting lunch. Reed questions Villa. Music.)

Reed: What do you think of socialism?

Villa: Is it a thing? I only see it in books, and I do not read much.

Reed: And will women vote in your new republic?

(Villa laughs and laughs and laughs.)

Villa: Do you mean elect a government and make laws?

Reed: Yes, like in the United States.

(Villa scratches his head. Offstage actor makes scratching noise.)

Villa: Well, if they do it up there
I don't see that they shouldn't do it down here.
But they have no sternness of mind.
They are full of pity and softness.
Why, a woman would not give an order
to execute a traitor.

Reed: I am not so sure of that, mi General.
Women can be crueler and harder than men.

*(Villa stares at Reed, pulling on his mustache.
Villa's wife enters with lunch.)*

Villa: Oiga, ven.
> Last night I caught three traitors
> crossing the river to blow up the railroad.
> What shall I do with them?
> Shall I shoot them or not?

(Señora Villa is embarrassed by the question, grabs Villa's hand and kisses it.)

Señora Villa: Qué sé yo. You know best.

Villa: No, I leave it in your hands.

(He grabs her hands and kisses her palm. She giggles and pulls her hand away, beginning to exit. She turns to Reed and Villa and makes her kissed hand a gun. Actor makes all the kissing, giggling, and shooting noises offstage.)

Señora Villa: Oh, well, shoot them.

(She points and shoots and exits. Reed and Villa stare and grin at each other.)

Did you hear these stories from other wetbacks, Martín?
Is that Villa in his twenty-two years as an outlaw bandido
and then as a guerrillero
in all your drawings?
Did you think,
upon hearing these stories,
if in fact you heard these stories,
"I should go home and be among my people
and not starve alone in this now-foreign place"?
Or were you already too far
crazed and destroyed
by this place of ghosts and steel?
You lost your goddamn Mexican mind and vagabonded
for fifteen years
What Martín did, where he lived
what happened to Martín Ramírez in those fifteen years
is not known
But the constants of labor and hunger
I'm sure were there.

In 1930, in a police sweep of downtown Los Angeles,
Martín is "captured" and jailed.

(Martín looks over his shoulder,
goes to run, and is caught,
handcuffed, and taken upstage.)

Diagnosed first as catatonic, then as
"a paranoid schizophrenic, deteriorated
and an incurable psychotic."

He went crazy from what kills us all.

Gave up language and hummed.

(Martín goes to his asylum cell upstage and chews bread.)

You stayed in the DeWitt State Hospital for thirty years.
Until your life ended.
When you began to draw is not known.
You made your own paper
from laundry slips, paper cups, and other scraps.

The "glue" you made from
mashed potatoes and water.
Bread and your own spit.
At the end of each day
your drawings,
your beautiful, beautiful drawings
were burned along with all the other inmate art
to keep the ward sanitized and hygienic.
But you hid yours from the fire,
on your person,
in your bed,
behind the radiator.

(The Candy-Striped Girl enters and takes painting. She exits and he removes
another folded piece of paper. Professor Tomar Pasto takes the stage and
writes on chalkboard, while an actor offstage makes the sound of chalk
across a blackboard.)

And then comes the day when you
and other inmates are taken
as show-and-tell to Sacramento College's
Intro to Abnormal Psychology.

You present the professor,
visiting Finnish psychologist
Dr. Tomar Pasto,
with a ream of paintings
from beneath your shirt.

(Martín hands one painting to Pasto and then keeps uncovering many more.)

Martín left us in 1960
or 1966.
Three hundred of his drawings
and all his hunger
survive.

Except that all of this is a lie.

(Martín and Tomar Pasto reverse offstage. Music plays. Martín reenters.)

The Return of the Repressed, like Amtrak, is never on time.

(Martín waits for train. Actors offstage create the sounds of an approaching train.)

Martín Ramírez was no mute.
Only a Mexican who spoke no English.
And had no one to speak Spanish with all those years inside asylums.

(The train sounds build to a roar. Martín falls as if felled by the speeding train.)

"Birthdays were the worst days."
Biggie Smalls

(Cast assembles as a group at a birthday party.)

(Each blindfolds themself and spins.)

(Martín rises, watches from a distance, sad and smiling.)

Martín Ramírez did not leave Mexico for California until 1925.
Two days after one of his daughters' second birthday.

(Before they remove their bandannas, Martín steals deer-like offstage.)

(The party sadly disperses.)

En el gallinero de la república

(Martín and three of the male actors enter in warrior stances, like bulls.)

Which means that Martín did not miss the Mexican Revolution.

(The four actors pair off and mount and prepare for a chicken fight.)

Rather, he was from a region in Jalisco
known as
the Henhouse of the Republic

(Their demeanors change, soften as they approach each other in the chicken fight. They dismount and run offstage as sissies and wusses.)

Martín, like his region, was Catholic and conservative.

(Martín enters and crosses himself and kneels to pray.)

And due to warfare,
where most of the Indian populace
of his area was decimated,
Martín was lily white.

(Two actors enter as if entering a battlefield and are quickly felled.)

(Martín rises.)

(Female actor enters and hands Martín a lily. Martín exits.)

(The dead Indians rise, nonchalant-like, and casually follow her.)

Martín arrived in 1925 to Northern,
not Southern California,
worked the rails and mines.

(Martín enters, begins to dig.

Two actors enter as cops, arrest Martín, all exit.)

In 1931 he was first picked up by the police
and entered his first mental hospital in 1935.

(Martín enters, draws.

Martín's wife enters from opposite side and receives drawing from mail carrier.)

Before his hospitalization Martín was already drawing.
Sending drawings with money home.

(She puts money in her bra, exits.

Martín stands, crazed and alone.)

This being the height of the Depression,
there was one doctor for six hundred patients.

(Other actors join as locos.)

Martín made his paper and continued to draw
and, with the other inmates,
watched movies on a projector
donated by a Hollywood production company
as therapy.

(All turn to screen and watch it like a movie.

Other actors exit. Martín is left alone and turns toward audience.)

In 1948 Martín entered DeWitt State Hospital
never to leave again.
He never did visit Tarmo Pasto's class, but Pasto did come to him.

(Pasto enters, evaluates both the artwork and Martín favorably.)

And while Martín's work was destroyed
because he was thought to have tuberculosis,
he did not in fact have it.

(Martín goes to cough, but instead smiles.)

In 1951 Pasto organized the first exhibit of Ramírez's work
in Sacramento and Martín's deer,

(Actor enters as deer.)

his horses,

(Actor enters as horse.)

and his foxy ladies

(Actor enters as foxy lady.)

delighted audiences and he continued to draw and draw.

(All exit except Martín.)

In 1952 a nephew visited him,

(Actor enters as nephew.)

stayed for two days, and asked Martín to return to Mexico.
But Martín preferred to stay where he was.

(Other actor exits.)

Besides this nephew Martín spoke Spanish with an Irish Catholic priest

(Priest enters, they converse, priest exits.)

And one doctor.

(Doctor enters, they converse, exit.)

And no one else
for all those years.

In 1963 at 5 a.m.
Martín Ramírez dies in his sleep
of a heart attack.

(Martín sleeps, then flings open eyes, dead.)

Not his wife, or three daughters,
one son, or twenty-two grandchildren
ever saw him again.

(Nurse enters and closes Martín's eyes, escorts corpse offstage.)

The myths of Martín were created by Pasto,

(Pasto enters.)

that asshole of a writer Octavio Paz,

(The pompous ass Octavio Paz enters.)

and art galleries in New York City,

(A curator enters.)

making some nice little mountains of money.

(Offstage, an actor spills coins as those onstage exit.)

Roll sound.

(Lights fade after the last coins spill.)

End.

APPETITES I HAVE INHERITED

Written for the Classic Film Project of Hero Theatre, this ten-minute play was presented at the Mack Sennett Studios in Los Angeles on September 7, 2013. Produced by Elisa Bocanegra, directed by Tina Sánchez, and performed by Ephraim López as Adán and David Leonardo Padilla as Adonis.

(Two impossibly beautiful brown men on an island shore. Adán, an actor in his thirties, reads a filmscript. He is serious, muscular, knowing. Adonis, a dancer in his twenties, uses binoculars to focus at a point offstage. Adonis is lithe, enthusiastic, joyful. Both are in costume: white short shorts or drawstring pants, no shoes, no shirts. The time is September 1962, and the setting is Mismaloya, a small island / rain forest off the coast of Puerto Vallarta, Mexico. Four maracas are also onstage.)

Adán: I could play this part.

Adonis: She approaches.

Adán: Has it been translated into Spanish? The play, I mean. Perhaps produce it in Guadalajara or, much better, Mexico City.

Adonis: Today she wears a white eyelet top. She must have bought it in town. The first day she visited she had on a very mod black-and-white swirl blouse with a red scarf over her coiffure. Very mod, Parisian or from London, perhaps.

Adán: I would be good in this part. They would have to make the priest Catholic, not Episcopalian, for these parts.

Adonis: I like the white, she could almost be Mexican in that top. Though her second-day visit, that was the stunner, a lavender embroidered beach top with matching scarf. Shoulder-length hair down, white capri pants.

Adán: What are you going on about?

Adonis: Her! *National Velvet*! *Giant*! *Cat on a Hot Tin Roof*! *Suddenly Last Summer*!

Adán: Suddenly this summer you seem to have lost your mind. Her eyes are violet; the top, though lovely, was more lilac than lavender. Focus, young one, we shoot soon.

Adonis: Focus on what? I have no lines. I play maracas, I chase and catch a lizard, play maracas some more. I'm still not sure if I'm Pepe or Pedro.

Adán: Todos somos Pepe.

Adonis: Yes, true, or at least whenever Ava Gardner calls, come running.

Adán: Good words to live by, especially on this shoot. This is your first film, no?

Adonis: Yes. A dancer by training, I've toured Latin America. Know ballet, folklórico, Graham.

Adán: The producer of this film is a Broadway big shot. Better you train your eyes and binoculars on him.

Adonis: Is it common for a visitor to sit next to the director while shooting? Is she giving him notes, you think?

Adán: Nothing about this shoot is common. Hollywood royalty in a Mexican beach town. They turned a little jungle of an island into a set of a desolate resort and built us and the crew accommodations. We have toilets and running water, hot and cold, that need not be boiled. That can't be true in your village.

Adonis: How do you know I am from a village?

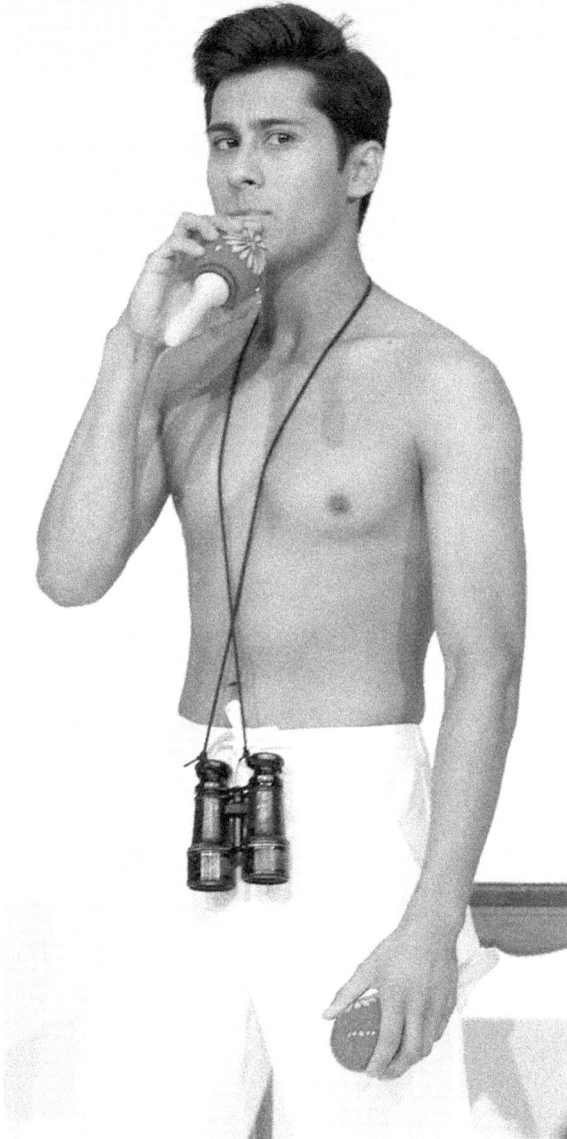

Diana Dalsasso, untitled
photograph, 2013.
Courtesy of HERO
Theatre.

Adán: You use your binoculars. I have my senses, sense memory, as I have been trained, and common sense that was beat into me as a child. *(Beat.)* A village not far from here, no?

Adonis: Yes, but how do you know?

Adán: You aren't comfortable with the lights or camera or the movie stars, but you enter this uncultivated land without fear. When we shot the chase, you fairly skipped through the thicket of ferns, roots, vines. And you grabbed that reptile like you would your own pet. I'm a city boy, Guadalajara. I know the rancho, but you are in your native habitat, jungle animal.

Adonis: I teach you to walk in the rain forest unafraid, if you teach me something.

Adán: Yes?

Adonis: Promise not to laugh.

Adán: Yes.

Adonis: When we had to fight the blond man.

Adán: That was a fun day of shooting.

Adonis: Yes, it was, but that made sense to me, the choreography of it. Hit duck spin. Like Cunningham, only more reasoned, less chance and balance work. But first we shot the scene where you served the blond man.

Adán: My one full line in the script.

Adonis: And you were so good. The way you leaned in and hated him but spoke the line smiling and glistening.

Adán: I glistened? Thank you for noticing. That's not my craft, just the heat. I am also not accustomed to your region's weather.

Adonis: Stop making fun.

Adán: Yes. OK. Go on.

Adonis: How did you hate that man and charm us at the same time?

Adán: Star quality.

Adonis: How arrogant.

Adán: No, just accurate. I know I have one line between the fetching, the punching, the maraca playing, and all the endless smiling. I wanted to make it count.

My role, and yours as well, is uncredited. Surely *National Velvet* and Ava Gardner and Anna from *The King and I* won't remember my name after we wrap. But the cinematographer, the camera operator, and much of this crew are the leading film-makers in Mexico. I want them to remember me, the way you need the producer to remember dancer you. *(He gets up close to Adonis.)* We, me and you, Pepe and Pedro, or, if this was an American film, Hazel and Missy, are being paid to play the happiest people alive. Servants. Now, I don't know what it's like in your village or even on tour with your dance company or within your family, but the servants I know are the angriest and most abused people I can think of, yet also the calmest and most charming. I funneled all of that into my line reading.

Adonis: All of that?!

Adán: All of that. But really, I am miscast. I should be playing the priest.

(Adonis laughs.)

Adonis: Now that is arrogant.

Adán: Yes, but true. He is good, once the greatest, and his voice remains amazing, but the Welshman has been a bit deep in the mescal and tequila, a bit too much method and a serious lack of discipline and control, which one needs to play a priest drunkenly spinning out of control. But that painter and the hysteric teacher, they are the ones to watch.

Adonis: Lolita is good.

Adán: Yes, but all starlet, all the time. Watch the difference in styles between the aunt and the painter, between American experimentation and visceral presence and British formalism and vocal craft.

Adonis: And the Mexican?

Adán: The Mexican what?

Adonis: School of acting.

Adán: Our training ground is in your bare feet, what your pinky toe remembers from being tickled by your mother, lightly and then later by a lover, with more force but still with the heat of love. It's in your strong calves and thighs, the work of hours of dance, but your Indian form could also come by that through other forms of honest hard work: in fields, in markets, in bars and bedrooms too. Mexican acting is Mexican living is Mexicans believing we are much, much more than servants smiling.

Adonis: You are an impossibly strange man. We have been shooting together for weeks. You and I. Pepe and Pedro. In sync. Running. Skipping. And shaking those damn maracas. All day long, you sit in sun or thatched shade, reading a script you have but one line in. And on this our last day, our first night shoot, you share all this with me? *(Beat. It gets quiet between them.)* The movie star, she leaves today too. That makes all of Mexico sad. Sad because, once again, we lose the world's attention and return to paying bribes to the PRI and boiling our water and making a pittance or swimming across the border to have America spit in our faces and ask us to clean that up and the rest of their messes, too. You, strange man in our strange land, make sense when it comes to acting but none when it comes to living.

(Adán laughs.)

Adán: You are right. What can I say? I am an artist, not a pragmatist.

Adonis: Yes, this is your problem as well as the problem of this production. I have already accepted the fact that I play maracas when I am but standing around waiting for Ava Gardner to give me orders. That I play maracas when drunk and brawling. That I shake my maracas when serving drinks. But how are we to make love, well, make out with Ava Gardner, in the ocean and play these maracas?

(Adán laughs, then kisses Adonis deeply.)

Adán: My last acting lesson: Kiss her but think of me.

(They kiss again, deeply. Adán exits.)

Adonis: Kiss Ava Gardner but think of him.

(Adonis exits.)

End.

SISSY

I feel the press of all that is around me here where I live,
at home among my people.
—Paul Robeson, *Here I Stand*

Sissy had its world premiere on June 13, 2008, at Company of Angels in Los Angeles, California, directed by Armando Molina and Tina Sanchez. The show was brought to USC for a performance with much of the premiere cast in 2009. In 2010, Rainbow Theater, a student of color theater program at UC Santa Cruz, did a workshop production, directed by Alma Herrera-Pazmiño. In 2006 a workshop production directed by Jorge Merced was produced at Pregones Theater in the Bronx. A staged reading directed by Robert Castro was a part of the New Theater For Now Festival at Culver City's Kirk Douglas Theater / Center Theater Group in April 2005. Pregones Theater awarded *Sissy* a 2004 Asuncíon Playwrights Project Award for queer Latino playwriting when it was given a staged reading and a workshop production in 2005, both directed by Jorge Merced. *Sissy* received a Best Latino New Play Award from the Center for Chicano Studies of UC Santa Barbara in 2004, where it received a staged reading directed by Luis Moreno as part of the UCSB Summer Theater Lab convened by Naomi Iizuka. Excerpts of the play were read at the Tribeca Theater Festival, directed by Michael Greif, as part of Tribeca's All Access Award for playwrights of color in 2004. *Sissy* won a

Panelist's Choice Award at the Edward Albee Theatre Festival in Valdez, Alaska, in 2000. It won a George Houston Bass Award for Best One Act from Rites and Reasons Theatre, Africana Studies, Brown University, and received a workshop production directed by Elmo Terry Morgan in 1999. *Sissy* was previously known as *July 19, 1979: The Tide Is High*. Sissy was initially developed in writing workshops at SF Mission District's Brava Theater Center taught by Cherríe Moraga and a playwriting workshop taught by Caridad Svich for the Latino Theater Initiative led by Luis Alfaro and Diane Rodríguez at Center Theatre Group.

WORLD PREMIERE / COMPANY OF ANGELS ENSEMBLE:

Sissy:	Xavi Moreno
Mana:	Kikey Castillo
Baby Brother:	Richard Azurdía
Ensemble/Multiple Roles:	Elisa Bocanegra, Lee Sherman, Ser Anzoátegui, Rudy Marquez, Kevin Vavasseur, Marcos Najera
Producer:	Kila Kitu, Dolores Chavez, and Ricardo Bracho

CAST OF CHARACTERS

Sissy:	A sissy turning twelve today
Mana:	Sissy's older sister
Baby Brother:	Their baby brother
Chapina Chaparra:	Mana's best friend
Negra Flaca:	Mana's other best friend
Neighbor Girl with Cancer:	The neighbor across the street
Cabrones Bros.:	Three asshole neighbors
Pig:	A local cop
Aunt Lovely:	Negra Flaca's aunt, a dusthead
Bus Driver with Mississippi Mud Tween His Toes:	An RTD Bus Driver
Doña Centroamericana:	Bus rider and cleaning lady
Herself:	Black drag queen
Cubanasa:	Cuban drag queen
Rica:	Puerto Rican drag queen

Overture—Paul Robeson and the Dream of a Disco Revolution

(As play begins, a curtain which is a clothesline with white sheets is removed to reveal our Sissy. He sits in a school chair and holds Paul Robeson's Here I Stand. *This play's epigraph, "I feel the press of all that is around me here*

where I live, at home among my people," is intoned by either Sissy in his most stentorian imitation of Robeson or a voice-over by another actor who can approximate that lush bass baritone.)

Sissy: This-here book is Paul Robeson's autobiography *Here I Stand*. He was the smartest man in the world. Could sing, act, write, march, and move the masses, as my parents and their friends like to say. But what I like best is how beautiful he is. I seen *Emperor Jones* which is some awful racist jungle king shit but he wear all gold in it and is more beautiful than the dad on *Good Times* and even Malcolm. I know I'm not supposed to think men are beautiful but that's alright. My daddy's got a record where Paul Robeson sings the "Internationale," I think in Soviet or Russian, and you ain't heard shit like it. It's better than Marvin Gaye's "Mercy Mercy" and Stevie's "Sir Duke" combined. It's like the core of the earth cracked open and out came his voice. My teacher told me I wouldn't be able to understand this book, but how would she know since all she wants us to do is sing that bullshit song "Getting to Know You" from that imperialist piece of crap *The King and I*. What kinda colored is Yul Brynner anyway? My other favorite brothers are Jim Thorpe, W. E. B. Du Bois, George Washington Carver, and Charles Drew. Dr. Drew is the blood who discovered blood plasma but when he got hurt in a car accident wouldn't no white hospitals treat him so he bled to death. Ain't that some fucked-up shit. In school they try to teach us about Mexicans like Father Hidalgo and Cesar Chavez, but they're too nice. I can't even imagine them cussing. Cantinflas is cool, but they don't got him in no books, I bet. Books is the best cuz they quiet—filled with words but not loud like this house. I like to read while baby brother watches TV and everybody talks cuz then I can imagine myself all alone in the words. Just fitting right there in the space between the period and capital letter. Plus, I wish I could write neat like book type so Mrs. Teacher wouldn't always be on my ass about my penmanship. What kinda shit is that? Books is quiet with nobody calling you joto maricón faggot sissy or yelling at you to come in off the street already. And hand-me-down books aren't as bad as secondhand cords. My daddy has a copy of *The Wretched of the Earth* by this French black dude. His copy has the official stamp of the Massachusetts state chapter of the Black Panther Party. I get to read it after I get through The *Autobiography of Malcolm X* and *The Communist Manifesto*. After I'm done reading all I can on Jim Thorpe, Paul Robeson, W. E. B. Du Bois, and Dr. Charles Drew I'm gonna check out this book on fifty exceptional Negro women including Madame C. J. Walker, Lorraine Hansberry, Marian Anderson, and Dorothy Dandridge. Mami says Rosa Parks wasn't just no tired criada but a organizer. Daddy says she was a communist, but that's what he says about everybody he likes. I don't know of any book on fifty exceptional Mexican mujeres, but with my mom and that lady Rosaura Revueltas who was in that movie *The Salt of the Earth*, that's two right there.

(Sissy crosses to bed, goes to sleep. He dreams. In this dream sequence Sissy has the birthday party he would have wanted. The backyard is lit like the Soul Train and Disco Fever sets. Mana, Baby Brother, Chap, and Negra are all present. The rap they do is a traditional double-Dutch introduction rhyme—syncopated to the downbeat.)

Everyone: Hey! Introduce yourself!

Sissy: I'm shy.

Everyone: Introduce yourself!

Sissy: I'm shy.

Everyone: Get in your car
And drive real far
Put your foot on the gas
And let Sissy kick ass!
Look at that booty!
Walk walk
Ain't it fruity
Walk walk

Know you want some
But you can't have none!

Sissy: Well, hold up! I'm ready.

Everyone: Well, introduce your damn self, then!

Sissy: My name is Sissy,
and I get busy
I got a mami
and a daddy
who in Mexico,
that's where they had me
yep, I got a green card
and a big ol' backyard.
But I ain't a mojado
oh-no-no-no
or a cholo

¿que, estas loco?
Cuz I'm the Sissy
who gets busy
So everybody
welcome to my
birthday party!

(Sissy approaches Mana.)

Sissy: I challenge you to a duel.

Mana: Say what? I ain't in the mood for kid games.

Sissy: Turning twelve today makes me a kid no more, pendeja.

Mana: Well, then, I ain't in the mood for no sissy games.

Sissy: I challenge you to a duel. Do you accept?

Mana: Can we use reinforcements?

Sissy: If you must. You're up first. Choose your weapon.

(Sissy snaps fingers two times. Baby Brother shows 45s to Mana. Mana picks record, shows it to Chap and Negra.)

Mana: Ready?

(They nod. Mana hands record to Baby Brother ceremonially. He puts it on. It is the Sylvers' "Hot Line." The Girls dance and lip-sync, with Sissy joining in doing the male parts. After Sissy and Girls do the Bump, Latin Hustle, etc., Baby Brother switches song. It's the Jackson 5's "Blame It on the Boogie," with Baby Brother doing Michael Jackson's lead part. The Girls and Baby freeze. Sissy approaches audience.)

Sissy: Here where no sound travels from, the sirens never stop but the pigs never arrive. Here we live without echo, so we have no history. Here in this city, Culver City. Here, listen.

(Sissy turns out headphones to audience, which blast Diana Ross's "The Boss." They unfreeze at the fast part, and the whole stage gigs for a few bars. They are interrupted by "La Internacional" sung in Spanish by adult, mainly male, voices. Sissy skates over to bed, dejectedly removes skates, and gets into bed. Sissy is then woken up by Daddy.)

Scene 1—Fuck You, Daddy

(Sissy is in his bed, the lower bunk of a bunkbed. His Baby Brother sleeps atop. Daddy enters. Spacing in Sissy's speech indicate that Daddy [shadow puppet, globo, light] "speaks.")

Sissy: Oh fuck. Daddy. {Daddy speaks.} Yeah, fuck you. {Daddy speaks.} Yeah. Ugh. I'm awake. Why am I awake? {Daddy speaks.} So? Why'd you wake me up? It's Saturday I ain't got nowhere to be except here. Well? {Daddy speaks.} It's my birthday. Ain't you got something to tell me? {Daddy speaks.} I got to what? Shit, why I gotta go? {Daddy speaks.} Fuck. Alright. Yeah, alright. {Daddy speaks.} You right. I should go with you to the store, so you get what I want. {Daddy speaks.} Shit, it's my birthday. *(Beat.)* Daddy, they gonna have birthday parties after the revolution? Or would that violate the principles of democratic centralism? {Daddy speaks.} I don't think that's a stupid question. You ain't gonna be able to convince the masses to revolt if you don't throw a party afterward. *(Beat.)* Or do we start over from zero after we won? Is that why el hombre nuevo is new? {Daddy speaks.} Daddy, do I have to have that Uncle Sam piñata? Why not a burro or something? Somoza would've even been better. {Daddy speaks.} Alright. I'll get up, but not till you tell me happy birthday. I've already been twelve for ten hours if you start from midnight and nobody in this family has told me nothing. {Daddy speaks.} Who cares if I was sleeping. Daddy, you're too logical sometimes. {Daddy speaks.} Thank you. Yes, I think it's going to be a good one. But Daddy? {Daddy speaks.} Just no revolution today. Only birthday. *(To sleeping Baby.)* Baby, levántate ya and wish me a happy birthday.

(Sissy exits, Baby sits up in bed.)

Baby Brother: But me I'm I'm the American baby. Born here. Fa-fa-quince minutes away. W-w-wwhen my mommy had me. And she didn't speak no English then. Not that she sp-spspeaks it all that good now either. When she was leaving the hosp-hosp-doctor they made her n-n-name ma-me. So she went w-w-w-with what she knew. Named me after my dadadadaddy. No ma-matter. Everybody calls me Bababy Brother, the one ba-born here, the one who stustustustutters. Sissy. He always ma-ma-making me do s-s-s-shows. He has me da-do things I d-d-don't like to do. Like dr-dr-dress up in mo-mo-mom-mommy's clothes. He is even bo-bo-bossier than my teacher or e-e-e-even Mana. He says—pu-ut on the red dress. No, the other shoes. Those don't go. I do-do-don't know why I do it. It is not fun. And w-w-w-w sissy and m-m-me always get busted for it. B-b-but its less boring th-than always pl-playing ka-kick the ca-can or hide andaanda go-go seek. Whe-

when he was littler and I was even way little Sissy would dress up anda do shows on the babalcony. He-he even got mommy to take his pic-pic-fuck. Foto. She hi-ides them in the foto al-al-scrapbooks behind other less Sissy pictures of Sissy. B-but now he likes to ha-ha-have me put on the dre-vestidas and dance around. I wouldn't mind so mu-much if he wasn't al-always correcting me. But sh-shit he ain't gonna take my foto.

(Baby gets out of bed, approaches Mana's loft-bed.)

Baby: Sis-sis-sis-Mana! Get up! We g-g-g-g-got to g-ge-ge-ge-ge-get ready for the pa-pa-party.

(Mana is already awake, writing in her diary and listening to Diana Ross's "It's My House." She ignores Baby.)

Mana: Dear dear me—yes me. Selfish old me. Me. Me. Me. It's 1979 the end of the Me Decade, but didn't nobody give me enough me, well to me out. *Selfish* must be a worse word to my parents than *wetback*. But I love that word—the way it sounds like it feels and rhymes with *attack*. I say it to myself every day. Sometimes about people I see or other kids at school. I ain't gonna lie. But also cuz I know that as long as there's that border, fence, and river they're gonna be some wetback bodies in the world. We aren't going anywhere. And so what if it's a racist word. And so what if I worry about me. I am something worth worrying about. Equal to if not more than some fuckin book or idea. Me—right here—the sister who dries her dreams out there in the backyard on the tool shack with her weed.

(Sister takes joint from diary, lights it.)

Scene 2—Bianca Jagger for Dictator of the Proletariat

(Sissy enters kitchen with People *magazine opened. Mami is a shadow puppet, globo, light, etc.)*

Sissy: Mami, look! {Mami speaks.} It's not cochinadas. It's Bianca Jagger on a horse! At Studio 54! {Mami speaks.} It's a club in New York. And last night I dreamt the backyard turned into my very own Studio 54 and I won the dance contest against Mana and everybody. {Mami speaks.} I'm not wasting my life away on pendejadas, it was just a dream. Don't be so serious and look at how beautiful she is. 'Magínate, ma, in a club on a caballo. Why I bet she thought she was Dessalines riding into Port-au-Prince to free Haiti from Napoleon's troops. Shouting "Liberté, Egalité, Fraternité!" *(Beat.)* I heard she's a socialist and supports the Sandinistas. They should make her a princess. Well, I guess they're anti-oligarchy. Maybe their minister of fashion. Maybe she'll open a club there. {Mami speaks.} 'Ama Mick Jagger isn't a prevert. It's pervert. And that song he did with Peter Tosh on *Saturday Night Live* is really good. (Sissy sings.) "We gonna walk and don't look back." {Mami speaks.} I know that show is on late porque es para adultos. Pero how am I gonna know what happens at Studio 54 and how Phoebe Snow and Linda Ronstadt sing "The Married Men" if I don't stay up and watch it? {Mami speaks.} I didn't buy the magazine, Doña Vecina was gonna throw it away. {Mami speaks.} No, it doesn't have an article on the Sandinistas. It's *People* magazine, not *The People*. {Mami speaks.} Why can't I read it? I do all my home-work, even the homework that you and Daddy make me do in the summer when nobody else anywhere in the world let alone this block has homework. We've al-ready gone over algebra, world history, and geography this summer and I seen all those Charlie Chaplin funny worker man films at Freedom Camp. Besides, today is my birthday and I should be able to read what I want. I'm going to go finish getting ready. You want to read the article?

Scene 3—A Sissy's Nightmare Gift

(Sissy is in his bedroom, finishing up his birthday "look." Daddy enters with present: a baseball mitt. Sissy cannot hide his shock and disgust.)

Sissy: You got me a mitt. For what? {Daddy speaks.} No, I am not. You're high, Daddy. {Daddy speaks.} Little League? It's too late to join for this summer. Plus, I don't even want to. Swimming lessons in the Piss Plunge are fine. {Daddy speaks.} Baseball camp? Ay, por favor, Daddy, I am not camping. They don't got phones. {Daddy speaks.} I know I know que you didn't have a phone or all that growing up in Mexico City. But Daddy, this is Culver City and I'm me, not you. And I don't like sports. *(Handing Daddy the mitt.)* Give the mitt to Baby Brother, since it was just his birthday and you didn't even make it to his party. Yes, I know what being on call is. Whose son do you think I am? The only doctor in this damn neighborhood. {Daddy speaks.} I'm not being bourgeois, Daddy. I'm just saying you can't all of a sudden decide to be typical. Like you can go from weekends of plotting the overthrowing of this government to baseball games and backyard birria. {Daddy speaks.} I know, Daddy. But we're not Cuban. Let Fidel play base-ball. I like Chinese jacks better. *(Sissy takes out Chinese jacks and plays.)* {Daddy speaks.} So what if it's for girls? I'm good at it. Want me to show you how? {Daddy speaks.} Why not? It's Chinese like mami's grandaddy and probably an invention of the Long March. {Daddy speaks.} I don't care, Daddy. {Daddy speaks.} OK, I do. I can't make boys like me. And I can't make myself like the things they like.

{Daddy speaks.} I know. Yes, I'm a boy. But not like other boys. {Daddy speaks.} I'm not being a "yo sé todo." But, Daddy, what other Mexican father on this street or neighborhood or even fucking zip code got a MD and a PhD? {Daddy speaks.} My point? Well, whose red diaper baby am I anyway? {Daddy speaks.} See, Daddy, you're mo'ded. You're so mo'ded, you're corroded, your booty exploded. *(Indicating Chinese jacks.)* You gonna play with me or not, Daddy?

Scene 4—Sissy's Own Private Barrio

(Sissy on his street, carrying in grocery bags from the car to the house. Neighbor Girl sits on her steps, the Cabrones Bros. hang in front of their house.)

Sissy: See this? This my street. A dead end, which is good cuz then you could play Kick the Can and touch football and whatever you want and not have to worry about traffic. Them boys talking are the Cabrones brothers, who don't talk to me much cuz I'm Sissy and they don't think cabrones and sissies have much to say to each other. That girl sitting on her front porch is the Neighbor Girl with cancer.

(Sissy approaches Neighbor Girl.)

Sissy: Hey, Neighbor Girl, what you doing?

Neighbor Girl: Nothing.

Sissy: Ain't you coming to my party?

Neighbor Girl: Maybe later. I'm doing something right now.

Sissy: Thought you wasn't doing nothing? Neighbor Girl, why you got that hat on? Did you cut your hair?

Neighbor Girl: Nah. It's falling out. The chemo.

Sissy: I'm sorry. My daddy says it'll grow back, and he knows cuz that's his doctor specialty. *(Pause.)* What you waiting on?

Neighbor Girl: My tio. He's gonna take me on a ride on his motorcycle cuz I'm feeling better today.

Sissy: So then afterwards you could come over. *(Beat.)* Where's your Cousin Quadroon?

Neighbor Girl: He went to his moms for the weekend.

Sissy: Really? I thought she didn't want to see him since he's living with all the Mexicans.

Neighbor Girl: Who told you that?

Sissy: Well, who do you think did, Neighbor Girl? Your Cousin Quadroon did.

Neighbor Girl: Oh. *(Beat.)* You want to hear something cool?

Sissy: Guess so.

   (Neighbor Girl puts on the tape player. It's "Rock Lobster" by the B-52's.)

Sissy: What's that?

Neighbor Girl: New wave. They're called the B-52's. Do you like it?

Sissy: Yeah, but how do you dance to it?

Neighbor Girl: That's even cooler. It's called the pogo. Look, I'll show you. *(Neighbor Girl gets up and pogos.)*

Sissy: Neighbor Girl, you look like a crazy white girl.

Neighbor Girl: C'mon.

Sissy: But I thought all you liked was disco and oldies but goodies?

Neighbor Girl: C'mon, Sissy. Dance with me.

Sissy: Alright.

   (Sissy joins her in dancing. The Cabrones Bros., who have been watching all along, bust up.)

Cabrones Bros.: Joto maricón fag!

Neighbor Girl: Fuck you, Cabrones!

Sissy: Oh, don't worry about it. They'd call me that even if I wasn't dancing. They just have to make sure and call me that every day.

Neighbor Girl: It doesn't make you mad?

Sissy: Sometimes. Other times no. I don't know anything different. *(Beat.)* You got any more of that new wave stuff?

   (Neighbor Girl's uncle drives up on motorcycle.)

Sissy: Well, I guess you gotta go. Talk to you, Neighbor Girl. Have fun.

Neighbor Girl: Happy birthday, Sissy.

(Neighbor Girl rides off. Sissy waves to her.)

Sissy: That was the Neighbor Girl with cancer who used to be the Neighbor Girl with long, long hair but it started to fall out once she became the Neighbor Girl with cancer. She's my sister Sister's other best friend besides la Negra Flaca y la Chapina Chaparra. Her family has the best parties on this street. And her cousin Quadroon is my age and blond and blue-eyed but mean like a Mexican boy but nice to me cuz he's new here and cuz I help him with his homework.

(Daddy enters, hails Sissy inside.)

Sissy: Si, ya voy. {Daddy speaks.} Nothing, Daddy, I was just talking to Neighbor Girl with cancer. Her tío took her on a motorcycle ride so she could remember what it was like to be the girl with long, long hair and have the wind blow through it. *(Beat.)* Daddy, know what I want? {Daddy speaks.} Some new wave. {Daddy speaks.} No, it's music. Yeah, it's cool. A band called the B-52s. {Daddy speaks.} No, Daddy, they're not militaristic. {Daddy speaks.} Invite them? *(Indicating Cabrones Bros.)* Do I gotta? {Daddy speaks.} Shit, alright, fine.

(Sissy approaches Cabrones Bros.)

Sissy: *(In one breath.)* My daddy said I had to invite you to my birthday party but don't be thinking I care if you come or not and why don't you go change before you come and buy me that record that I was dancing to as a present and don't even try to sneak any beer.

(Sissy turns to walk away from Cabrones Bros.)

Cabrones Bros.: Joto maricón faggot sissy!

(Sissy turns his head back to them.)

Sissy: That's my name. Don't wear it out.

Cabrones Bros.: "Don't wear it out." Just a stupid lil faggot.

(Cabrones exit, laughing. Sissy is crushed and vulnerable on this, his very own street.)

Scene 5—The Gender Rollercoaster

(Backyard. Sissy has his headphones on. Mana, Chapina, and Negra listen to a radio playing the Ohio Players' "Love Rollercoaster." A child, represented by a doll, is off in the corner.)

Sissy: I should have been born a girl. Then it would be boy girl boy girl boy in my family instead of boy girl boy sissy boy. Then when I'm mistaken for a girl at the dental clinic, on the bus, in public restrooms, by men on the streets, it would, I would no longer be a mistake. Then Mana wouldn't send me away when talk with La Chapina Chaparra y La Negra Flaca just got good.

Mana: Listen. See. Did you hear it?

Negra: I didn't hear, boo.

Mana: Yeah, right there. That's the sound of some girl screaming who died on a rollercoaster.

Chapina: Sounds like something else is happening to her.

Sissy: Like what?

Mana: Go away, Sissy. *(Girls freeze.)*

Sissy: If I were a girl my name would be Savannah Assata Turner and Tina Turner would be my mom. I once got real enojado with my moms and told her I wanted Tina Turner to be my mom instead of her. I was five years old at the time. She still talks about it. It wasn't that I didn't want my mom to be my mom, it's just that I wanted my dad to take me to the *Tommy* concert The Who was doing at Griffith Park but he wouldn't cuz of all the acid freaks and marijuaneros that were going to be there. I bet Tina Turner's daughter if she has one got to sit backstage and watch her mother shake it to the left and shake it to the right while she screamed *"I'm the Gypsy the Acid Queen, pay me before I start, the Gypsy I'm guaranteed to tear your soul apart."* And I bet lil ol' Savannah even has her own wigs and shimmy shimmy dresses to do *Proud Mary nice and easy and then do it nice and rough*. But my all-time favorite song is "Ooh Poo Pah Doo" where my mom Tina talks about making *some strange noises in your ear* and how she *ain't gonna stop 'til* she *creates some disturbance in your mind*. I am the disturbance in so many people's eyes. But if I were named Savannah Assata and Tina Turner's daughter, folks would just compliment my plaits and my nice, non-ashy shade of redbone.

(Girls unfreeze.)

Negra: I don't hear shoot.

Mana: Listen. *(Pause.)* How would you know, Chap?

Chapina: Know what?

Mana: About the sound of something else.

Chapina: Malo and I are getting married.

Negra: For real?

Mana: For why?

Negra: Don't be so cold blooded.

Mana: It was just a question. How's about I rephrase it: Why you marrying that motherfucker?

Chapina: He ain't a motherfucker, bitch. He's about to be the father of my child.

Negra: Oh my gosh!

Mana: Father? He ain't even a man. And even if he was, no one gets named Malo for being good. And I ain't a bitch, Chap, I'm your friend. Or don't you need them anymore now that you got a baby coming and that fool running you?

Chapina: Sister, you don't know nothing. You're still a fucking virgin.

Mana: So? So were you at the beginning of the summer.

Chapina: Things change.

Negra: They sure do. Could we change the topic of conversation?

Mana: So, what you gonna name her? Mala?

Negra: How come you know it's going to be a girl?

Mana: Just a feeling, a what's-it-called.

Sissy: A intuition.

Mana: Get out of here, Sissy. Go tell Mom we're out of ice. And pick up that kid.

Chapina: Whose is it?

Mana: I don't know. But she don't need to hear all this. Vete, Sissy.

Negra: You gonna baptize her Catholic?

Chapina: I'm not sure. Malo's mom is a Jehovah's Witness and his dad is a santero.

Mana: Pinche gusanos.

Negra: But your dad's Mormon and your mom is Catholic.

Chapina: They don't know … and don't tell them. Mana, can I stay here this summer?

Mana: Good fucking lord.

Negra: As often as you take the Lord's name in vain …

Mana: Sissy, what are you still doing here? Go tell Mom about the goddamn ice! And grab esa niña también. Ya.

Sissy: Alright … alright. Congratulations, Chapina. Could I be the ring bearer?

Mana: Don't you mean the flower girl? Go, Sissy. Now!

Chapina: Thanks, Sissy. But I don't know if I'm gonna be having a wedding. I just had my quince, and that was real expensive.

(Mana glares at Sissy.)

Sissy: I know, I'm going. The kid, the ice, anything else?

Mana: Don't come back.

Scene 6—Approaching El Panameño

(Sissy enters the kitchen, a baby balanced on the hip he does not have.
The kitchen is represented by a symphony of Spanish-language female voices
chopping, cooking, and laughing.)

Sissy: ¡AMA, necesitamos mas hielo! Ma que there's no more ice. {Mami speaks.} Daddy can't go, El Panameño's truck is blocking him in. {Mami speaks.} ¿El Panameño? He's playing dominos with the Puerto Rican independentistas, and talking to some white girl. I mean some internationalist. {Mami speaks.} You want me to tell him that? *(Puts hand on his free hip and sucks his teeth.)* {Mami speaks.} I wasn't sucking my teeth, I was just breathing. *(Sucks his teeth again. She hits him.)* Oh, why you got to be hitting folks? {Mami speaks.} I wasn't talking back. Here, if Ima go tell ese negro borracho, you got to watch this kid. {Mami speaks.} I don't know whose it is either.

(Sissy hands over baby, goes to backyard. El Panameño sits with the White Girl, I Mean Internationalist on his lap. He is playing dominos.)

El Panameño: Domino!

(Panameño and White Girl stand and dance to Patti LaBelle's "Teach Me Tonight [Me Gusta Tu Baile]." Sissy shadows them and dances as he delivers his monologue.)

Sissy: *(Addresses El Panameño. Sucks his teeth.)* Negro, please. You ain't so new. But you act like it, sitting spread-legged and Panamanian as you need to be. You ain't so special just cuz you were born black and non-English-speaking. But that does real well for you in this world where common brothers get passed by. Plus, it keeps you from having to wear daishikis, which we all know, Pan-Africanism or not, ain't nothing but a dress. But you ain't a sissy. I am. Along with a faggot-maricón. So what? At least I ain't one of those white girls so impressed by a Afro-American from Central America who could read and write in two languages. Shit. You won't pay me no attention cuz there's that gringa trying to impress you with her anti-imperialist stance and loose hair. But you just wait. I'll get my turn.

(Sissy taps El Panameño on shoulder.)

Sissy: Panameño, my mom said to stop flirting and go pick up some ice.

Scene 7—A Gun, a Stick, a Rock, a Gang

(Backyard. Mana, Negra, and Chapina still converse. Cabrones Bros.: One wields bat, the other ties bandanna and spins him.)

Negra: They're gonna break the penada.

Mana: Piñata, negra, pi-ña-ta.

Negra: I don't speak none of that Messican.

Mana: Well, girl, you better learn. I know black. I don't feel like candy, and that's not what I feel like breaking right now, either.

Chapina: Why can't you be happy for me, girl? I want the baby and Malo wants me.

Mana: Have your baby, but don't ask me to trust him.

(Sissy enters, with ice and child.)

Sissy: I get stuck running errands and they're breaking my piñata without me. Fuck turning twelve! I wish I was never born! I'm running away.

(All except Mana and Sissy freeze.)

Mana & Sissy: I was born in Mexico City and I'm still trying to make sure Culver City don't kill me.

Mana: Then my dad decided to come to the US cuz he heard there was a revolution happening here. It's eleven years later and, well, I am still waiting

Sissy: And like those kids in Soweto in 1976 I am ready to take up arms right here and right now. Not to be taught in my own language like those surafricanitos since

Mana: Spanish belongs to my mom and daddy and the rest of the padres on this street and English is owned by white people.

Sissy: The speak I speak best is my own Sissy language that no one wants to hear.

Mana: I want a gun, a stick a rock a rag that used to be a T-shirt stuffed in a jug of Gallo or a oil can cuz Culver City is trying to kill me and the rest of the girls what live here. Not cuz why my daddy thinks, we don't got jobs so we ain't workers and not even cuz of what the paper calls the gang problem. This city is gonna kill me not cuz I gangbang or cuz I'm dusted and want to fly but because my eyes don't blink all the way and I can see out of my squint the snipers on all the rooftops. After all us niñitas—little girls who'll be the walking dead before they get to be women. I need a gun, a rock, a stick, a gang.

Sissy: Like those kids in Soweto toy-toying through their shantytowns.

Mana: A gang that instead of claiming their women, an alley, or corner claims this whole world here in Culver City as safe for bitches who want one day to be more than just that.

Sissy: I refuse to die in anybody else's language.

Mana: *(Pause.)* I really do think she's gonna have a girl.

Sissy: I really should have been born a girl. Then it would be boy girl boy girl boy in my family instead of boy girl boy sissy boy.

Mana: I hope it's a girl. But she's still making a mistake.

Sissy: Then I would no longer be a mistake.

> *(All unfreeze, candy rains down, and in the mad dash for it our Sissy makes his escape.)*

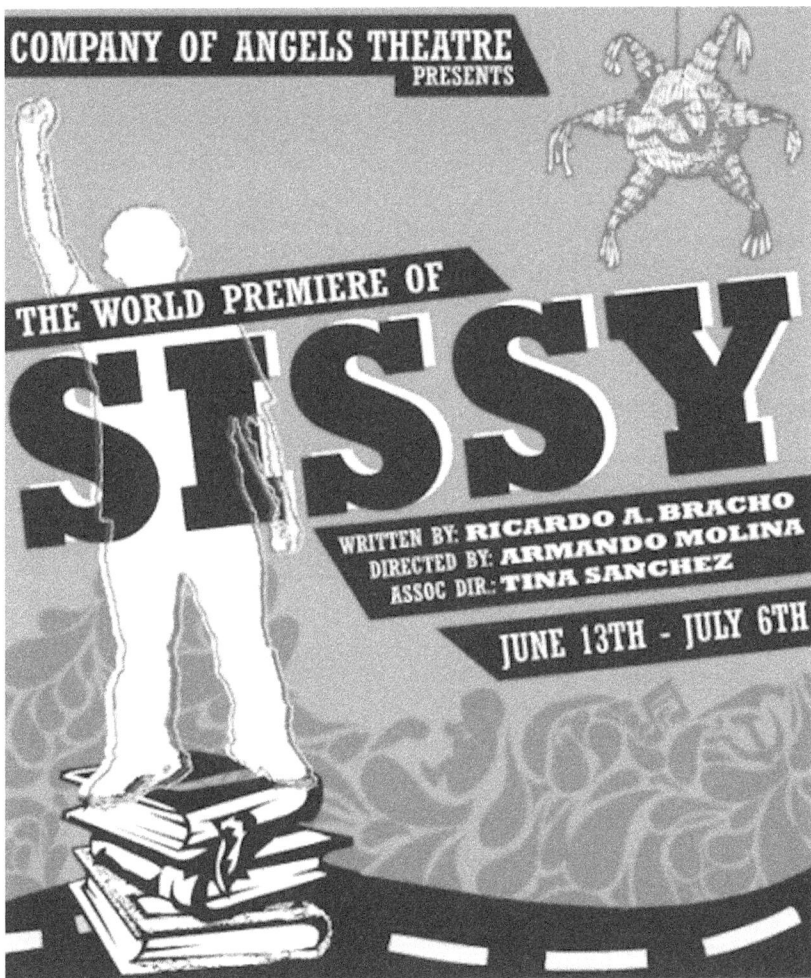

Xavi Moreno, poster for *Sissy*, 2008. Courtesy of Company of Angels.

Scene 8—Enter the State and the Shermhead, Exit the Sissy

(Sissy at the bus stop. Pig circles Sissy.)

Pig: What are you waiting for?

Sissy: The bus.

Pig: Why?

Sissy: This is a bus stop, sir.

Pig: Where are you from?

Sissy: My mother's barriga.

Pig: What? Is that some fuckin new gang slang?

Sissy: I ain't in a gang.

Pig: Ain't? Sure do talk like it, punk. Where do you live?

Sissy: Here.

Pig: You live at this bus stop, idiot?

Sissy: No.

Pig: No, what?

Sissy: No, I don't live at this bus stop. No, I am not an idiot.

Pig: Do you want to get taken in, smart-ass?

Sissy: No.

Pig: Then answer my question.

Sissy: You'll need to ask one. Mostly you've been barking commands.

Pig: I already asked you, where the hell do you live?

Sissy: Look, if I say I'm from where I'm from, then you'll ask me if I'm in the gang and I'll say no and you won't believe me. We do this all the time, sometimes more than once a week.

Pig: That's cuz you're always loitering around, young man. Stay off the street. Go home, lil momma's boy.

Sissy: Well, at least you're listening. I told you a long time ago I was from my momma's belly. If you gonna bother Mexicans all the time you should learn some Spanish, badge number 321889 whatever your name is.

Pig: You know my name.

Sissy: And you know mine. Know where I live. What else do you need to know about me?

Pig: That you're not out here breaking any laws.

Sissy: I'm twelve fucking—

Pig: Watch your mouth, punk.

Sissy: I'm twelve years old today, sir, and I only recently started taking the bus home by myself or walk home from school without baby brother. I have a backpack that has books in it. Even in the summertime. Nothing spectacular.

Pig: Spectacular? How old did you say you were?

Sissy: Old enough to use a thesaurus. Look, you got all the information you need from me tonite to fill out whatever forms you got to fill out. Quotas, I think they're called.

Pig: What did I already tell you about being a smart-ass?

Sissy: I know. But both times it's been my mouth.

Pig: That's what's gonna get you in trouble.

Sissy: Maybe. But mostly it keeps me out of it. Anything else, officer?

Pig: Too smart for

Sissy: A Mexican?

Pig: A kid.

Sissy: Yeah. I guess that too.

Pig: Get off this street. That's the last time I'm telling you before I give you a ride somewhere else.

(*Pig exits. Sissy hears someone from offstage. It is Lovely, Negra Flaca's aunt, who is drunk and high on* PCP. *She smokes a joint and holds a bottle of cheap booze.*)

Lovely: Zumminah umminah uminah yeah yeah. He gone yet?

Sissy: Oh, shit, it's just you. I thought you was gonna be an undercover cop. What's up, Aunt Lovely?

(*Though Lovely cannot focus on him, she is trying to figure out who Sissy is. She stumbles over to him and, holding on to him, tries to take in his face.*)

Sissy: It's me, Sissy, Sister's lil brother. You know, your niece Negra Flaca's friend.

Lovely: Uuuhhhhhh. Yeeaaaahhhh. Whaaaaat?

Sissy: How can you smoke that angel dust, Lovely? You know it's part elephant tranquilizer and part battery acid.

Lovely: Uhmmmmm. Taaaaastyy.

Sissy: I just turned twelve today and ran away for ever and ever.

Lovely: Huuuuuuuh? Haaapy birthday, baaby. Got any cakeeeee?

Sissy: Nah, I'm traveling light. Hey, where's your Baby Boy who holds you up when you're this fucked up?

Lovely: Whhooooo?

Sissy: Your son, Baby Boy? The one you hold on to like how you're holding on to me when you're too fucked up on sherm and Night Train to stand up on your own.

Lovely: My baaaby? Where is my baaaaby?

Sissy: I bet you left him at Negra's mom's house. Well, here comes my bus. Take care of yourself and watch out for that Pig.

Lovely: "I'd like to teach the world to sing in perfect harmony."

(Bus arrives at stop with passengers and the Bus Driver with Mississippi Mud Tween His Toes at the helm.)

Sissy: You go to Hollywood?

Bus Driver: Why, hello and how do you do! Sure do! That's a whole quarter for you.

(Sissy deposits a quarter he pulls from his shoe.)

Bus Driver: Welcome aboard the Rollin T. Davis, otherwise known as Rapid Transit Disappearance, properly known as the Rapid Transit District. My name is Bus Driver with Mississippi Mud Tween His Toes. We'll be going from Culver City through Palms, down Pico to Fairfax. Make a stop at *Ro*deo Drive.

Doña: Ro*deo*.

Bus Driver: Well, it's *Ro*deo if you rich but *Ro*deo if you poor. That there's the Donna Centroamericana.

Doña: Doña.

Sissy: Mucho gusto, Señora. *(To Bus Driver.)* Can you let me know when we hit Hollywood?

Bus Driver: That'll be self-evident, my son. Have a seat.

(Sissy takes seat. Bus Driver takes off. "Hollywood" by Rufus with Chaka Khan plays, which the Bus Driver and Doña Centromericana lip-sync to Sissy.)

Scene 9

(Back in the backyard, Mana and Negra Flaca do the Hustle to Herb Alpert's "Rise.")

Negra: Where's Chap?

Mana: She went home to sneak some clothes out. She's not stretching any of my stuff with that pansa.

Negra: After all that huff-n-puff, you gonna let her stay here?

Mana: Better here than Malo's. Sides, I don't have any sisters.

Negra: You got Sissy.

Mana: You could have him.

Negra: Where is he? Ain't he gonna open presents?

Mana: I haven't seen him. *(Pause.)* Let's go find him.

(Mana & Negra exit. Baby Brother enters, looks around, does the Hustle. The Cabrones Bros. #1, 2, & 3 enter cracking up.)

Cabrones #1: Following in your brother's faggot footsteps?

Cabrones #2: Where's your Mana marijuanera?

Cabrones #3: Where's the beer?

Baby Brother: I I I I I do-do-don—no sé.

(Cabrones crack up and exit, Baby Brother fumes.)

Scene 10—In the Court of Her Majestic Majesty Herself

(Herself struts her stuff, humming "Lotta Love." Sissy gets off bus.)

Sissy: Oh, I love that song. Isn't that Nicolette Larsen? Her hair is almost longer than Crystal Gayle's.

Herself: Well, my brown eyes will never be blue, and I wasn't singing to you.

Sissy: I'm sorry. I'm Sissy. What's your name?

Herself: Herself.

Sissy: Herself? What kinda name is that?

Herself: Oh, and you really got room to talk. Boy, what you doing out here? Isn't it well past your bedtime?

Sissy: I don't got a bedtime or even a curfew, my father thinks they're fascistic.

Herself: You better get your ass home. You certainly don't belong here.

Sissy: How you know?

Herself: Open your eyes, child. You too well-fed to have been out here long. 'Sides, you don't look like you could handle it. *(Pause.)* Now move on with yourself, I'm working.

Sissy: Working?

Herself: Yes, I am clocked in.

Sissy: You call singing on a corner work? That's not labor. My daddy is a communist, I know labor.

Herself: Well, I don't care what your daddy is, unless he's my next trick. But yes, this-here corner is my office. I call it the Booty Boutique and you either gonna steal my business or scare it away. So, get on with your sissy-self.

Sissy: Nah, I came to see The Life!

Herself: The Life? Child, you would have to be born first.

Sissy: Huh?

Herself: Here, look. *(Herself pulls compact from purse and pushes mirror in Sissy's face.)* Look. Not a moment of roughness in you. Go home. Your face won't survive this street. *(Pause.)* Damn shame.

Sissy: What is?

Herself: You is. That face. Not a moment of hard in all that baby fat, and as young as you might be and as virginal as you clearly are—there's nothing innocent in you. *(Pause.)* Scary.

(Silence. Sissy and Herself stare at each other. The silence is interrupted by the offstage hooting of La Cubanasa & La Rica, who enter with flourish.)

Sissy: Who those hoes?

(Herself slaps Sissy's shoulder.)

Herself: They might be just that, but respect your elders.

La Cubanasa: Ay, mulata, no sabía que you babysitted.

La Rica: Que kinky. What you do? A little romper room scene?

La Cubanasa: Vámonos, Herself. Let's do show, then, ho.

Herself: A show? I ain't dressed for it!

Sissy: *(Interjecting.)* Hi. I'm Sissy.

La Cubanasa: Eso es obvio.

La Rica: *(To Cuba.)* Ay bruta. *(To Sissy.)* Encantada. Yo soy La Rica y ella es La Cubanasa.

Sissy: ¿Cuba? ¿Vienes de paraíso?

La Cubanasa: No, amor, de Cienfuegos.

Sissy: It's just that I heard so much. My dad and his compadres debate all the time about Martí, Che, el foco, tropical socialism.

La Cubanasa: Deja de hablar de todo esa mierda.

Sissy: Y mama y las otras camaradas hablan de Vilma Espín y Haydee Santamaría. I love Blancanieves y Rosita Fornés.

La Cubanasa: Who doesn't love a good vedette? Ay que niña soviética. Look, I trying to enjoy my new American life de libertad. I need a drink, ladies. This kid gonna have me flashing back to el UMAP.

Sissy: ¿El que?

Herself: Well, someone's gonna have to buy me a drink or pay for cutting into my trick time.

Sissy: Where are you from?

La Rica: La otra ala, Puerto Rico.

Sissy: Oh, do you know Lolita Lebron?

La Rica: No, I ain't never been to that jail. C'mon, pollito, we'll cho you the net.

Herself: The ropes, bitch, it's the ropes.

La Rica: C'mon, let's take her to la discoteca.

Herself: How we gonna get this child in?

La Cubanasa: Eso es fácil. We just say he my cousin y que es un midget.

La Rica: I heard que enanos tienen pingas enormes.

Herself: Heard? I saw you pick one up last night.

La Rica: He wasn't no midget, just bajito and I had on my big plataformas.

La Cubanasa: Ya jineteras. I had enough of all this talk. ¡Quiero disco!

Scene 11—Lift Ev'ry Voice and Lip-Sync

(Inside the disco, the Emotions and Earth, Wind & Fire's "Boogie Wonderland" is blasting. Herself, Cubanasa, & Rica say hello to everyone. They hide Sissy behind them, who keeps on trying to peek out in complete amazement.)

Herself: Child, behave yourself.

Sissy: I am, I ain't said a word or touched or broke a thing.

Herself: But your eyes are about to roll out they socket. Act cool.

La Rica: Si, compórtate bien y no te pierdas.

Sissy: Why everybody gotta be my mom all the time?

La Cubanasa: Hey! I only old enough to be your older sister.

Sissy: Great, just what I need, another one of those.

(They show Sissy to a front-row seat.)

Herself: Sit your happy ass here and don't talk to anybody or even look at them too long. Especially any men!

Sissy: But that's all there are here.

Herself: Well, that remains to be seen. Just you never mind and wait for your aunties to do their show.

Sissy: Can I perform too? I played the Reverend Doctor Martin Luther King Jr. last year. I know the "I Have a Dream" speech by heart.

La Cubanasa: No empiezas con más política, chica.

La Rica: Here. *(Rica hands Sissy a tambourine from her purse.)* You keep the beat for us, nena.

Herself: This song that my sistas here are gonna help me do has got a special message to Cubanasa's midget cousin who's then catching his bus home. ¡Viva La Sissy!

Rica & Cuba: ¡Que Viva!

> *(They perform Labelle's "Say Goodbye to Hollywood." Sissy exits and waits at bus stop, humming along to their song, playing his tambourine wildly.)*

Scene 12—Sick for Home

> *(As he arrives at bus stop, Sissy reencounters Doña Centroamericana.)*

Doña: Oiga, pollón, done con tus aventuras so soon?

Sissy: Yeah, it's cool n all out here. But it's getting cold and I'm getting hungry and if my mom notices I'm gone, damn . . .

Doña: You got scared?

Sissy: Yeah, I guess I did. Where you going?

Doña: To clean my own house now. I clean this one and another after I get done with cleaning and cooking y cuidando for norteamericanos que son dirty y not nice.

Sissy: Dang, you work hard.

Doña: Yes, I was teacher en mi país and now I janitor, jardinera, cocinera, y maestra para casi no money. And like you, I sick for home.

Sissy: You mean homesick?

Doña: Si, eso.

Sissy: Then why not go back like I'm about to?

Doña: War.

Sissy: Oh.

(Pause.)

Doña: I had a brother like you.

Sissy: Like me how?

Doña: Listo y lindo. Like you and the others around here. *(She points with her mouth, smiles, makes a butterfly shape with her hand, and puts butterfly hand on Sissy's shoulder.)* Is OK, hijo. Or will be when you a man.

Sissy: Like your brother?

Doña: He not live to be man. The junta kill him when he eighteen. *(Her butterfly hand flutters again and then crumples and becomes a fist.)*

Sissy: I'm sorry, Doña. That must make you sad.

Doña: Triste, sí. But is OK, because cada caterpillar becomes beautiful mariposa.

Sissy: But Doña?

Doña: ¿Sí, hijo?

Sissy: Do the butterflies ever win the war?

Doña: Debes learn to fly faster than the bullets. *(They both laugh.)* Hay viene el gua-gua. Let's go home.

Bus Driver: Fancy seeing you two again. All aboard the Rollin T. Davis, properly known as the Rapid Transit District, also known as the Rapid Transit Disappearance. Culver City is our destination and our destiny.

Scene 13—The School of Hard Spanks and Racialized Geography

(Sissy returns home, finds Mana with hands on her hips, Baby Brother with rake in hand. Mami and Daddy globo / shadow puppet / light source berate and whup Sissy's ass all the way inside his home.)

Sissy: Ouch, hey, not so hard, OK, I know, I was just playing down the street, I wasn't being rude or elitist, I was just thinking. OK, OK, I get it, I'm sorry.

(Sissy is spanked off the stage, Mana follows laughing, Baby Brother begins to rake the yard.)

Baby Brother: Ch-ch-ch-chapparal. E-e-e-verybody s-says el-el-el-Los Angeles a d-d-d-desert. But it's r-r-r-really a a a chapparal. A almost d-desert. They s-s-sa-

say it d-d-d-don't ma-matter but it d-d-do. A-a-a-ask the the Indians who-who-who lived here f-f-f-primero. They knew could-couldn't too-too-too much live or gr-grow here. N-n-not e-e-enough wa-wa-wa-agua. I ga-guess na-nobody told the Indians fa-further down. F-f-f-pinche Mexicas. I kn-know all this c-c-cuz ge-ge-geography anda anda anda anda w-w-world history are my my favorite s-s-s-sub-sub-topics at school. Also cuz in th-th-this ho-ho-casa you got to to be able to con-con-con-t-r-i-b-u-t-e to conversation. So I kn-know about ma-ma-maps. Sis-sis-sis-sissy he go-got a b-b-better ma-ma-ma-membery for the ca-ca-capitol of st-st-states and st-st-stu-stu-shit. B-but I know r-r-ro-ro-rocks anda anda anda fos-fos-shells. In-in-in adentro del caracol th-th-that isn't the s-s-s-sound of the o-o-o-o-mar b-b-but history. That what my daddy say. He say it it it the s-s-s-sound ofa ofa pe-pe-people voting with their fa-feet. Bu-bu-but hehehe wr-wrong to-too. It is the sound of his-his-history. Ofa ofa dinosaurs b-being born anda dying off anda anda Me-Me-Me-Mexicanos co-co-co-coming to this co-co-coun-país and whe-whe-when this wa-was Mexico todavía. Anda way before that cuando era india y n-n-n-nada mas anda anda they knew it was a ch-ch-chapparal and couldn't to-to-too much things li-li-live here. And st-still don't.

Scene 14—Floating On

(Mana is in bed, which is a loft inside the garage. She is smoking a joint and singing along to "Float On." Sissy is outside her window, raking. Climbing up the stairs to her bed, he begins to speak. Mana has put out her joint but still sings along.)

Mana: "And if you feel that this is you. Here's what I want you to do. Take my hand."

Sissy: Sis . . .

Mana: "Come with me, baby, to love land."

Sissy: Sis . . .

Mana: "Let me show you how good it can be sharing your love with Larry."

Sissy: Mana!

Mana: What?!

Sissy: What are you doing?

Mana: Nothing. Get out.

Sissy: Something wrong with you? You drunk?

Mana: Nah. A little buzzed. What would you know about getting drunk? Always trying to be grown.

Sissy: I was born that way.

Mana: What . . . high?

Sissy: Fuck you . . . grown.

Mana: Nah, you were born chillando. Cried so much as a baby you'd throw up. Get hit for throwing up on daddy's shoe or in the car and cry some more. Terco.

Sissy: Like my Daddy.

Mana: But loca like mom.

Sissy: She ain't so crazy.

Mana: No one in this fucking family is normal.

Sissy: The Party don't require normal.

Mana: Fuck the Party.

Sissy: This party was pretty good. What do you do up here?

Mana: Nothing. Everything. Think. I don't know. I wish we were religious. Catholics.

Sissy: We are. Marx is Daddy's god.

Mana: Marx ain't nothing but a German Jew.

Sissy: And Jesus was a African one. What's the difference?

Mana: Mexican.

Sissy: You're tripped. Did you smoke dust?

Mana: Jesus is for Mexicans. Not all this progressive shit.

Sissy: The Sandinistas work with all those radical priests. Liberation something or other.

Mana: Why does everything have to have a name, a fuckin party-line in this house?

Sissy: Cuz Daddy loves it. Historical materialism, he calls it.

(*Baby Brother enters.*)

Baby Brother: Fag. Asshole. Fag. Asshole.

Mana & Sissy: What?

Baby Brother: The . . . the . . . the . . .

Mana: Spit it out. Don't stutter.

Sissy: It's a hesitation, not a stutter. What is it, baby?

Mana: I don't see why you're defending him. It wasn't me he was calling faggot.

Baby Brother: The Ca-Ca-Ca-Cabrones stole all the leftover beer.

Mana: We'll be right there, baby.

   (Baby exits.)

Mana: Hey, sissy.

Sissy: What?

Mana: I was just gonna tell you happy birthday, fucker.

Sissy: Oh, thank you. I mean fuck you. Let's go see what those Cabrones did. Ma's gonna kick my ass.

Coda: Cabrones' Comeuppance

(Cabrones' are passed out drunk, empty beer bottles surrounding them. Mana, Sissy, and Baby Brother run in and Mana, noticing crashed-out Cabrones, shushes her brothers. They huddle and giggle. Lights fade. When lights rise, Baby Brother is finishing tying up Cabrones with a mangera. Mana is putting lipstick on each of them. When they are done, they exit, Mana relaying lipstick to Sissy, who writes "SISSY WAS HERE" on their foreheads. When done, giggles, goes to exit, thinks again, runs back, and kisses each one. Raises his fist and then busts up. "Los Angeles" by X rises.)

This Party Ends.

A SISSY LEXICON

The twentieth century, when the future looks back on it, will not only
be remembered as the era of atomic discoveries and interplanetary explorations.
The second upheaval of this period, unquestionably, is the conquest by the
peoples of the lands that belong to them.
—Frantz Fanon, "First Truths on the Colonial Problem,"
in *Toward the African Revolution*

I thank the scholars, artists, and friends noted next to the definitions they contributed for being good comrades in deed and word. Terms are in order as they appear in the play.—Ricardo A. Bracho

PAUL ROBESON (1898–1976): Black Shakespearean actor and singer of Negro spirituals. A civil rights activist and lawyer, he fought against Spanish fascism with the Abraham Lincoln Brigade in the Spanish Civil War. He was named All-American in football for Rutgers University and played professional football. A scholar and staunch supporter of the Soviet Union, son of a runaway slave, picketed the White House, and refused to sing in front of segregated audiences. Robeson learned twenty languages, started a crusade against lynching, and wrote an autobiography called *Here I Stand*. (Natalie Smith Parra)

BLACK PANTHER PARTY FOR SELF DEFENSE (BPP): Founded by Bobby Seale and Huey P. Newton in Oakland in 1966. Without a doubt, the BPP transformed the struggles for the liberation of Black and other oppressed people globally. For this fact, members and leadership were surveilled, imprisoned, and assassinated. As the tenth point of their ten-point Party Platform declares, "We Want Land, Bread, Housing, Education, Clothing, Justice And Peace." And we still do. (Ricardo A. Bracho)

THE WRETCHED OF THE EARTH (1961): The revolutionary treatise written by the Martinican-born philosopher of the world Frantz Fanon (1925–61). There is no other single work that has come close to offering so useful a guidebook for the twentieth and twenty-first centuries. Tells us why all colonial occupiers/settlers better "get the fuck out now!" or be killed, cuz there's a new force in town and it ain't never going away: in a word, *decolonization*. Everybody:

> Arise you prisoners of starvation,
> Arise you wretched of the Earth,
> For justice thunders condemnation,
> for a better world's in birth …
> —Eugene Pottier, "The Internationale" (1870s)

(Randall Williams)

JIM THORPE (1888–1953): Born in Prague, Oklahoma, in 1888 when it was still Indian Territory. Thorpe was voted the greatest US athlete of the first half of the twentieth century by the Associated Press in 1950. A member of the Sac and Fox nation, his Indian name was Wa-Tho-Huk, which loosely translates as "A Path Lighted by a Great Flash of Lightning," or simply "Bright Path." Thorpe excelled in track and field, football, baseball, lacrosse, and ballroom dancing. He won gold medals at the 1912 Summer Olympics in the pentathlon and decathlon. He was on the US team, although American Indians would not be recognized as dual citizens of this nation-state and their sovereign tribes until 1924. His record scores in the pentathlon would stand for two decades, but he was stripped of these awards when it was learned that he had played professional baseball on summers off from college—a common enough practice in his day, but unlike others, he did not play under an alias. He later played baseball for the New York Giants, Cincinnati Reds, and Boston Braves; football for the Canton Bulldogs and all-native Oorang Indians; and basketball with the World Famous Indians. He lived his later life in abject poverty and as an alcoholic. He died in Lomita, California, in 1953, a year before Native Americans were given the right to vote. His Olympic medals were reinstated thirty years after his death. (Ricardo A. Bracho)

W. E. B. DU BOIS (1868–1963): Born in Great Barrington, Massachusetts, the son of a Haitian man and a descendant of Elizabeth Freeman, who successfully sued Massachusetts for her freedom. The Father of Pan-Africanism and founder of the NAACP, he joined the Communist Party at the age of ninety-three. The first Black man to receive a BA from Harvard University, he wrote over four thousand articles, books, and treatises, including the important *The Souls of Black Folk, Black Reconstruction in America, John Brown,* and *The Philadelphia Negro.* He died in Accra, Ghana, as a citizen of that independent African nation and of the left-decolonial-liberationist world. Always pronounce the *s* in his last name. (Ricardo A. Bracho)

GEORGE WASHINGTON CARVER (CA. 1864–1943): Born into slavery in what is now Diamond, Missouri. He, his mother, and his sister were stolen by night raiders and taken to be sold in Arkansas. Orphaned in the process, the infant George developed whooping cough and, when returned to the Carver plantation, could not do field work. He wandered the fields, learned about the various wild plants in the process, and became known as a child as the "Plant Doctor." His adamant dedication to pursuing knowledge eventually led to his enrollment at Iowa State Agricultural College, as the first Black student and later as the first Black faculty member. Eventually he took a position at the then five-year-old Tuskegee Institute and would remain there for forty-three years. He famously tussled with founder Booker T. Washington and submitted many letters of resignation. At Tuskegee he taught other former enslaved people farming techniques and developed a mobile school called a Jesup Wagon to bring education to the fields. In applying the scientific method to the labor of the small farmer, as an early proponent of sustainable agriculture, in working to dismantle the practice of monocultural cotton production and in developing hundreds of recipes and products from peanuts and sweet potatoes, Carver more than earned the moniker "Black Leonardo da Vinci" given to him by *Time* magazine in 1941. (Ricardo A. Bracho)

DR. CHARLES R. DREW (1904–50): A surgeon and medical researcher whose work greatly improved blood storage, which led to the development of large-scale blood banks during World War II. Dr. Drew protested the segregation of blood by race, correctly noting that it had no basis in science, and was the first Black surgeon to serve as an examiner on the American Board of Surgery. His death in a car accident has long been attributed to having been denied care by a White hospital, but another Black doctor involved in the accident has refuted that assertion. (Ricardo A. Bracho)

FATHER HIDALGO (1753–1811): Founder of the Mexican War of Independence and "Father of the Country." This Roman Catholic criollo priest learned many native Mexican languages and became actively involved in the Mexican independence movement against the Spanish Empire. Tipped off by Josefa Ortiz de Domínguez that the Spanish troops had intelligence on the planned rebellion and were on the move, Hidalgo rang the church bells at dawn on September 16, 1810, in the village of Dolores. The gathered Indios and Mestizos, who were expecting a mass, instead heard Hidalgo's demand for independence, what has become known as El Grito de Dolores, in which he exclaimed, "Long live nuestra Virgen de Guadalupe, death to bad government, death to the Spaniards!" (Ricardo A. Bracho)

CESAR CHAVEZ (1927–93): Revered leader of the United Farm Workers who worked to unionize and better the working conditions for farmworking labor in California, and whose grape boycott and hunger strikes gave him and the cause national prominence. In the context of the left politics of this play, Chavez is a liberal reformist for his lifelong allegiance to the Democratic Party and strategy of Gandhian nonviolence. Many on the left see him and the UFW as reactionary for purging communists and non-Mexican members early on and for later stances against undocumented farm labor. (Ricardo A. Bracho)

CANTINFLAS (1911–93): The Mexican actor who epitomizes comedic genius and whose mode of broad caricature, sophisticated wordplay, and trenchant satire is evident in the work of El Teatro Campesino, Cheech & Chong, Culture Clash,

Fulana, Chicano Secret Service, and Pocho. Mario Moreno began his career in the '30s in traveling shows (carpas) and dabbled in minstrelsy before creating the persona Cantinflas, whose sartorial and aesthetic conventions of a thinly groomed mustache and baggy pants tied with a rope were meant to evoke the pelado, urban campesino slumdweller. Charlie Chaplin called him "the greatest comedian in the world," and Miguel del Río called him "the Mexican dictator of optimism." He earned a 1956 Golden Globe for Best Actor in a Musical or Comedy for his lead role in *Around the World in Eighty Days*, which was his US debut, and that year was the world's highest-paid actor. (Ricardo A. Bracho)

MADAME C. J. WALKER (1867–1919): Born Sarah Breedlove into a former slave family. Walker became known as America's first Black woman millionaire by developing hair care products for Black women and also worked to have lynching declared a federal crime. (Ricardo A. Bracho)

LORRAINE HANSBERRY (1930–65): The first Black woman to have a drama produced on Broadway, *A Raisin in the Sun*, and the youngest person and first Black person to win a New York Drama Critics Circle Award. (Ricardo A. Bracho)

MARIAN ANDERSON (1897–1993): Brilliant Black opera singer who was routinely excluded from US venues under Jim Crow segregation. Anderson was raised in a working-class family in South Philadelphia and toured extensively throughout Europe, where she was embraced by audiences, critics, and composers. A contralto who was the first Black person to sing at the New York Metropolitan Opera, she is best known for her 1939 Easter Sunday recital on the steps of the Lincoln Memorial before a live integrated audience of seventy-five thousand and a national radio audience of millions. This open-air recital was organized after she was denied permission to perform to an integrated crowd in Constitution Hall by the White supremacist organization Daughters of the American Revolution. Filmmaker Cauleen Smith contends, "Marian Anderson and Albert Einstein were dear friends. She had to stay at his house whenever she sang at Princeton because there were no hotels that accepted 'coloreds.' I suspect she and Al, that ole sly devil, were lovers." (Cauleen Smith, Helen Jun, and Ricardo A. Bracho)

DOROTHY DANDRIDGE (1922–65): A '50s-era Black entertainer noted for her nightclub and cabaret acts, her sultry screen presence, and her stunning looks. She was the first African American nominated for an Academy Award as Best Actress of the Year (*Porgy and Bess*, 1959). Unfortunately, it was not her time. Limited screen roles, family and personal tragedy, failed marriages, and bankruptcy left her dead of an overdose in 1965. (Keith M. Harris)

ROSAURA REVUELTAS (1909–96): Mexican actor best known for her stalwart and inspiring performance as Esperanza Quintero in *Salt of the Earth* (1954), the only US film ever to be blacklisted. Based on actual events, *Salt of the Earth* portrays the poverty, racism, and inhumane working conditions circumscribing the lives of Mexican American miners in Silver City, New Mexico, who staged a thirteen-month strike against Empire Zinc Corporation. The miners, and eventually their entire families, struggle to organize a union. The film is noted for utilizing the community of New Mexican miners as its actors. Rosaura's portrayal of Esperanza, wife of a miner, leaps to the forefront of the film when the men are forbidden to picket by an injunction. Amid the doubts of their husbands and the animosity of the Anglo mine owners, the miners' wives take to the picket lines to carry out the work of resistance. *Salt of the Earth* also benefits from its vanguard inclusion of a feminist critique: Esperanza underscores to her husband Juan that the oppression he endures from the mine owners and bosses parallels the oppression wives face in their lives as Mexican Americans and women. In this, the film achieves emotional and social depth as it demonstrates the interdependent nature of hierarchies. Blacklisted screenwriter Michael Wilson, who gathered his material from the actual New Mexican miners, wrote the screenplay. Herbert Biberman, who served time for contempt against the US House Committee on Un-American Activities and was branded as one of the infamous "Hollywood Ten," directed the film. The production and distribution of the film faced a systematic blockade by Hollywood elites, who worked diligently to kill the project. Tactics included alerting the Immigration and Naturalization Service to Rosaura's involvement. Eventually, officials arrived during filming, challenged her documentation, arrested her, and deported her to Mexico. The film was completed by using a stand-in for Rosaura and doing clandestine postproduction work with her in Mexico. Unlike its interdicted US reception, the film found acclaim in Europe and won the grand prize from the Paris Academy of Film. The Academy awarded Rosaura its Best Actress honor. She never again worked in Hollywood, and later in life she went on to become a writer. (Irma Mayorga)

DEMOCRATIC CENTRALISM: Marxist-Leninist precept, most strongly identified with the Soviet model but also practiced by various sectarian left organizations, that a revolutionary communist organization, hereinafter "the party," must be organized based on the collective experience of the party. The leadership decides on new positions (a new line), which all party members are then bound to put into practice. The logic goes: Only if all put the same line into practice can the party find out if the line works; if each member of the party goes their own way, there will never be a strong, unified party. (Natalie Smith Parra and Ricardo A. Bracho)

EL HOMBRE NUEVO (NEW MAN): Concept articulated by Che Guevara. Che proclaimed that a (socialist, anti-imperialist) New Man, with no ego and full of ferocious love for the other, had to be created out of the ruins of the old (capitalist, colonialist) one. (Natalie Smith Parra and Ricardo A. Bracho)

SOMOZA: Not the delicious puffy pastry, but the brutal dictatorship that ruled Nicaragua for more than forty years. There were actually three Somoza dictators —a dynasty of a father and two sons—who ruled Nicaragua consecutively by means of repression and torture. All three were trained as dreaded National Guardsmen by the United States, and ruled the country either directly, as presidents, or indirectly, as heads of the National Guard. The first, Anastasio Somoza García, came to power originally in 1937, after having ordered the assassination of democratic reformer and guerrilla leader Augusto C. Sandino during peace talks, and deposing President Juan Bautista Sacasa. Famously, FDR is said to have remarked of this first Somoza, in 1939, "He may be a son of a bitch, but he's our son of a bitch." Luis Somoza and Anastasio Somoza Debayle ruled the country after their father's assassination in 1956 by the poet and patriot Rigoberto López Pérez. In 1967, after the death of Luis, Anastasio Somoza Debayle came to power and reimposed the iron-fist policies of his father's era. More ruthless than the first Anastasio, Somoza Debayle was overthrown by the Sandinistas on July 18, 1979. He fled to Alfredo Stroessner's dictatorial Paraguay—the only place that would take him—where he was assassinated (or, as we prefer to say, ajusticiado!) by a righteous cell of the Argentine Ejército Revolucionario del Pueblo. (María Josefina Saldaña-Portillo)

THE ME DECADE: The sociocultural shift in the United States away from the politicized activism of the 1960s to the privatized self-indulgence of the 1970s, characterized by an apolitical focus on self-help, self-awareness, and self-consciousness. The term was coined by a New York novelist, Tom Wolfe, in 1976 and critically invokes the 1970s as a period of ahistorical self-absorption in which spiritual gurus, therapists, and religious cult leaders reigned within the national social landscape. (Helen Jun)

JEAN-JACQUES DESSALINES (CA. 1758–1806): Born in either Guinea or Nigeria, captured and enslaved, and brought to cut sugarcane in Saint-Domingue, which we now know as Haiti. In 1791 he joined a slave rebellion that would lead to the Haitian Revolution, which made Haiti the world's first Black independent postslavery nation-state. On January 1, 1804, Dessalines declared Haiti an independent nation, naming it after its original Arawak name. Given the titles of governor-general-for-life and emperor of Haiti, he declared Haiti an all-Black nation and refused to allow Whites to own land or property. Though he tried to maintain sugar production without returning to slavery, his system of agrarian militarism put all Blacks into either compulsory field labor or military service, while he placed mulatto light-skinned elites in positions of bureaucratic power. (Ricardo A. Bracho)

THE SANDINISTAS: The groovy, armed guerrilla faction of a much broader social movement in Nicaragua during the 1970s that overthrew the dictatorship of Anastacio Somoza Debayle in 1979. Though this movement is often referred to generally as "the Sandinista movement," the term *Sandinista* more specifically refers to actual members of the Frente Sandinista de Liberación Nacional (Sandinista Front of National Liberation), or FSLN. The FSLN represents the union of three different armed guerrilla movements that formed independently among peasants in the rural countryside, urban workers, and student leaders during the 1960s. In the early 1970s, these three groups banded together, formed political alliances with civilian opposition groups, and successfully led the overthrow of Somoza. The party of the same name then proceeded to preside over the Nicaraguan country through free and fair elections for the next decade. During this period, the Sandinista-led government virtually eliminated illiteracy, reduced the country's mortality rate considerably, instituted land reform and rural credit, and promulgated a constitution that defined a family as "any group of people living in solidarity under one roof." How cool is that? (María Josefina Saldaña-Portillo)

THE LONG MARCH: Arguably ill-advised military action of the Chinese communist army in the fall of 1934 in battle with Chiang Kai-shek's Kuomintang. Against the protests of Mao Zedong, Russian military strategists launched a full-scale retreat from Jian-Xi to consolidate a communist stronghold in Hunan, ordering the Red Army to carry everything it could, including furniture, typewriters, and printing presses. After forty-five thousand of the slow-moving soldiers were killed off by January 1935, control was handed to Mao, who led the Red Army through some of the world's most treacherous terrain, and after 368 days, ten thousand soldiers—approximately 10 percent of the original number—reached their destination. Considered a miraculous physical feat, the Long March consolidated the political leadership of Mao, who regarded the bravery and endurance of the Red Army as emblematic of the indomitable spirit of anti-imperialist struggle. (Helen Jun)

GUSANOS: The pejorative term that pro-revolution Cubans applied to the wealthy and middle-class Cubans who fled Cuba after the revolution. English translation: "worms." (Natalie Smith Parra)

SOWETO IN 1976: Began with the arrival of the Dutch in the Cape of Good Hope (1652). Materialized this time on June 16, 1976, when thousands of schoolchildren walked out en masse to protest the mandated use of Afrikaans as the language of instruction: "If we must do Afrikaans, Vorster must do Zulu." Twenty-nine children were killed that day, and the next day all of South Africa was ablaze. With the older generation of anti-apartheid activists either dead, in prison, or in exile, a new generation had emerged to change the course of the country, led by Steve Biko and the Black Consciousness Movement. The era of peaceful struggle and negotiated settlements was over, and this new generation learned the language of armed struggle, which didn't translate into Afrikaans. (Randall Williams)

JOSÉ MARTÍ (1853–95): Maestro. poet, patriot, journalist, translator, martyr, leader of Cuban independence from Spain. A fervent anticolonialist, Martí advanced the most important conception of our culture, published in its most concise fashion, in his 1891 article "Nuestra America." Martí's solidarity with our aboriginal cultures was absolute, and although he spent some years in exile in New York, this Cuban exile was not seduced by "civilization": "Everything I have done to this day, and everything I shall do is to that end[,] . . . to prevent in time the expansion of the United States into the Antilles and to prevent her from falling, with ever greater force, upon our American lands" (letter to Manuel Mercado, 1895). Compare these last words of Martí with those of his bourgeois nemesis, Domingo Faustino Sarmiento: "We shall catch up to the United States. . . . Let us become the United States." Burn Sarmiento, read Martí. (Randall Williams)

EL FOCO: Designates the unitary focus of guerrilla operations and became the basis of a theory of revolution in which guerrilla warfare plays the critical role—inspired by the success of the Cuban Revolution (1959). First developed by Che Guevara (*Guerrilla Warfare*), it received its most extensive theoretical elaboration in the work of Régis Debray (*Revolution in the Revolution?*). El foco can be thought of as the "detonator" or "spark," but the ultimate effectiveness of the explosion depends on the depths and form of the political crisis into which the bomb is inserted. (Randall Williams)

TROPICAL SOCIALISM: Term used, both in the positive and as a pejorative, to describe the specific contours of socialist governments and movements in the Global South of the Americas (i.e., Latina América, the Caribbean, and any ghetto/barrio/rez in the United States). The term encompasses the left ideologies that emerge from within (post)colonial slavocracies and geopolitical territories with significant African and Indian communities and insurgent histories. It is commonly associated with the Cuban Revolution, but has also been ascribed to the Bolivarian Revolution in Venezuela and is known as *socialismo moreno* in Brazil. (Ricardo A. Bracho)

VILMA ESPÍN (1930–2007): President of the Cuban Federation of Women from its founding in 1960 until her death. Espín acted as a messenger between the revolutionary movement on the island and the 26th of July Movement based in Mexico City. In Mexico, she met Raul Castro, whom she married in 1959. (Ricardo A. Bracho)

HAYDÉE SANTAMARÍA (1922–80): One of two women to participate in the revolutionary attack on the Moncada Garrison, in which 180 rebels attacked the military barracks in Santiago de Cuba. Tortured and jailed, upon release she edited and organized the clandestine publication of Fidel Castro's "History Will Absolve Me." In 1956, she led an urban uprising in Santiago de Cuba, and in 1958 she helped form an all-female revolutionary platoon. In 1958 she was sent to Miami to organize for the movement, and in 1959 she returned after the triumph of the revolution. She founded and headed the world-important cultural center, Casa de las Americas, and died by suicide in 1980. (Ricardo A. Bracho)

BLANCA NIEVES: References the interpretation of Snow White and the Seven Dwarves performed by the National Ballet of Cuba under the direction of Alicia Alonso. (Ricardo A. Bracho)

ROSITA FORNÉS (1923–2020): Born in New York to Catalonian parents, and taken to Cuba by her mother and Cuban adoptive stepfather at the age of two. In Cuba, she began a sixty-eight-year singing, dancing, and acting career that earned her the title "La Gran Vedette de Cuba." Her attempts to perform in Miami were often met by Molotov cocktails. Although she admitted to a longtime affair with Cantinflas, she never confirmed the rumors that she had affairs with the Cuban dictator Fulgencio Batista and Argentine revolutionary Che Guevara. (Ricardo A. Bracho)

UMAP: Unidades Militares de Ayuda a la Producción, one of the many blights on the history of already existing socialism. These were prison camps in Cuba that from 1965 to 1968 forced gays, Jehovah's Witnesses, Catholics, and Protestants to hard labor in a misguided effort to reeducate them of "bourgeois and counter-revolutionary values." The camps were closed after internal pressure from Cuban citizens and the National Union of Artists and Writers and after British writer Graham Greene was sent to investigate. Nicaraguan poet Ernesto Cardenal's excellent book *En Cuba* features interviews with prisoners and guards. Cuban sexologist Monika Krause contends that the camps were not indicative of socialism but antisocialist in their ignorance of and aversion to homosexuality and a moment of true sadness in the history of Cuba. (Ricardo A. Bracho)

LOLITA LEBRÓN (1919–2010): Puerto Rican nationalist leader who was imprisoned by the US government for storming and shooting up the US House of Representatives with two others on March 1, 1954. She unfurled the Puerto Rican flag, shouted, "Viva Puerto Rico Libre!" and, by her own account, shot into the ceiling. At the time of her arrest, she stated, "I did not come to kill anyone, I came to die for Puerto Rico!" She served twenty-five years in prison and was pardoned in 1979 by Jimmy Carter. A lifelong independentista, she served sixty days for protesting the US Navy occupation of Vieques. At the International Tribunal on Violations of Human Rights in Puerto Rico and Vieques, she ended her deposition by stating, "I had the honor of leading the act against the US Congress on March 1, 1954, when we demanded freedom for Puerto Rico and we told the world that we are an invaded nation, occupied and abused by the United States of America. I feel very proud of having performed that day, of having answered the call of the motherland." (Ricardo A. Bracho)

HISTORICAL MATERIALISM: The most important revolutionary-scientific-analytic form ever conceived to understand human economic activity as a series of dialectical processes: between humans and nature, and between humans and humans (social relations). Formulated by Marx, the concept demonstrates how materialism—the selfish preoccupation with goods and money—is not natural but historical, and describes how to destroy it and establish cooperation and mutuality through revolutionary struggle and collective economic activity. The point of this science is not simply to understand the world, but to change it. Now that's a science we can all use. (Randall Williams)

PUTO

a virus contaminating the collective body of the city
in the wake of his delirious journey through it
—Juan Goytisolo, *Makbara*

For She Who Walks in the Shadow of Capitalism, Celia Herrera Rodríguez

Puto was first developed in Center Theatre Group's 2007–8 LA Writer's Group, convened by Literary Manager Pier Carlo Talenti. On April 6, 2010, UC Santa Cruz's Cantú Queer Center held a staged reading at the Stevenson Event Center. It was directed by the author with visuals by Dino Dinco and casting by the author with Sean San José of Campo Santo of San Francisco, and it was produced by Tam Welch and Toro Castaño of the Cantú Queer Center. On April 20, 2011, Virginia Grise and the author codirected a staged reading at Company of Angels in Los Angeles. Marc David Pinate directed a workshop production with a student cast at the Theatre School of DePaul University in Chicago, which opened on October 4, 2011. At the invitation of Hiram Pérez of Vassar College's Latin American and Latino/a Studies Program, Bracho directed students in a staged reading on March 23, 2012. Chicago's Urban Theater Company included a staged reading of the play in its Real Aggressive Writing Series, directed by Juan Castañeda, on May 13, 2013. Producer David Anzuelo included the play in the Bright Untamed Festival, where it was directed by Daniel Jacquez at INTAR Theatre in New York on

August 25, 2014. A stage reading was held on November 9, 2014, at the Bonaventure Hotel in Los Angeles as part of a remembrance of José Esteban Muñoz at the American Studies Association's annual conference. It was directed by Bracho with a talk-back facilitated by Richard T. Rodriguez. Cherríe Moraga directed a staged reading of the play at Stanford University on May 5, 2015.

Juana María Rodríguez, Randall Williams, Sean San José, and Virginia Grise provided dramaturgy for various drafts of the script. Center Theatre Group's Literary Department, specifically Pier-Carlo Talenti and Mike Sablone, made the play possible via the Playwright's Group, and other writers in the group were keen and warm first readers, especially Josslyn Luckett, T. D. Mitchell, and Kate Rigg. Actors who greatly contributed to the play's development include Elisa Bocanegra, Catherine Castellanos, Mariella Saba, Omar Metwally, Raul Castillo, Victor Vázquez, Ser Anzoategui, Alexis de la Rocha, Selene Santiago, Norman Zelaya, Ricky Saenz, Taylor Hawthorne, and Ruben David Adorno.

CAST OF CASTOFFS

Puto:	A photographer, a player, a counterfeiter, a currency trader on the brown market.
Ovíd:	An unemployed professor / art historian. Puto's best friend and strongest critic.
Smiles:	A leader / cadre member of the awakened cell CREW (Communist Revolution Every Weekend). Boy, is he beautiful.
Knees:	A beekeeper, an ex-con. A butch dyke. Nuff said.
Officer Carlos Moreno Jr.:	Otherwise known as Charlie Brown-noser.
Dalton:	An artist. Never met a reflective surface he didn't enjoy seeing himself in.
Kid:	Twelve, with a bullet and a stack of books.
Sol:	Kid's mom, Puto's comadre, a former movement leader.
Bello:	A horny boy.
Lunar:	RUCAS leadership (Revolutionary Underground Chicas Against the State). Never been seen not wearing hoops or lipstick.
Transam the Transman:	A magician and successful artist.
Lady Bus Driver:	A DASH driver.
Hornera:	Baker and gunrunner.

Diosita La Putita más Regia:	Trans-mujer performer, puta, y revolucionaria.
Rabbit:	Leader of SWARM (Southwest Armed Resistance Movement).
Tortuga:	Rabbit's man, he don't talk much.

(The time is May 2019 in a parallel reality. The Bush family has assumed an imperial monarchy [the Koch Brothers and Monsanto take credit]; the Border Wall has been finished between the United States [California, Arizona, New Mexico, Texas] and Mexico [though the Apache wage impressive war against both nations]; industrial farming and prisons in the Central Valley have merged to form massive agri-prisons; the illegal immigrant, the felon, and certain aligned artist-intellectuals/poet-philosophers have been de-citizened [or denied the option of citizenship, in the case of migrants] and are unable to assemble or use dollars and have restricted mobility. They form a permanent, generational servant class, since immigration to the United States has come to a standstill due to rabid antiterrorist state terror and because who would want to get caught up in all this ish.)

(The setting is Los Angeles, California, the city and the county; Homeland Defense Paramilitary Zones: Eastern Containment, Boyle Heights, and Pico Rivera Catchment Areas; Zona de Lago de Plata, Echo Park Catchment Area; Surf Zone, Santa Monica Catchment Area; Rampart Cops Zone, MacArthur Park Catchment Area; and where the Angeles Forest meets the Mojave Desert, Wild Mexican Indian Territory.)

(The sounds, murmurs, susurrations, hard breathing, creaking of bed, dirt talk, banging of headboard, creak of mattress, rustle of sheets, laughter, and knowing that is two men fucking. These men know each other, know what the other likes, like to dare each other into new acts, positions, intensities, intimacies. The sex culminates. They are more low groaners/soft moaners than screamers—this isn't porn, after all. The movement subsides, the sounds become speech and then spoon-sleep.)

Scene 1

(Lights rise.)

(An empty bedroom in a Lincoln Heights apartment. The room should indicate on some level that the inhabitant is Mexican, homosexual, and an artist/photographer but not in overreaching or clichéd ways.)

(Offstage.)

Puto (voice-over [vo]): *(Puto's voice.)* Babe, what do you take in your coffee again? I have half-n-half, soy, raw sugar, brown sugar, some contraband honey. Smiles? *(Puto rushes on stage, into bedroom holding a package of flour tortillas in one hand, corn tortillas in the other.)*

Puto: Hey, sleepyhead, flour or corn? Smiles? *(Puto rushes around.)*

(No sign of anyone else.)

Puto: Smiles? Smiles!

(Blackout.)

Scene 2

(Lights rise. The room has been lightly ransacked since the last scene. Puto sits, his body still, his mind frantic. He makes a call on his cell.)

Puto: Meet me. At the café. NOW!!! *(Dial tone.)*

Ovíd (vo): OK, freak. *(Lights out.)*

Scene 3

(A cranky Ovíd drives to meet Puto.)

Ovíd: Hijo de la gran puta Puto. Like nobody else has problems en este mundo mierda norteamericana. And that elitist sangana Puto has it the easiest, dual citizenship before the binationalization of the economy, before they finished building the border wall so he rides around just hoping Homeland Paramilitary stop him. A fuckin' aboveground gig as an art photographer—fuckin' indianist porn if you ask me, but since I am neither a gallerist nor a curator nor a collector, no one does. And since I am an unemployed and unemployable immigrant art historian, they aren't going to be asking anytime soon. Boys, shit, well, he isn't hard to look at and the money belt of dollars, euros, and yen don't hurt. But like I have to stop my thankless, workless day for his bullshit. This shit better be good.

Scene 4

(Homegirl Café. Sunlight coming through windows. Ovíd n Puto at table with coffee mugs. Puto is paranoid, Ovíd is amused by it.)

Ovíd: So?

Puto: Did you bring it?

Ovíd: What?

Puto: Your little tape recorder thingamajig?

Ovíd: I always carry it. What's goin' on with you?

Puto: Give it to me.

Ovíd: OK. Calm down. Just begin at the beginning. *(Ovíd hands him handheld recorder. Puto grabs it, hits record.)*

Puto: Today, the 20th of April, 2015, the year of someone else's lord, I execute my last will and testament. *(Ovíd grabs the recorder.)*

Ovíd: What the fuck, Puto? I said start at the beginning, not at your untimely end. Just breathe. Then begin at the beginning.

Puto: I walked into the room to ask him, flour or corn, and he was gone.

Ovíd: Who? What?

Puto: Smiles. Tortillas. They didn't steal the tortillas. Just him. And my laptop.

Ovíd: Who stole him? Or did he just take off with it himself? I told you about hanging out with him and his CREW. Communist Revolution Every Weekend, mi culo, bunch of hoodlums.

Puto: They do important political work.

Ovíd: And you do him?

Puto: Sometimes. He's sweet. C'mon, he Smiles in his Sleep.

Ovíd: Seems he disappears that way too.

Puto: Yeah, and I'm next. Just like my name, Puto, I am fucked. Fuck!

Ovíd: Calm down. You're still not making any sense.

Puto: I began at the beginning as you instructed, Profe.

Ovíd: Begin before that. Before the troubles.

Puto: The War? The Drought? The bee extinction?

Ovíd: No, sonso, focus on the trouble at hand. Before you found him missing. What led him to be in your bed. The quotidian, the mundane.

Puto: Huh?

Ovíd: Just hit rewind, fool.

Puto: OK.

(Puto hits rewind on the tape recorder. Time rewinds.)

Scene 5

(The day before, April 19, 2015, the year of somebody else's lord. Puto's apartment. Puto has camera, Smiles stands in bathrobe. Set lights.)

Puto: OK. Drop the robe.

Smiles: I thought we were gonna work first.

Puto: This is labor. Here, put these on.

(Puto hands Smiles cleats, which Smiles puts on. Smiles then lies down, simulating that he is dead. He wears a Mexican soccer outfit and lies on a piece of astroturf in a pose lifted from Jesús Helguera's El Niño Héroe.*)*

Smiles: Why I gotta do this?

Puto: I'm helping you with your work, you have to help me with mine. So what's up?

Smiles: Knees is getting out of prison tomorrow, needs a new name, dollars, pesos, a job if you got one.

Puto: I could use an assistant. Why's Knees so important?

Smiles: Knees is the bee's knees, a beekeeper on our side. Knows how to keep 'em, charm 'em.

Puto: I see. And Knees won't go work on one of those private apiaries in Malibu, La Jolla, or Santa Barbara?

Smiles: Nah, Knees is an outlaw from way in the day and, as a Mexican immigrant con, can't earn dollars anyway. Knees been down a long time, much of it in the hole.

Puto: For?

Smiles: Some trumped-up gang-related nonsense. But Knees maintained one of our first underground orchards. Knees is the business.

Puto: Fuckin' farmers posin' as gangsters.

Smiles: And you got me posing like some goalie with a concussion, foo. Besides, the more food we can grow, the more land we reclaim, we won't need dollars, pesos, micas, passports. As long as we control the production, distribution of resources and defend the land and its O.G. inhabitants . . .

Puto: Yeah yeah yeah, I was in that same study group. OK, now I need you to play dead. Stop smiling. Dead. Not asleep. You are the heroic one. The one who gives his life for his nation. Gives life to the nation. Damn, you are beautiful. OK. Last shot. Now come and let's get you out of that costume and into my bed.

Smiles: We still got work to do.

Puto: I can talk and plot and negotiate horizontally.

(They embrace. Puto kills the lights.)

Scene 6

(Puto n Ovíd at café.)

Puto: And there I stood, tortillas in hand, and there he wasn't.

Ovíd: Well, it was hot, but not clarifying. Now what?

Puto: Now I have to go back home. I have a shoot in a few. I'm meeting Dalton and shooting him, he's going to portray three boys in that Gauguin painting, the one where they are sitting at the table with fruit and knives.

Ovíd: You reference such exoticist crap.

Puto: It pays the bills, or provides the best cover for it.

Ovíd: Hey, can I come by later and borrow your leaf blower?

Puto: You don't have a yard.

Ovíd: No, I just need to pose as a day laborer in order to make it past the Westside Border Patrol on Western. I need to go to the library.

Puto: No worries. I can also give you a real good counterfeit library card so you can actually check some out. A leaf blower with a PhD. God, I love this country.

Ovíd: And it hates you right back.

Scene 7

(Back at Puto's place, darkness. Knees sits, wearing the scrubs they give you upon release from prison. The manila envelope containing Knees's possessions is on her lap. She holds a jar of honey to the light. Puto enters apartment, brings up light on a dimmer switch. Knees slowly stands.)

Knees: Hello, I'm Knees. Smiles sent me.

Puto: I'm Puto. Smiles is gone.

Knees: I see.

Puto: And so is my laptop.

Knees: Anything else?

Puto: No.

Knees: Did you notice the dust in your apartment?

Puto: Pardon?

Knees: Look.

(Knees leads Puto by his shoulder they peer at the shelves.)

Knees: The dust, everything has been unsettled, moved about an inch to the right. You got creepy crawled, mijo.

Puto: Creepy crawled?

Knees: Some Manson Family shit. Charlie would have the girls break into people's houses while they were sleeping, move everything in their place a few inches, and exit without stealing anything or getting caught.

Puto: My stuff is gone.

Knees: Yeah, well, this wasn't Squeaky Fromme. Probably the WASP Ring ordered it from the inside. They don't want you working with us, especially with me.

Puto: So what are we gonna do about that? My livelihood is on that computer. My legal one, anyway. And Smiles's mom is gonna creepy crawl my face when I tell her he's missing.

Knees: She's movement. And she doesn't need to know. Not yet. We need to man up. And you need to calm the fuck down.

(The sound of buzzing approaching.)

Knees: Shit.

Puto: What?

Knees: The Ring is sending their minions. Wasps trained to kill. We need hoodies and to secure all the windows. Take all the meat out the fridge lay it on the floor. Fuck. C'mon, Puto, we gotta move. *(Knees exits to begin prepping.)*

(The buzzing becomes louder and louder.)

Scene 8

(Buzzing but at a low volume.)

(Knees n Puto stand in hoodies, with cans of empty insect repellent.)

Puto: Now that was fucked.

Knees: Yeah, but we got through it. Let's go. What should we take with us?

Puto: The safe, knife, gun. My cameras and equipment are already packed.

Knees: Anything of sentimental value, homes?

Puto: That got taken this morning.

Knees: We'll work on that, compa. Let's grab that shit and head to a safe house I know in Whittier.

(Puto dims the light to off. They exit. Buzzing dies.)

Marc David Pinate, *Puto* production flyer, 2011.

Scene 9

(A parking lot in Pico Rivera. Puto n Knees each hold a Styrofoam tray of nachos. Knees has nachos con carnitas, fresh avocado, no sour cream or cheese. Puto has pollo, extra everything.)

Puto: This isn't a safe house in Whittier. It's Casa García in Pico Rivera.

Knees: And nothing makes me feel safer or more back home than these nachos. Just eat while I think.

Puto: So like were you in a men's or women's prison? Not being rude, just that you're pretty butch, didn't know if you were trans or anything.

Knees: *(Looks at him hard.)* Eat.

Puto: OK, just making conversation.

Knees: Look, mijo, the less you know about me, the better.

Puto: Why's that?

(Knees puts down her food, looks him dead in the eyes, pinches Puto hard.)

Puto: Owww, what the fuck, Knees!?!

Knees: If that's how your pussy ass responds to a little pinche pinching, what happens when Homeland Security gets a hold of you? The less the better, entiendes?

Puto: Understood.

Scene 10

(Driving, the sense that Puto n Knees have been quiet for quite some time. Flickery lights, the sun coming in from between trees overhead.)

Knees: OK, tell me about you. And turn right at the light.

Puto: But I thought we weren't supposed to share info.

Knees: I can handle a lot more than being pinched. I need to know more about your role in the movement. How it is we got here. Left here.

Puto: Well, I'm a photographer. I have galleries in Europe and in New York.

Knees: Stop bragging. I mean, what you do for us?

Puto: Oh, I guess I'm what the O.G. call a fellow traveler, not a member of CREW, but a useful ally, you know, in what they do.

Knees: I know what we do. What do you do?

Puto: I teach the class on Revolutionary Aesthetics and the Sublime.

Knees: Come again? Keep going straight for a while. Say more about your class.

Puto: Well, it's sorta a combo creative writing and critical viewing workshop, art history and practice class—kinda how to make art in the movement that isn't all murals and Que Viva! politics.

Knees: And?

Puto: What you want, lesson plans? The usual suspects—Genet, Fassbinder, Poniatowska, Said, Césaire, Mendieta, González-Torres.

Knees: No, it's just that, well I don't see why the enemy would be after the arts & crafts teacher.

Puto: Snap! That was harsher than your pinch. I sell all one needs for a new identity, national ID and the like. Uhm, oh yeah, I am also the unofficial giver of names.

(Knees looks confused.)

Puto: I give every member of CREW their party name. Like, I gave Smiles in his Sleep his name cuz he does that, and everyone else once they have finished their initial study groups and move into cadre work. Everybody but No Nick Will.

(Knees scratches her head.)

Puto: You don't know Guillermo? Well, he didn't like Memo to the Murderers, though he writes the best aboveground editorials, or Billy the Bolshevik on account of his vaquero steez and Leninist affect. So he's No Nick Will until I can come up with something that will stick.

Knees: Witty. But man, none of this makes you particularly important, Puto. Take this left.

Puto: Uhm, I've slept with a lot of CREW. The aforementioned Smiles and No Nick, had a group thing with the Maguey Brothers—they aren't really related, just good with cultivating succulents and medicine—Tres Flores, the CREW's barber and horticulturalist,

Knees: Well, clearly, you've earned your nom de guerre.

Puto: And you know I am, well, the reason I can't be a regular member is cuz of my day job as a currency trader and counterfeiter on the brown market. I move pesos, yen, dollars, euro.

Knees: That makes you useful, but not necessarily, well, it's not like it makes you loyal or trustworthy, and CREW trusted you with me and Smiles, leadership, so, no that ain't it either.

Puto: Oh, maybe it's cuz, well, the only really secret thing I do is handle communication between CREW and RUCAS.

(Knees's eyes brighten.)

Knees: Revolutionary Underground Chicanas Against the State.

Puto: Well, it's Chicas now instead of Chicanas cuz they have some other non-Mexican women involved, but yeah, them. You heard of 'em?

Knees: Heard of? Shit, I founded that shit when the men tried to deny us weapon training at the first Southwest Armed Resistance Movement meeting.

Puto: You were at the first Swarm? Damn, you are gangsta. Well, then, you know how the cells work, no direct communication, only one point person from CREW, me, deals with one designated contact from RUCAS. So, anyway, I have to deliver some notes to Lunar at a party I am faux crashing tonight.

Knees: Who's that?

Puto: She's this hot-ass chick, I gave her the name Lunar cuz of the beauty mark

Knees: She has above the left side of her beautiful mouth. That's my ex. This makes more sense. Where are the notes?

Puto: Taped beneath my balls. I pretend I am her coke dealer, we go to the bathroom, I— (*Knees cuts him off.*)

Knees: No more details. Go to that party and do whatever else you were gonna do today, in the exact order you were gonna do it, only don't go back to your apartment, ever again, actually.

Puto: But Ovíd is gonna come by later to borrow my leaf blower.

Knees: Stop here and stop him, but don't communicate by phone. Ovíd?

Puto: He's an academic, not movement, his moms gave him that name, not me.

Knees: Oh, yeah, and wash your truck.

Puto: Why? Will that put the Wasp Ring off my scent?

Knees: Nah, dude, your shit is just dirty.

(*They both laugh.*)

Knees: And tell Magda—Lunar, tell her Eva Crane sends her a box of bees from the other side.

(*Puto squints.*)

Knees: Don't ask, do tell.

(*Puto drives off. Knees steals away.*)

Scene 11

(Sunset Junction. Puto reaches a Homeland Defense checkpoint. Officer Carlos Moreno swaggers over.)

Officer: *(Without looking up.)* Citizen?

Puto: Dual.

Officer: ID, please.

(Officer looks up, realizes it's Puto, and can't help but smile.)

Puto: *(Reaches into glove compartment, hands him a wad of documents.)* Here you go, Officer Charlie Brown-noser.

Officer: *(Smile erases.)* Don't be calling me that on the job, Puto.

Puto: But it's your job that got your nose so brown, turned Carlos Moreno into Charlie Brown-noser.

Officer: It was either this or being a guard at one of the agri-prisons. Who wants to live in the CV?

Puto: Dude, you live in Fontana. Can I have my passports and IDs back, Officer?

Officer: 'Sides, Puto, not all of us went to college, got art careers n pinchi Mexican and American citizenship.

Puto: No, true that, Carlitos. But there's a bunch of fools we used to hang with at Circus, Chico, shit even Midtowne Spa that aren't fuckin' Homeland Security. So . . .

Officer: So what, Puto? I got a job, insurance, and the security that my mom and tías won't get deported. I can even marry a paisa and get his chunt-ass citizenship.

Puto: Well, I hope you and your PANista lover have a wonderful life together. Are we done here?

Officer: So what business do you have on the other side of Western, citizen?

Puto: A photo shoot, Officer. Though I needn't tell you that, my IDs assure me safe passage through all catchment areas. Hell, I could even live in the Hills with a thousand chunt lovers and paisa beloveds if I agreed to pass them off as my servants. We all got choices, Carlos Moreno Jr., and yours was to become Officer Charlie Brown-noser.

Officer: And I got my eyes n nose on you.

Puto: Sniff away. It's Christian Dior Eau Sauvage. Mixed with my own scent of, what did you used to say I smelled like, Carlitos Güey?

Officer: Canela n sweat, Suavitel n tortillas.

Puto: You could have been a poet, but I guess you can't write deportation tickets in haiku.

Officer: That's enough. You have two hours to do your business in Catchment Area #1, Citizen. Think you can get it all done in two, Puto?

Puto: Oh, it takes a lot longer to do me, you remember that, don't you, Officer Brown-noser?

Officer: I remember a lot of things, Puto. You just remember that I know all that I know.

Puto: And you remember what you forfeited for that uniform and job security, and we'll be even, amor.

Officer: Enjoy your day, Citizen. Homeland Defense takes pleasure in defending you and your country's borders, possessions, and interests.

Puto: The displeasure is all mine.

(Puto roars off.)

(Officer glares, adjusts his package.)

Scene 12

(Santa Monica. Puto at Dalton's door. Knocks and door opens.)

Puto: Dalton?

Dalton: Sign the release hanging on the door, Puto.

(Puto grabs the clipboard with attached release and signs without reading it. Dalton is in underwear at his computer, a variety of webcams on him. Puto's demeanor is markedly different. He is his aboveground art market-self in this scene.)

Puto: Hey, Dalton, how goes it?

Dalton: Good. Did you bring the wigs and the knives? I went and got the papaya.

Puto: I want to take it a different direction. Why aren't you wearing any clothes?

Dalton: Since when has that ever bothered you? It's for this piece *Muse*, and camera 4 needed me shirtless, and camera 1 wanted me in tight underwear. But I am pretty sure camera 3 is my gallerist, cuz he's asking me to do all this sick-ass shit.

Puto: When's the show?

Dalton: Three months. But camera 2 wants me to eat pie every day for two weeks, very Wayne Thiebaud meets Nayland Blake, so I wanted to do this shoot before I get fat. So what are we gonna do instead of the homage to Gauguin?

Puto: An homage to Xanadu. I want you to pose as the mural in Venice that Olivia Newton-John emerges from. I guess underwear will be fine. Can you get up from your post, Dalton?

Dalton: Yes, that would thrill camera 3. *(He stands and adjusts some of the cams, and Puto begins to photograph him.)* Man, I already told my gallerist I ain't no damn Chris Burden or Marina Abromafuckinvic. Weight gain is about as self-immolating as I am gonna get. Hey, Puto, did you sign the Citizen Artist Act?

Puto: I'm sure my gallerist did for me.

Dalton: How is Veronique?

Puto: Still a double zero. I imagine she is hungry. You got any pie?

Dalton: No, but we could go get it after we are done.

Puto: Don't you have to stay here for the cameras?

Dalton: Nah, I just leave them on—some of them prefer my absence. So we could go to Norm's. How much time did you get allotted?

Puto: Fuckin' only two hours, and I got to go pick up the kid next.

Dalton: You still do that?

Puto: Every week.

Dalton: Puto, you better find out if Veronique did sign those papers. Your career's gonna be fucked if she didn't.

Puto: I'll be fine either way. I still got reps in Paris and Antwerp and Moscow. Singapore and Mexico City are lining up. I'll be fine. There, that's enough shots. So should I email this to you or to the gallery?

Dalton: To them.

Puto: Oh, shit, I forgot, my computer is being funky, can we upload them to yours?

Dalton: Sure. Then I can pick which ones to send.

Puto: But isn't the whole point of this show that you are the muse for other artists?

Dalton: Yes, but it doesn't mean I am any less of a control freak.

Puto: Hey, can I leave my camera and equipment here with you, Dalton?

Dalton: Sure, Puto. Is everything OK?

Puto: Yeah, why do you ask?

Dalton: Well, normally when I see you, you rip off my clothes, and now I am not even wearing any, and you didn't even kiss me hello, cop a feel, maul and molest me even a lil bit.

Puto: Sorry, just have a lot on my mind. *(Recovering his professional composure.)* This project and the soccer martyr series.

Dalton: Oh, how is that going?

Puto: Good. Shot that kid Smiles the other day.

Dalton: He still fine as ever?

(Puto doesn't answer.)

Dalton: *(Walks over to Puto, grabs him.)* Hey, Puto, dude, you OK? You high, man? I got some Valium.

Puto: Oh, that would be cool, for later. Nah, I ain't high, just got a lot on my mind.

(They find each other in each other's arms. They kiss.)

Puto: Thanks for that. I feel much better now.

(They hug. Puto holds on.)

Dalton: You sure you OK? Dude, you shouldn't get all worked up. It's only fuckin' art.

Scene 13

(On Brooklyn Ave in Boyle Heights. Puto is parked in his car dozing. He dreams.)

Scene 14

(Kid approaches sleeping Puto.)

Kid: Gotcha!

(Puto slams awake, in full panic, tries to catch his breath.)

(Kid hops into the car.)

Kid: Man, you look like h-e-double-hockey-sticks. What's the matter? And why are you early? You're never early. I thought they were lying when they told me you were already here. What's the goings-on?

Puto: First off, conversations begin with "Hello," "How are you," "How was your day."

Kid: Oh, I am fine, my day was so-so, thanks for asking.

Puto: Do you have any lunch left, Lil P?

Kid: Nah, I traded with cousin Gordis. He had tacos de papa n chorizo.

Puto: That's why he's Gordis, mija. And he's not your cousin.

Kid: Well, if you hadn't made me call his real uncle Tío for all those years, we wouldn't be play cousins. But you did, so too bad, he's my cousin now and real funny. His mom's tacos beat my mom's homegrown salads, fruits, n veggies any day. She sent me to school with a beet salad. Guácala.

Puto: Gordis wanted to eat beets?

Kid: Well, I told him it made your poop turn purply red so he wanted to see if it was true.

(They both laugh.)

Kid: Mom says she needs some more dollars.

Puto: Yeah, I know, I got it on me. How's study group?

Kid: OK, but why do the women of socialist feminism have to have such f'd up names? Alexandra Kollontai, Rosa Luxemburg, Shulamith Firestone, Sheila Rowbathawa.

Puto: Rowbotham, but I suppose you're right, Peanut.

(Silence.)

Kid: P?

Puto: Yeah, Lil P?

Kid: Can I have a yen or a euro to show the kids at schools?

Puto: No, but I got some two-dollar bills for your collection. They know what I do?

Kid: No, well, some like Gordis have an idea, but look at his family.

Puto: Not his familia, just his uncle, and yes, I regret that you called him Tío. Stupid fuckin informant.

Kid: Uhm, language. There's youth in the car, P.

Puto: Sorry, Lil P. But Gordis's Tío, his actions hurt a lot of people.

Kid: You?

Puto: Not directly. But yeah, it hurt what we are trying to accomplish.

(Kid laughs.)

Puto: What?

Kid: Your stomach growled. Can we go have high tea?

Puto: Not today, mija. Another day, I promise, high tea and the opera or the symphony, and a full day downtown, no time allotment restrictions or anything. But yeah, I am damn hungry. Mind if we hit a King Taco on the way home?

Kid: I already had Mexican.

Puto: So did I, but that seems like a century ago. And that's really all there is in our catchment.

Kid: Big P?

Puto: Speak, cacahuate.

Kid: So what is it we are trying to accomplish again?

Puto: Baby, I wish I knew. Oh, I know, Al n Bea's, how's a french fry burrito sound?

Kid: Better than beets.

Scene 15

(They are finishing up their food in the patio of Al n Bea's, have books and papers spread out.)

Puto: So, how would you apply what Luxemburg is saying about the general strike to those early anti-anti-immigrant marches, Peanut?

Kid: Uhm, different, like cuz the marches were marches. Even if people did take the day off from work during the first few years, they didn't really shut down the city. What's it called, the infra?

Puto: Infrastructure. Yes, you're cooking with gas, Lil P. Yeah, so even if they exposed the mass class of undocumented workers as truly massive, the marches did not organize those marching or allow for their spontaneous organizing to occur. So what would she call that?

Kid: Reformism?

Puto: You got it, peanut butter cookie. And it's a failure in leadership. Though we might argue with her over national liberation she saw the need to learn to farm and to control land base as intrinsic to fending off starvation in the city and one of the ways to make the Revolution permanent and the dictatorship of the proletariat long lasting. Your teacher making you memorize her last written words?

(Kid nods.)

Together: "The leadership has failed. Even so, the leadership can and must be recreated from the masses and out of the masses. The masses are the decisive element, they are the rock on which the final victory of the revolution will be built. The masses were on the heights; they have developed this 'defeat' into one of the historical defeats which are the pride and strength of international socialism."

Kid: "And that is why the future victory will bloom from this 'defeat.' 'Order reigns in Berlin!' You stupid henchmen! Your 'order' is built on sand. Tomorrow the revolution will already 'raise itself with a rattle' and announce with fanfare, to your terror:"

Together: "I was, I am, I shall be."

Puto: *(Clapping.)* A+, Peanut.

Kid: OK, now we're officially late. Mom will be mad. You gotta take me home so I can do my real homework.

Puto: What they got you doing now?

Kid: I am on the high-end industrial service and hospitality track still. So I have to make a bed with hospital corners in under five minutes and see how high a quarter will bounce off of it.

Puto: You're kidding me, Kid.

Kid: I s-h-i-t you not, P.

Scene 16

(El Sereno, one of the jewel streets. Sol is in her small vegetable garden in her yard, hum-singing something, like "Misty Blue" or Meshell's "Faithful." Kid bounds up to her and Puto hangs back. Mother and daughter kiss.)

Sol: Hey, kid.

Kid: Hi, Mami, sorry we're late. Big P was helping me with my homework.

Sol: You were making his bed?

Puto: Not that homework, our kind of study.

Sol: Oh, good, I guess. Mija, take these in and set them to soak in the sink.

Kid: OK, Mami.

(Puto caresses Kid's face with the back of his hand.)

Puto: Bye, baby.

(They hug and she bounds offstage. Throughout this time Sol has not looked up at Puto. There's a terseness to their interaction, silence and anger and duration and hard love. Sol returns to her gardening, and Puto keeps his distance.)

Sol: You not staying for dinner, P?

Puto: Nah, just ate and got a lot to get done today.

Sol: We need money.

Puto: I know, G, the kid told me. It's all done. I gave her my money belt.

(At this Sol stops what she is doing, stands up, brushes herself off, and meets Puto's eyes for the first time. The tableau should feel like a duel. She speaks, slow but sure, but the fear and anger are rising.)

Sol: You did what?

Puto: I kept some, enough. It's just that I'm going out of town—some business in New York that might lead to work in Milan, so, just to make sure you've got things covered.

Sol: Bullshit.

(Silence. Stare-down. Puto breaks first.)

Puto: OK, you got me, G, some shit's come up, gone down, whatever, whichever way it goes. I don't know, things are f'd up. Big time.

Sol: What gives, Puto?

Puto: I'm not altogether sure, but I am handling it, G.

Sol: That's not my name . . . anymore.

Puto: This one time, forgive me my nostalgia, Sol. But G may be called into action in the very near future. *(At this, he approaches her and pulls his gun from his waistline.)* So, here.

(At this, Sol slaps him. They are both surprised and stung by it. Stare-down recommences. Sol breaks first.)

Sol: I have a child in my home. Or in the process of losing your goddamn fuckin' mind have you forgotten that important fact, Puto?

Puto: It's for that very reason, for her, I give you this now.

(He holds out gun. She understands now, takes it and, like a pro, slips it in her waistband.)

Puto: Well, that's it. I probably won't be able to pick Kid up next week. You make sure and give her all my love.

(She touches his face, where she slapped him, with the back of her hand. They hug hard and for a moment. Sol breaks it and regains her composure, returns to her garden.)

Sol: You just make sure to be back week after next and pick her up a lil trinket from your travels.

Puto: Fo sho. OK, G, Sol, I'll be seeing you.

Sol: Don't make promises you don't plan on keeping.

Puto: I'll return, good as new, hopefully better than before.

Sol: You better get going, packing and whatnot.

Puto: Yeah.

> *(Once his back is turned, Sol stands and watches him leave. Sings, hums, gathers her tools and herself, and exits.)*

Scene 17

(Puto arrives at Ovíd's house in Pico Union and finds Ovíd n Knees in surgical masks seated at a table using Q-tips to swab pollen from potted plants. There is a tray of test tubes.)

Puto: Hello?

Ovíd: Hola, Puto. You got here just in time for chumpe.

Knees: *(Not breaking concentration.)* Sup.

Puto: Why is my leaf blower on your front stoop, Ovíd? Why are you guys, well, one, together, and two, in Richard Prince nurse drag?

Ovíd: Señor Rodillas is teaching me pollination processes. Fascinating stuff.

Knees: Japanese method.

Ovíd: Did you know that since the '90s all those Asian pears in their little-lattice cradles have been pollinated by people, not bees?

Knees: Tried out a new pesticide. It was too toxic, flatlined the bee population.

Puto: Great, you have been going through back issues of *National* Fucking *Geographic* while I have been trying to find my boyfriend and my GODDAMN ART CAREER.

Knees: Smiles is more your fuckbuddy.

Ovíd: Amantes, very '70s.

Knees: Símon.

Puto: And I have just come into an episode of better jokes & gardens.

(Knees and Ovíd laugh.)

Knees: That was a good one.

Ovíd: I am going to make us plates. (Ovíd exits.)

Knees: He's nice. You have a nice life, Puto.

Puto: I had a nice life. But now is not the time for pithy commentary, Knees.

Knees: Duh. But you shouldn't meet the external conditions of crisis with a morass of personal contradiction.

Puto: Huh?

(Ovíd enters with glasses of ensalada.)

Ovíd: I think Knees is saying your whining is very undialectical.

Puto: Since when did the two of fuckin' you get on the same page? Knees, he's not movement. Is this conversation even straight up and proper to be having?

Knees: No, there are some lessons and formalities still to come.

Puto: Have you jumped him in?

Knees: Nah, you and I both know it takes at least five members to jump in a newbie.

Puto: Well, these are crisis times. 'Sides, you count for at least four.

Knees: Duh. You ready, primo?

Ovíd: Uhm. Ensalada?

(They sit him down.)

Scene 18

(Ovíd seated. Puto n Knees swirl around him.)

Puto: Chapter 8 of the Immigration and Nationality Act:

Knees: To commit an act that the actor knows, or reasonably should know, affords material support, including a safe house,

Puto: Ovíd do you give us permission to be in your home?

Ovíd: Sí. Siempre tienen casa en mi casa.

Puto: OK, but not comadre style. I mean do me n Knees

Knees: And whoever else we confer honor and status to have entrée to your home?

Ovíd: Yes.

Puto: Especially in situations like this, when things are hot?

Ovíd: Yes.

Knees: *(Back to memorized list.)* To commit an act that the actor knows, or reasonably should know, affords material support, including transportation.

Puto: Can we trade cars or, better yet, can you give Knees a ride anywhere Knees needs to go?

Ovíd: As long as it's in my catchment. I am on restricted status, remember, denaturalized but not deported due to my "sympathies."

Knees: For real?

Puto: Ovíd is pretty gangsta for a poet-scholar.

Knees: We'll compare verse later. OK, to commit an act that the actor knows, or reasonably should know, affords material support, including communications,

Puto: OK, I got this. Ovíd, tell Knees to hurry the fuck up so we can go find my piece.

(They laugh.)

Knees: Point taken. To commit an act that the actor knows, or reasonably should know, affords material support, including funds.

Puto: Ovíd, can I have a couple of bucks?

Ovíd: ¿Qué puta, Puto? You're the rich one.

Puto: OK, but say I wasn't and I really needed some money to say, I don't know, blow something up, would you give it to me?

Ovíd: Sure.

Knees: Moving on. To commit an act that the actor knows, or reasonably should know, affords material support, including transfer of funds or other material financial benefit.

Puto: Here's a hundred euro, Ovíd. Can you give it to Knees?

Knees: Then make it dollars, I want these Air Jordans I saw on Brooklyn Ave.

Puto: Fine. Here.

Knees: Well, the last part is all beyond you at the moment, but here goes: To commit an act that the actor knows, or reasonably should know, affords material support, including false documentation or identification, weapons (including chemical, biological, or radiological weapons), explosives, or training-for the commission of a terrorist activity; to any individual who the actor knows, or reasonably should know, has committed or plans to commit a terrorist activity; to a terrorist organization described in clause 6, 1 or 6, 2.

Puto: And CREW, RUCAS, whoever we forthwith pass through your doors with, will be members of a terrorist organization, as defined in clause 6, 1 or 6, 2. Understood, Ovíd?

Ovíd: Yes. Except for the clause 6, 1 and 2 part.

Knees: We can go over that later. So how this goes is we commit to all of this and then we agree to never, ever, under any circumstance admit to it. If or when you get caught, plead guilty to whatever you get caught for as an individual, not a gang member or whatever else they try to pin on you for violation of RICO statutes. Don't cop to any federal crimes. We do our time in state prisons, more opportunity for organizing.

Ovíd: I have to agree to all this to fertilize my flowers?

Knees: Yeah.

Puto: Pretty much.

Scene 19

(Over pan con pavo n Pilseners, Puto n Knees plot. Ovíd is abuzz with domestic activity.)

Ovíd: *(Bringing out guacamole con huevo duro.)* So do I have to start dressing like Knees now that I am a communist criminal?

Puto: That's criminalized communist, but no.

Ovíd: Oh, good, and do I get me one of those Marxist cholo boyfriends now?

Knees: Not in the welcome package, but I guess Puto here will don you with a new moniker soon enuf.

Ovíd: Can't wait. Well, the quesadilla's almost ready. I have had such a surge in nationalist culinary sentiment ever since I have been internationalized. *(Ovíd exits.)*

Puto: He's a mess. But we're a pretty good team.

Knees: Yeah. You're solid when not so self-involved.

Puto: This involves me, Knees. Smiles is my heart. I can take more pictures. There's nothing damning on that computer except for a few X-rated vids n pix.

Knees: What next?

Puto: The potluck, Lunar.

Knees: Leave me your truck. Take public transpo, stay in crowds.

Puto: Fine. But that means you got to wash it.

Scene 20

(Puto on the MTA, heading north on Alvarado, seated. Bello comes by and very unsubtly hangs on to the handrail in front of our hero, his track-panted crotch all up in Puto's face.)

Puto: Uhm.

Bello: What's crackalackin, Puto Por Vida?

Puto: You know me?

Bello: Only from them internets. I'm bello y bellaco.

Puto: *(Leaning back, using his hands as a frame to look at Bello's face.)* Oh, shit. *(Stands and they shake hands.)* Mucho gusto, Bello.

Bello: So where we getting off, fool?

Puto: Oh, word?

Bello: Word is bond. You finer than even you think.

Puto: Haha. You good.

Bello: I'm better than it. That's what's up.

(Face-off. The shit is hot between them. They are basically both imagining each other naked and committing various perverse acts. One and then the other breaks the spell and remembers they are on a public transportation system that mainly serves LA's servant classes.)

Bello: Can't go to my mom's.

Puto: My place is . . . getting fumigated.

Bello: Then? C'mon, Puto, tell Papa, where you getting off?

Puto: Damn, any day but today, I'd say next stop, shit, I am tempted to say right here, right now, but today, fuck, Bello, it just isn't that day.

(Train stops. Puto squeezes past Bello. There is some light grope or rub action.)

Bello: You sure about that, Puto?

Puto: I'm so not.

(Puto exits. Back doors close. They stay lock-eyed, return to dirty reverie. Bello blows Puto a kiss. Bus rides off. After a beat, Puto does same.)

Scene 21

(Echo Park, above Sunset. A lesbian of color potluck: The food is delicious, the music dated and so-so. Lunar stands with Transam as Puto approaches.)

Transam: *So how does she reconcile her work on land and blood nationalism with her position as a poststructuralist feminist?*

Lunar: (Shrugs.) Day wear, evening wear.

(They knowingly laugh.)

Puto: Hey, Magda.

Lunar: God, it took you long enough. Will you excuse me, for just a moment?

Transam: Hey, I know you.

Puto: You do?

Lunar: Well, Puto does get around.

Transam: Yeah, uhm, but not from LA. The Creative Capital retreat?

Puto: Could be. Haven't been for a few years now.

Transam: No, no, no, it was at Watermill. You got in all that trouble for having an orgy with the janitors.

Puto: With the cater-waiters, actually. And it was no trouble at all. I made a mint. Every photo that documented said orgy sold on the spot, and it drove up my going price point. Magpie, I invited the guests to watch and shoot, had cameras everywhere. Sarah Jessica Parker bought the one Stephanie Seymour shot. I think Björk and Matthew Barney bought each other's.

Lunar: Aww, que cute. Well, small world. Puto, this is Transam.

Puto: Oh yeah, Transam the Transman. Nice to see you. Sorry, I didn't recognize you.

Transam: No worries. I was just beginning to transition then.

Puto: You still do that magic act?

Transam: Yeah, Packing the Divining Rod, but I got off the Drag King circuit.

Puto: Very cool. Hey, can you excuse me and Mag here for a minute?

Transam: Oh, of course. She said her candyman was en route, had no idea it would be you.

Lunar: I'll be right back, babe.

Transam: Don't do too much of the devil's dandruff.

(They kiss.)

(As they walk away from him . . .)

Lunar: You're late.

Scene 22

(In the bathroom. Lunar retouches her makeup in the mirror.)

Lunar: What the fuck, Puto? You can't be this late again. I've had to feign interest in these bitches and their butches for far too long.

(Puto starts to strip off his clothes, turns on shower.)

Lunar: What the hell are you doing?

Puto: Taking a shower. I stink.

Lunar: Well, sorry your trade didn't let you shower at his place, but don't be late, and give me those notes, asshole.

Puto: I smell like fear, not fuck. *(Reaching into his boxers. Pulls out glassine bag—opens it and hands notes inside to Lunar.)* Here. *(Slips them off, steps into shower.)* Oh, and Eva Crane sends you bees from the other side.

Lunar: You met Knees? What the fuck is goin' on? *(Reading notes.)* These notes are all about you. Shit.

Puto: Hey, any other movement people at this party?

Lunar: Nay, this is a more check-writer, bumper-sticker crowd. They think their art careers and nonprofit jobs or academic appointments mean they are activists.

(They both crack up at that.)

Puto: Well, I need something else to wear. Could you get me something, Lu? Oh, and by the by, Knees is hot.

Lunar: Who you telling? Knees is like Malcolm or Pancho Villa, came to consciousness on the inside.

Puto: So why you ain't still together? What's up with you and Transam?

Lunar: Knees is the strongest strategist I know, but that much time inside just doesn't leave a lot of person, you know?

Puto: I guess. And Transam—wasn't he just in the Whitney?

Lunar: And Documenta. Yeah, I am just fucking him until he comes out as a fag, which will be any day now, I am sure. Did you see how he sweated you?

Puto: Well, I am fine and famous. Hey, and could you fix me a plate?

Lunar: I'm supposed to be your coke client, not your bitch.

Puto: Girl, you can take me apart in critique–self-critique about being late and sexist and what have you, but I really need this shower and some food to go, and could you get me something cute to wear? Any of these FTMs up in this piece wear Opening Ceremony, Rick Owens, or Carol Christian Poell?

Lunar: Actually, I have just the thing.

Scene 23

(Puto wrapped in a towel, looking in the mirror.)

Puto: It's not all gonna be OK, but dude, you have got to be OK with whatever goes down. This shit is real.

(Lunar knocks and then, without waiting for a response, opens the door, with a pair of folded dickies, a wife-beater, and a short-sleeve collared shirt. Clothes should look like what Knees had on in the scene with Ovíd and Smiles's pre-soccer-uniform outfit.)

Lunar: See, what'd I tell you, Transam is a total fag. He wanted to bring you these clothes.

Puto: Lunar, this isn't bespoke. A wife-beater? C'mon, now, at least a Nice Collective T.

Lunar: You can't say "wife-beater" at this kind of party.

Puto: This is CREW wear.

Lunar: And according to the notes you had affixed to your taint, I am to induct you into inner circle. Luckily I went to the peso pulga and stocked up. Put it on, Puto. Your mission doesn't end here.

(Puto dresses as they talk.)

Puto: No shit, Lunar. I still have to find Smiles.

(Lunar's hand goes to her hip and her eyebrows go up.)

Puto: Yeah, I lost him. Sorry.

Lunar: Well, this takes precedence. You got to move some stuff out of LA.

Puto: To?

Lunar: I don't have those instructions. You have to go get them at the map point.

Puto: Map point?

Lunar: Yeah, like in the rave days.

Puto: Shit, I used to go with the promoters or at least the DJ. I have never been to a map point en mi puta Puto vida.

Lunar: Well, you got to go to MacArthur Park. There's a habibi store on the northeast corner of the park.

Puto: The map point is an Arab-owned liquor store? Isn't that a lil obvious?

Lunar: No, next to it, the Guatemalan panadería. They make excellent empanadas and run guns. And I don't know where exactly you're going, but you're gonna meet Rabbit.

Puto: No way. Are you serious? Thought she was just a movement myth.

Lunar: No, she's real, all right. A lil natural-fibery for my taste, but then again she probably finds my push-ups and peep-toes thoroughly retrograde. OK, you gotta get going.

Puto: I need a ride. Knees kept my truck.

(Lunar laughs.)

Lunar: Well, you won't be getting it back anytime soon, but she'll get it back to you in much better condition. Knees likes under the hood of a car more than she does panoch. Well, almost.

(Puto laughs.)

Lunar: But I can't give you a ride. Transam is gonna perform and then we have to hear about the tenure battle of some woman of color professor. Yawn. Reformist hoes.

Puto: You bringing Transam into the movement?

Lunar: Nay nay nay. He's well on his way to artfag stardom. And, well, not for nothing, and present company somewhat or at least temporarily exempted, but we can't really trust your kind.

Scene 24

(Puto walks to idling DASH, Echo Park to Pico Union. Lady Bus Driver is smoking a joint, listening to music on earbuds, and singing along.)

Lady Bus Driver: "You must be a special lady and a very exciting girl, you gotta be a special lady cuz you got me sittin' on top of the world, sittin' on top of the world!"

Puto: Uhm, excuse me.

Lady Bus Driver: Oh, say what? Don't be sneaking up on folks, man. That's thirty-five cents or thirty-five thousand pesos, depending on your identity papers and whatnot and what have you or don't have you. *(She waves him on.)*

Puto: I have a twenty.

Lady Bus Driver: That'll work. *(She stuffs bill in her shirt front pocket.)*

Puto: Hey . . . forget it, keep it.

Lady Bus Driver: I was just singing my theme song. You got a theme song, boo?

Puto: Uhm, it used to be "Daddy's Home." "Your daddy's home to stay."

Lady Bus Driver: Oooh, you nasty.

Puto: Yes, ma'am. It's a sure-fire panty dropper. Can you not stop where there aren't folks waiting for the bus? I'm kinda in a hurry and I'd be much obliged, Miss.

Lady Bus Driver: Yessir. Where ya headed?

Puto: MacArthur Park. Why?

Lady Bus Driver: Just want to get on the good foot. You're on the ride-or-die DASH, last bus of the night before catchment lockdown goes down. And Mama's got to get to her zone to get into her zone, ya feel me?

Puto: Special lady, special night?

Lady Bus Driver: That's it. You strange for a vato. Polite and sweet smelling like you boys often are. But off. Ya know?

Puto: I'm not a

Lady Bus Driver: Oh, don't worry, I work for the city, true, but belong to one of the few unions left that offers sanctuary to our immigrant members. Fuck this piece-of-shit racist motherfucker crackerverse government.

Puto: What you said.

Lady Bus Driver: Right, right.

(They bump fists.)

Puto: But I'm really not gangsta.

Lady Bus Driver: Well, then, you better give that boy his clothes and swagger back, son.

Puto: Precisely my intentions, Miss.

Lady Bus Driver: Ain't you formal. My name's Lady.

Puto: Mine's, well . . .

Lady Bus Driver: You can keep it lo-pro, baby. Cuz you may not be a hood rat, but you clearly out here doin' dirt, not that I got one iota of a problem with that. Let's take this town, boo, a few skipped DASH stops through the posturban neo-plantation at a time.

Puto: Best words I've heard all damn day.

Lady Bus Driver: That's cuz you haven't had any Al Green in your ears. "I'm so tired of being alone, I'm so tired of on-my-own, won't you help me, girl, just as soon as you can."

Puto: *(Speaks, not sings, these lines.)* "People say that I've found a way, to make you say, that you love me. But baby, you didn't go for that, me, it's a natural fact, that I wanna come back, show me where it's at, baby."

Scene 25

(MacArthur Park. Noche en el barrio. Puto walks into panadería, chimes go off. Hornera/o is there with trays of conchas.)

Puto: Buenas noches.

(Hornera/o nods in response.)

Puto: ¿Hay empanadas?

Hornera/o: Sí, tenemos de camote, piña, manzana, y de crema.

Puto: ¿Y cuál recomienda para una jornada larga?

Hornera/o: Lo que usted prefiera.

Puto: *(To himself.)* I didn't get a password. Uhm, pues mi amiga Lunar dice que

Hornera/o: *(Stops.)* Los de crema entonces. Pero van a salir del horno unos frescos en unos minutos. Usted debería esperar en el parque. En la bandshell abandonada.

Puto: Pues bien. Y te pago ahora o . . . ?

Hornera/o: No, te doy una bolsita gratis compañero, Puto.

Puto: Mil gracias.

(Hornera/o gets on cell phone, hits key, has conversation in Quiché.)

Hornera/o: Are'k'o chi'—A qa'stzij are' sab'laj utz che we chak ri'? *(Translation: Yeah, he's here. You sure he's the best for this job?)*

(Hornera/o walks into back of shop. Puto lingers.)

Hornera/o: Con prisa, Puto.

Puto: Sí.

(Puto runs out.)

Scene 26

(Puto wanders around bandshell at MacArthur Park, humming, nervous and aimless, paces.)

(Smiles enters, laptop tucked under his arm, wearing an amalgam of his own clothes, some of Puto's and part of the soccer uniform Puto posed him in.)

(They lock eyes and then run to each other.)

(Puto n Smiles make out passionately, endlessly.)

Scene 27

(Coming up for air.)

Puto: You.

Smiles: What?

Puto: You scared me. What did they do to you?

Smiles: Shit, didn't nobody do nothing to Smiles. Heard a noise, knew it wasn't you, I booked. Grabbed what I thought was important.

Puto: You didn't grab me.

Smiles: No, I didn't. Someone needed to be there for Knees, and I needed to see what you were really made of, Puto.

Puto: You were testing me? What kind of shit is that, Smiles?

Smiles: The kind of shit that ends you up in that outfit, comrade.

(They smile.)

Smiles: You look good in it, mijo.

Puto: Really? Thanks, I feel good. But if I am really in this CREW now, we are all gonna start using my tailor. Just a few darts would really shape up this silhouette. *(Pause.)* Now what?

Smiles: Well, aren't you here waiting for something?

Puto: But I found you or you found me. It ends here, doesn't it?

Smiles: No. You and I, we're not the goal. You know that.

Puto: Then I really do need to know something, Smiles.

Smiles: Ask me any question, I'll tell you no lie.

Puto: Flour or corn?

(They resume their infinite kiss.)

(Knees walks up.)

Knees: Get a room, 'ey.

(Puto n Smiles break kiss. Smiles n Knees shake hands and hug.)

Puto: Is MacArthur Park always this jumping? Are you having me followed?

Smiles: Not exactly. We've just been expecting you for a long-ass time, brother.

Puto: Fair enough. Last question: What have you done to my ride, Knees?

Knees: Not a thing that didn't need doing. Washed and waxed it, went to my home-boy's shop, and looked at some dubs. Don't worry, you're getting an even bigger truck tonight. It's parked on the corner of Rampart & Seventh. Here the keys.

Puto: Do we have time for a few at the Silver Platter?

Knees: Me n Smiles do, but you best be on your way, mijo.

Smiles: Yeah, Knees is correct, as ever. Hey, what should I do with your laptop, man?

Puto: Take it to Ovíd. Tell him to email the shots of you to my gallerist in New York.

Knees: No, you no longer have a gallerist. That you no longer exists, Puto.

(Silence. Puto is clearly despondent.)

Smiles: Sorry, babe. It won't be like this forever.

Puto: Yes it will. I'm no longer in the art world. No more grants, no more gigs, no more openings, no art patrons. No champagne or even fuckin' cava or caviar or contraband honey. I bet I can't do anything fun and illegal like counterfeiting and money trading either anymore. Now I am just a garden-variety faux gang-banging revolutionary arms runner. Shit, I should just rechristen myself Santo.

Knees: Try Whiner. No mames, Puto. Like you really care about your career other than the ass it gets you.

Puto: Another thing I have not gotten all damn day.

Smiles: I'll throw you a big huge orgy upon your return, pa.

Puto: OK, fine, but there better be some new recruits I haven't seen or had.

Knees: *(To Smiles.)* And his game really works on all of you?

Smiles: Knees, man, all I can say is once you finally get him to shut up, the shit is on.

(Smiles n Puto kiss goodbye. Knees n Puto pound.)

Knees: The directions are in the glove compartment.

(Knees n Smiles exit. Puto stares at the keys in his hand for a second, looks around, and then books.)

Scene 28

(Stage as split screen. One side: Puto is driving. Other: Ovíd, Knees, n Smiles are drinking at Redz. We hear a cell phone. Puto feels it beneath his seat and cautiously drives and grabs it.)

Puto: *Jesus, what now?*

Ovíd: Y como me hablas. Your oldtimey comadre y newfound comrade.

Puto: Ovíd, is this more bad news? Or more riddles? I'm over either.

Ovíd: No, we—well, it was my idea, but Señor Rodillas.

Knees: Hey, Putz.

Ovíd: She says hi. So does Sonrisas.

Smiles: Ora, I like it, more adult than Smiles.

Puto: You can't have my trade or my nicknaming position, regardless of how long I may be off on this pinche aventura.

Ovíd: Tranquilases vos. We're just here at Redz tomando en tu honor, pensando en ti. Mira hay alguien que quiere decirte "hi." Oiga, Diosita!

(Diosita la Putita más Regia shimmies up, getting ready to hit the lip-sync stage wear.)

Puto: Diosita, finally, a sane friend. How are you, loca?

Diosita: Good, beetch. Y tú, mi amor? Tus compadres dicen que estás de vacaciones.

Puto: Something like a vacation, yeah. You good, mi mujera? It's been a minute. We need to talk when I get back. I think I found a new love or art form or, well, I don't know what it is, but it is big!

Diosita: Well, ju know I love the big ones. Bueno, mi lindo, you cash me up cuando regreses. I am going up on tarima ahora. I do your song, mijito.

Puto: I don't have a song.

Diosita: Well, con que me contaron la bucha y los bellos estos, you do now.

Puto: With what they told you? What did they say, Diosita?

Diosita: Enuf. I have a lot more under mi minifalda than eben ju know.

Puto: No doubt. Todo love.

Diosita: Ciaocito.

(She hands the phone back to Ovíd.)

Ovíd: Here. Listen.

Narrator: Damas y Caballeros, presentando Diosita la Putita más Regia! Aplauso!

(Knees and boys clap y tiren gritos. Diosita grabs the mic.)

Diosita: Antes de empezar, quiero decir algo a mi público. Sí, people, you are my gente. We come to this place casi every night. But tonight será special, never forget it. Or me. Esta canción es para mí Puto, y cada puta y puto presente. *(She lip-syncs the whole of Diana Ross's "Remember Me" with Knees, Ovíd, and Smiles joining as backup.)*

Scene 29

(At the nexus where the Angeles Forest meets the Mojave Desert, Puto parks, walks some distance. It is night, and the sky is a million stars. He shivers from a cold generated more by fear than air.)

(From the darkness, a voice.)

Rabbit: I've got a gun trained right on your left nut. I'm not that good a shot, but you'll lose something in the general area if you take one more step.

Puto: *(Freezes, raises his arms in the air.)* Is that you, Rabbit? Lunar, Knees, Smiles sent me. I come bearing guns or something.

(Rabbit turns on a porchlight. Seated is Tortuga, swaying in a rocking chair, a rifle across his lap.)

Rabbit: Brother Puto! We weren't sure you'd make it.

Puto: Neither was I.

(Rabbit relaxes, props gun on side of house, goes to Puto and hugs him deep.)

Rabbit: You must be tired, comrade. We've laid out a bed for you. Some champurrado. This is Tortuga.

(Tortuga nods, almost imperceptibly.)

Puto: Shouldn't we unload the truck?

Rabbit: En la mañana. You sleep now.

Puto: Thank you. *(Suddenly finds himself crying.)* Thank you so much. I'm not sure for what, but thanks.

Rabbit: Shhh, mijito, you come in and sleep.

(Puto sleeps and dreams.)

Scene 30

(Morning. Outside their home, Rabbit and Tortuga do their morning prayers, a pipe ceremony. They each take turns inhaling and blowing the smoke in the four directions and inaudibly praying. Puto awakens from his deep slumber and walks out on to the porch, dressed like he was in the very first scene, chonies and a T-shirt and barefoot. He stops himself from talking, bows his head.)

Rabbit: Today we bathe you in blood, mama. And I don't mean you, Mama Tierra, I mean my ma, mommy, Mirtha Ramirez Solares, buried just north of here. I am not sorry for what is to come, mother, only saddened you are not here with me, us. Ho.

Tortuga: Ho. *(Noticing Puto.)* Mira costilla, ya levantó el Puto.

Puto: Not el Puto. Just Puto.

(Smiles all around.)

Puto: Is there something I should do? I've never . . . I don't . . .

Rabbit: Relax, Puto, you're going to be with us for a while. *(Standing up.)* I bet you're hungry. Tortuga's making chilaquiles this morning.

Puto: Yes, I am, but . . .

Rabbit: *(After a pause.)* You'd like to see what's in the truck?

Puto: Yes, if I may.

(Rabbit exits, Puto is uneasy, Tortuga is silent and calm. Rabbit reenters with a wooden crate.)

Puto: That's it? That's a weapon of mass destruction?

Rabbit: Indeed.

Tortuga: La reina.

Rabbit: The queen of the hive. We understand you name things. You'll have to come up with one bien linda for her. We're going to have to go hike into the forest once it cools down and darkens a bit. I'll show you how it's done.

(The sound of gunfire and bombs going off in a deep distance. Tortuga smiles, Puto panics.)

Rabbit: Not to worry, mijo. That's our side.

(Tortuga stands, and he, Puto, and Rabbit stare off into the sound of armed revolt. The queen bee's buzzing is the last sound.)

A BLACK AND A BROWN

Written for "What's Going On? A Virtual Play Festival" live-stream events held on August 1 and 8, 2020, via YouTube, Facebook Live, and the Company of Angels website to mark the company's sixtieth anniversary, the uprisings in response to the murder of George Floyd, and the then ongoing COVID pandemic and quarantine. Bruce Lemon directed this five-minute play, Julianna Stephanie Ojeda was producer, Rogelio Douglas III played "A Black," and Alex Alpharaoh was "A Brown."

―――――――――――

(While we rage and a plague spreads, "A Black" and "A Brown" fill out an online Marxist questionnaire on interpellation and state-mandated death.

A Black is dark-skinned, lean to muscular, the threatened threat embodied. A Black is professional, intellectual, and enraged.

A Brown is smaller, lighter, less rage, more hood, more love. A Brown wears his Dodger blue heart on his sleeve.)

A Brown: A Black sits at his desk on his Zoom. A Black is at his desktop, his screen has four open windows: one has the Johns Hopkins site on COVID to the US map of confirmed cases, another has a YouTube Fred Hampton speech, another a William Robinson recent article on the global police state. Beneath these three, and on mute, he has PornHub open to a search of group action. A Black really misses group action.

A Black: A Brown has laid out at his desk a mix of toys, instruments, talismans, weapons: a kaleidoscope, a knife, a harmonica, a necklace, a compass, an hourglass. A Brown stands away from the desk in chonies. A Brown is doing a lucid dreaming exercise over and over: looking at the palms intently, then flipping them over, one, two, then three times. Asking the palms:

A Brown: Am I awake?

A Black: Eyyy, B. You ready?

A Brown: Born that way.

A Black: *(Reading from questionnaire.)* What is the first racist pig murder, beating, act of state brutality and overall white barbarism you remember seeing, reading, or hearing about? The Rodney King video? Amadou Diallo? Sean Bell? Trayvon Martin?

> *(A Brown does one more round of lucid dreaming hand-turns. Staring intently into his hands, he does not say, "Am I awake?" Instead, these words rush out:)*

A Brown: *I was four. Or five. But it wasn't on* TV *or* Twitter. It was on the landing between my family's and next-door neighbor's apartments. Two pigs batoned and kicked a man, a boy really, A Black, lean and dark, lovely like you, while my mother and his sisters screamed at them to stop. They didn't.

> *(A Brown does the lucid dreaming exercise.)*

Now you. *(Reading from the questionnaire on his screen.)* When was the last time you were stopped by the pigs? What was the context and outcome?

A Black: Last fire season, so like, what, eight to ten months ago. I was getting off the redline, heading home, from another day of being composed, efficient, polite, and respectful even to disrespectful motherfuckers who cross the street when I am coming, decline to ride in elevators with me, never bother to learn my name or to tell me apart from the other Black guy. A day, in short, like any other. Some broke-ass white boy in a broke-down ride needed help pushing his car into an auto shop on Western and Franklin. Good Samaritan that I am, that my grandmother raised me to be, I put down my bag, rolled up my shirtsleeves, and obliged him. The cops that stopped us before we had pushed it three inches could not believe that it was his car, not mine. And that I had no record.

A Brown: Bro, you have a record.

A Black: Expunged. And all those arrests at protests and demos don't count and happened in other cities. Moving on *(he reads from questionnaire)*: Have you or anyone you've known been pepper-sprayed, batoned, kettled, beat down by the pigs while protesting?

A Brown: C'mon, now, bro bro, everyone you or I know has witnessed or experienced this. The first time, I was around ten, and being the sissy / lil mama that I was, I was handing out the sandwiches I had help make to those protesting down Broadway in some anti-state, pro-immigrant worker march. I saw a cop, take his baton and crack a woman, a Brown one, across her head with it. What I most recall is how the sound reverberated, had physical volume, shape. What I was most impressed by is that it did not stop her from fighting back.

(A Brown returns to his lucid dreaming exercise.)

A Black: OK, baby, we gotta take a break from this online Marxist questionnaire on interpellation and state-mandated death. Cuz I gotta ask you, cuz, what the hell kinda hex, ceremony, Mexican sissy witchery is you doing?

A Brown: They don't call me the Bolshevik Bruja for nothing.

A Black: Nobody calls you that, bih. Anyway, the jazz hands juju?

A Brown: Lucid dreaming exercise. They help you to remember your dreams, intervene in recurring nightmares, continue your dream from the night before, disrupt the divide between being awake and the dreaming life. You're sposed to space the exercises out, but now is a time of crisis. We are at the precipice of so much. The first surrealists, all communists, believed that utopia would emerge from the unconscious, strategy from the dreamworld. That "the revolution begins at night."

A Black: I think that answers all the questions posed to us. And I know that after tonight's protests, I'm definitely going to give you something to dream lucidly about. I love you down, Brown.

A Brown: See you on these streets, our streets, soon. I love you back, Black.

(Zoom session ends.)

"I DON'T DO PLOT, I DO IDEOLOGY"
Interview with Jennifer S. Ponce de León
December 4, 2015

Jennifer S. Ponce de León: *In your talk "It Is the Libido," which you delivered at Stanford in 2008, you laid out your critique of several of the discourses and types of politics with which academics have often associated you and your work, such as cultural nationalism and other identity-based politics, queer of color critique, and the discourse of intersectionality (which you have described as "essentialism by other means"). In that talk, as well as in your plays and other texts, you clue us in to the intellectual, political, and aesthetic traditions that inform your writing and life praxis, and that you vindicate and extend through these. In "It Is the Libido" you said, "I'd like to form a praxis that could incorporate, in dialectical friction, antihumanism and whoring; a heart that belongs to Fanon, Marx, Luxembourg, and Genet, as well as a fanboy's interest in the Bolivarian Revolution, FARC, the Intifada, and the mythmaking of conceptual prog-rockers, the Boricua and Chicano LA Tejanos, the Mars Volta." Can you speak more about the genealogy of your work and your thinking?*

Ricardo A. Bracho: Well, I was born in 1969, so I come after the break: Paris '68, Mexico City, the Stonewall Rebellion. We are, my generation, the children of those movements. In my particular circumstance, I am a child of the Latin American left, a red diaper baby, an inveterate Marxist-Leninist—and none of those things I see or operationalize as identity, as a way to feel about myself and others, but more so how [Jean] Genet talked about what writing was when he said it was a way to "return to society by other means."[1] I think in our particular moment of both identity proliferation and what I call the soft-core politics of being a young student, there's a lot of feeling about feelings, and those are suddenly now people's politics. I don't think so. I am terribly twentieth century. I'm a capital *M* Marxist. I guess my idea that decolonization happens with guns is considered terribly statist. I don't care. That is my folded-arm stance in relation to the current state of affairs. I hope it's not like "Get off the lawn, I'll wet you down with my hose!" I'm cranky, but I don't want to be grumpy. So, yeah, that is my originary moment when I burst on the scene natally. Then, in my adolescence, into adulthood: There's AIDS, there is the antiapartheid movement in the US, there was the defense of Nicaragua and El Salvador in US-based solidarity movements that were so compelling to me. But those movements and my engagements with them don't ever end up being just a way to write poetry about myself, which I think ends up being this position that is queer of color critique, a kind of new cultural nationalism that is called Chicano Indigeneity, and the facile way people invoke intersectionality and then move on to be just terribly typical bourgeois. I want another way, I guess. I think that we should fight with each other more.

Then we hit the late '80s and early '90s, and I moved from LA to Berkeley to attend [the University of California at] Berkeley, and there are these faculty diversity movements, various tenure cases for academics of color on campus. But really, much more importantly, the Gulf War and the Rodney King beatdown and pursuant rebellion. Throughout that I was in an organization called Roots Against War, which was a people of color, people of the Global South political organization that ran the gamut of Marxists, Maoists, some cultural nationalists—that was definitely the tension within a portion of the leadership—various Third Worldist perspectives, feminists. And that was just a really good way to launch into the world with some articulated and strategic rage.

Then there was the gay men of color group, which was partially a movement around AIDS policy. There were various poetry anthologies, and a particular nexus around writing on the East Coast among Black gay men had a really profound effect on me. Also: meeting Assotto Saint, Donald Woods, David Warren Frechette, and Craig Harris—all of whom I met in and around the time in my life when I went to conferences a lot. So, there was the first *Out/Write* Conference in 1990. My friends Lisa Hall and Keith Harris put me on the Chicano panel, but a lead organizer kicked me off because I wasn't known enough. Cherríe Moraga, who was on the panel, was very, very nice to quote me.[2] And then the Audre Lorde conference in Boston, "I Am Your Sister," also in 1990. Jacqui Alexander invited me to run the workshops for the men. I think those moments were particularly impactful. And taking a class with Cherríe at Berkeley; I took a theater class with her, and then a creative writing class, and started to be invited to do poetry readings in San Francisco. I looked around, and I was just getting these [invitations] 'cause I was the only one [Chicano gay writer]. Rodrigo Reyes, who had been a poet and organizer in San Francisco, passed in the early '90s; Francisco X. Alarcón had moved away; Arturo Islas had passed. So, that was terribly foreboding, and I don't like isolation. I am not a good representative of people; I contradict myself by the time I get to the end of a paragraph. So I did not want to be the only one. And that's really why I started teaching creative writing workshops for various kinds of groupings, like youth or gay men of color or Latino gay men.

Ponce de León: *The next thing I want to ask you is about transnationalism and internationalism. In a conversation with Jorge Ignacio Cortiñas and José Esteban Muñoz that was published in* Trans-global Readings: Crossing Theatrical Boundaries, *you talk about the viability of the translocal instead of the transnational,[3] and in your text "A Proclamation of, by and on Negation," you note, "I am an internationalist and a localist, not a transnationalist."[4] Please talk about, first, your critique of the idea of transnationalism, and second, the importance of internationalism to the politics of your work. Then the third part of that question is: What do you think is needed in the discourses and institutions of theater to better support an internationalist politics like yours?*

Bracho: I think that kind of "transnational" moment in academe has faded because the only entities that are truly transnational are corporations. Refugees and exiles and straight-up migrants who just wanna go somewhere new don't retain the nation in that crossing, unless you just want to be horribly nineteenth century and sentimental about it. I remember hearing Noam Chomsky on C-SPAN or whatever, it was when that transnational thing was big, and he was saying that we should not have abandoned the international, and the "we" he meant was the left. That was an error, and it's an error that we should correct so that we can straighten up and fly right. I don't know what the move to call something "transnational" does for movement, does for affinities, does to help people through the brutal economic and different language processes that are taking place because of globalization.

I was raised in internationalism. I was a child of overeducated people whose neighbors were also Mexican immigrants, gardeners, and maids. Belgian miners and Black project organizers and various South American intellectuals and political folks were always coming through my front door. When I worked in HIV and AIDS [prevention] in San Francisco at an organization called Proyecto ContraSIDA, that's how I modeled the work I did—and not in this facile way of "I want it to be like home." I wanted it to feel like Heathrow, but without the surveillance. The movement of people that is consciously disruptive to the flow of capital is what I think the work needs to be about, and not *El Norte* or something.[5] I don't know what that means for theater, because the basic problem of American theater—and American theater is grossly basic—is that our US bourgeoisie is neither discreet nor charming, but they are our subscriber base. I'm forty-six years old; I should not be the youngest person I see when I go to a play, but I am often.

Ponce de León: *Now, this goes back to the first question I asked, where I quoted you speaking about the dialectical friction between the different intellectual and aesthetic traditions with which you align your work: I want to talk about the way your works speak to the formation of subjectivity that happens through contact with socialist and anticolonial thought and practice, as well as through experiences of popular culture, sexuality, and forms of pleasure and sociality found in spaces of consumption that are very proper to capitalist urbanity. I think that your plays* Puto *and* Sissy *most clearly show such dialectical frictions. I want to know how this is related to your ideas of left and liberationist politics and the cultures through which they remain vital and are transformed.*

Bracho: I remember hearing Norma Alarcón giving a talk at some seminar in Berkeley, and she had one of those moments where you know a thing, the fabled epistemic break. She was going through Hegel into early Marx, and she was talking about the class for itself, the class in itself. And then she went through what Marx lopped off in taking Hegel's subject for itself and the subject in itself, which was the subject for others. And that sort of tripartite identity formation has always been the model for me with character building. Usually as I write, I'm in the doing of it, either by pen or by fingerprint. So, a character comes named: They are a subject in itself. They have some wherewithal because they are not pre-discursive, so they are a subject for themselves. And then the work of the writing of a play is trying to figure out how they are a subject for others, including those others on the stage and the audience or the reader. I think that's where the fun and my working through of my politics happen, if that somewhat answers your question. People want you to say that voices and spirits come into you. I don't know why. But you really can't bring up Hegel to a literary manager in the US. So these are thoughts I keep to myself or share with you mainly.

I was recently teaching a one-day theater workshop at the Kirk Douglas Theater for the Center Theater Group. It's in Culver City, where I was raised, and what my play *Sissy* is all about. I was telling a group of young people that part of the mystification of writing is about its professionalization and specialization.

The reason we are like, "Oh, voices come and talk to me and I'm merely a vessel," is to say, "Oh, that one can talk to God, but that one can't"; it is only to keep the supply finite and rare, and thus to be paid better. Because if it's something that everyone can do, then everybody should.

Ponce de León: *I think part of my question has to do with what you said before about your crossed-arm stance of being a "Marxist with a capital M." Within dominant US cultural discourses that denigrate those Marxist and socialist political and intellectual traditions that you claim, there are so many stereotypes about what those alignments mean for artistic production. That is, there is the idea that they dictate a specific aesthetic. But your work has nothing to do with those stereotypes.*

Bracho: Yeah. I remember, one of the reasons I wrote *Sissy* was because a good friend of mine, Richard Castaniero, told me I hadn't written a Chicano play yet because I hadn't written a play about the Chicano family [*laughs*]. That hurt my feelings. Even though I like to pretend I don't have them, I do. So, I was like, "Oh, I'm gonna show you," and I really wanted to. That's why the first part of the play, which takes place in the backyard of the house, not only happens in 1979, but it happens in the bilingualism of the Chicano Theater movement of that time, which was not the bilingualism of my street: You know that thing where everything gets translated. So there's that, "Ma, we need some ice, que no hay hielo," or whatever the line is in *Sissy*. That is not how I spoke, but that was the discourse of Chicano theater. And yet things are a little awry in the version of Aztlán depicted in *Sissy* already in that there are Black people, Central Americans, and then once he [Sissy] leaves and goes on his quest for La Mancha to see what he encounters in the streets. (I realize that in nearly every play I do a scene of interpellation.[6] In *Sissy,* that is that moment with the cop.) Then Sissy enters a world with Central Americans, which is almost all in Spanish, and then he gets around some—although they would be "transgender sex workers now"—they are drag queen hookers in 1979, and he gets around queenspeak, which he does not know yet. I wanted to really shake the foundations of the house of cultural nationalism in Chicano discourse there. Also, another thing about popular music: It is also to have fun. Rosaura Sánchez said that she found it too irreverent. But I don't know any other way to be here in late capital other than to poke fun at it, 'cause it's not going away quite yet, and I don't wanna be a bad time. I make entertainment; I'm not too highbrow for it.

Ponce de León: *About* Sissy: *There are these two cultural subject-making forces in the play. On one hand, emanating from the father, who is disembodied in the play, you* *have Sissy's education in revolutionary Marxist and anticolonial thought, and the connection to organizing with the copy of [Frantz] Fanon's* Wretched of the Earth *that was from the, I think, Oakland chapter of the [Black] Panthers . . .*

Bracho: Exactly. It was the Massachusetts state chapter.

Ponce de León: *. . . and the father is also a source of masculinist subjectivation who has a certain obliviousness to Sissy's own desires (giving him the baseball glove and so on). Then, on the other hand, you have the popular culture of the '70s, which you see both Mana and Sissy inhabiting as they are assembling their senses of self. Sissy finds a language of expression in it. One of the things I like about the play is that it doesn't set these up as conflicting or as following a generational divide, because Sissy takes up both of them with equal enthusiasm: He is as excited about reading his father's copy of* Wretched of the Earth *as he is about going to the drag show in Hollywood. Having seen so many stories that represent these different types of cultural influences as unassimilable to each other, or where their difference is narrated via one generation trashing what came before it, I love the different approach we see in* Sissy.

Bracho: Yes, exactly that. So, I remember when Pedro Lemembel was passing, you and I had a series of both email and phone conversations. I never took his critique of *el nuevo hombre* as a disavowal of the politics that produced it.[7] We should have that internal mechanism. We don't have to formalize it as critique–self-critique, in the way it happens in some Marxist, Maoist, feminist circles, but we should think about the bullshit we do, and how both subjects and movements get produced. The thing that Sissy also encounters are the Cabrones brothers: the sort of masculinist thing that these streets provide. And that's the encounter. But even in the critique of those boys, I don't want them to go away, 'cause the away they go to is jail (which is the problem with hate crime legislation, 'cause that's just going to tack more onto the tail of that fucking bid inside).

Also, the thing you said about the excitement of Fanon, the excitement of a first drag show: I don't know how else to have a spectacle of frisson that not only keeps an audience interested but keeps movements alive. I don't know why we pretend that it isn't really fun to take over the streets. It's a fucking good time. And yet we want this seriousness. I really do think we should just dispense with our overuse of adjectives like *radical* and *revolutionary*. We don't live in those conditions. The best we can hope for, as Ruth Wilson Gilmore said one time I heard her speak, is "antireformist reform." So that's where we're at, but we want people to be properly radical or revolutionary, which means self-serious. There's this idea, particularly in the queer and trans movements, that lesbian feminism was a bad time. I'm like, those dykes were having a fucking ball, come on!

Ponce de León: *I want to ask you about that within* Puto. *You have these motive forces in the play: both the underground revolutionary movement, and also sex, desire, and love. Talk about why revolutionary subjects in the play are also explicitly libidinous subjects and moved by that as well.*

Bracho: I think because this is my most direct engagement with [Sigmund] Freud. Some people ask what inspires a play. I don't really work off that model (it's a little too Enlightenment for me), but I always have an essay or two that I'm working something out with. So, with *The Sweetest Hangover*, it was "Is the Rectum a Grave?" by Leo Bersani and [Gayatri Chakravorty] Spivak's "Can the Subaltern Speak?" And for *Puto*, it was the Red Army Faction's "The Urban Guerrilla Concept," which is, I think, clearly Ulrike Meinhof's brilliant writing, and Freud's essay "In a Time of War," written on the eve of World War I, which he opposed. He didn't make those kinds of global political pronouncements often in a text 'cause he didn't tend to periodize them in such a finite way. But he really takes up in this short essay what the libidinous can do to the social. I think we do ourselves and our movement a lot of harm if we don't get to talk about that instinctual life. Puto, until the morning after where the play begins, is all about and embodies that instinctual life of a certain kind of artist-intellectual, the class I am. I often write characters who are artists because I do believe in self-critique, and because we shouldn't pretend like we aren't middle class and that we go to conferences and we stay at hotels, and have all the little bennies that come from being art-poor, basically. Puto, the character, is all about that. Then, as the day transpires, his desires keep on getting interrupted. Like in that exchange with Bello, the Black Honduran boy on the bus: In his everyday gay life, Puto would get off that bus and be about it. But it's a little delay. He's still gonna get some eventually—although I don't think Rabbit and Tortuga are down for a three-way by the end [*laughs*]. His desire is not going to be taken off the list of demands when they write the manifesto, and nor should any of ours.

Ponce de León: *When writing* Puto, *were you thinking of it as being in conversation with, or as a counterpoint to, other kinds of representations of revolutionary subjects?*

Bracho: Well, yeah: It's a slap. There is a flattening effect in the idea that we have of revolutionary subjects. I don't think the Zapatistas don't fuck. The machine gun, the shoulder strap: It comes off when the clothes do too. But we tend to be overdetermined in our discussions around violence by the racialization of criminality and by the state's brutal violence, so then it's just about "Black-on-Black crime" and such. I oppose that. *Puto* remains unproduced, mainly, I think, because of those politics around sex and violence. But I was writing it in a playwright's group at the Center Theater Group that one of HBO's *True Blood*'s head writers was in, and that show was full of sex and violence—but it wasn't about revolution, it was about Gothic decay.

Ponce de León: *When were you writing it?*

Bracho: Was it 2007 . . . When was that second May Day March for Immigrant Rights? 'Cause that was when you and I went, and that was really the abysmal point of inspiration. There were two marches in Los Angeles that year because, I guess, the organizers had gotten into a pleito [fight]. So we went to the one downtown. It was all fucking American flag-waving. It was terrible. I remember that at the end of it, me, you, the filmmaker Jim Mendiola, the journalist and scholar Ruben Mendoza—we also bumped into Harry Gamboa [Jr.], and it was this odd little crystallization of Chicano art stars. That got me thinking. Then, by the end of that day, the second march ending in MacArthur Park, where I now live, ended in state violence. The LAPD had just gotten tricked out with all this new drone equipment and stuff and they were ready to play, and they airbag shot journalists on camera for a march that was ending—it was at its moment of dispersal. Nearly every LA riot is generally a cop riot. And then I remember when we had that discussion over at Adrian Rivas's Gallery 727 afterwards. And Hugo Hopping was saying that I couldn't require immigrants to have more critical politics around waving the US flag, and I was like: Well, I wasn't *requiring* anything of them, but yes, I can because yes, they do. They don't need me to tell them so.

Ponce de León: *Absolutely. And I see that play as a critical counterpoint to the consolidation of the image of the "good immigrant" in media discourse—that is, as a humble, pacified worker or student . . .*

Bracho: Well, it's all Dickens: It's poor Little Dorrit and her rule. And the reality of the thing: I live in LA's densest neighborhood, MacArthur Park. It is also probably the most Mayan barrio in the US; most of the people are trilingual. And I see what Rosa Linda Fregoso and other feminists talk about: the parentification of children. It is not cool that five-year-old girls are mommying their two-year-old siblings, and I see that all day long. Not in actuality, but in our rhetoric around the "Latino family" we want to glorify and sanctify the mother. And we don't need me, 'cause there is that good thing that is Chicana feminism to point out the absurdity of that.

Ponce de León: *Considering the moment when you were writing* Puto, *why did you decide to set it in the future, in a dystopian LA that's actually not so different from reality?*

Bracho: I like genre. You're supposed to write tragedy to think you're some kind of playwright somebody, but that's overblown. None of my work is realism. I am thoroughly antirealist 'cause realism sucks. And those conventions keep us in our place. I really wanted to talk about that moment and place and how the way to uncover that violence is to lift off its veneer and let it fully express itself. So, if the state's racism that's coming at us and that has produced BLM or the UndocuQueer movement, if we unmask it and let that grossly flourish, then we have the state as it is at the onset of that play. I really like to be free of autobiography. That's why I wrote one called *Sissy* (even though it's lies.) I'm not interested in memoir; I don't find myself that interesting. And since I'm not a literary critic who's doing a psychological reading of me and myself, I don't have the motivation, "Oh, why is this here? Why is that there?" and knocking that down to the mimetic. It really minimalizes the reach of one's politics or aesthetics, and I need a lot of space for mine, 'cause I'm mouthy.

Ponce de León: *You mean a kind of biographical approach to interpreting your work?*

Bracho: Yeah. If I wanted to be on a reality TV show, I would try to be on one. There are the mundane knowable things like, oh, I'm a whore. Big whoop. But there isn't this sort of psychological reveal in the text. We should work harder. And I mean the "we" of the audience.

Ponce de León: *So, my next question is partly about* Puto, *also about* The Sweetest Hangover. *In many of your plays, but perhaps most noticeably in these two, the familiar scripts of bourgeois moralism are completely absent. What I mean is that the plays aren't about exposing these ideologies or arguing against them; they simply accord them no space. Instead, the plays put us headlong into a world that's organized by other values and forms of sociality, which require no explanation. It seems to me that the social relations and values depicted in your plays are not defined by their difference from bourgeois mores, heteronormativity, Whiteness, et cetera. Instead, they just are, and don't require comparison or justification. Do you see that as a particular kind of aesthetic strategy?*

Bracho: A thing that you and I were reading around that moment of *Puto* was that reprint and translation of Félix Guattari and Suely Rolnik on the micropolitical [*Molecular Revolution in Brazil*]. They went on that tour at the very right time in postdictatorial Brazil, and [talked with] a range of people, from favela organizers to gay activists and also São Paulo urbanity. What they formulate around the micropolitical and also this notion of becoming: waking to everyday life. You are seeing people becoming, so then you form an analysis that fits it. So, it's becoming woman, becoming trans. And Puto, traveling through the day, he meets people. People readily show themselves to you in life. But in a play, they don't have a lot of time, and if that character's not going to come back, we don't have time to spend with them in the kitchen until family secrets are revealed, which is the normative mode of American theater that I want to burn down. So, I think *Puto* is that bullet. Oh, I mixed the metaphor—I'm sorry! *Puto* is not the bullet, *Puto* is the match.

Ponce de León: *OK,* Puto *is the match . . .*

Bracho: Well, no, because the play is at least formed around the bullet. Because I remember when I was living in Highland Park, somebody had graffitied the word *puto,* but then they had also graffitied a penis, and I was like, "Oh, that's interesting," 'cause you would just hear that word, and you see it a lot in LA. And then a bullet's trajectory is not straight; it has an arc. And I was like, "the arc of a play." And that play is all about arc because it starts in one place and goes to another in a very compacted amount of time. And then that curve also has material manifestation in a certain kind of uncut penis. So, all of that went together to sort of form the bullet.

Ponce de León: *I'm wondering if it's correct to call what we see in* Puto *a utopian aesthetic because it doesn't seem like it's referring to an elsewhere. The possibility it points to seems more like something in-process or something that's underground.*

Bracho: Yeah. When I saw her speak, an audience member asked the sci-fi writer Octavia Butler about *Parable of the Sower,* which is a far uglier dystopia in California than what I imagined in *Puto.* She said the trek that the character [Lauren] goes on from the South to the North was about her grandmother's migration—from the Midwest, not the South—to LA, to the Pasadena/Altadena area. So, we've already been there, and I'm talking about that colored "we" that we inhabit. So, if there's nothing new, then let's show it. Migration and decolonization: These things aren't metaphors. Luckily, I think. So, let's see where we have been. As a genre, sci-fi or speculative fiction really allows for that, which is why China Miéville, the great socialist writer of England, works so well in it.

Ponce de León: *What about the world of* Sweetest Hangover*: Do you think of it as utopian?*

Bracho: I think homosexuality and vice have been intertwined, particularly in the Global North, since the nineteenth century. So, this world of the illicit, what

José Esteban Muñoz in his essay "Feeling Brown" refers to as the "anal economy" (there's a section on it, but I really wanted him to call the whole essay "This Bridge Called My Crack"): I think it's a weird kind of safety valve.[8] The actual place where much of that play takes place is now a parking lot for the San Francisco Giants. I also think, particularly for urban gay men of color, ephemera is our institution. So, after-hour spots—they used to do break-ins, rave break-ins where you took over a warehouse—or the squatter movement, which we really don't have in the contemporary US in the way that you have in Europe and Latin America: Those are all really interesting anti-state formations that don't always—in Latin America they do, but here, they don't always—have an articulated state critique. They are the politics of resentment and a good unstructured time. They don't always force them into the sentence of manifesto, which I'm fine with.

Also, that club life. Richard Dyer has this great essay, "In Defence of Disco," and he's talking about London's gay left in relationship to the general left. So, the general left was listening to rock and roll, and we're all shaking it with a tambourine in hand at the gay club. There comes a problem with that. So, I think that's part of it. Also, the thing about house music—and Tricia Rose talks about this with hip-hop—is the relationship of communities to technology and the machine. The underworld was a vast network—and I'm not talking the political one, I'm talking nightlife in the '90s. And all I wanted to be was that. The Black gay community has a saying, "You're a child of life." And I knew that I was that, but I wanted to be a *legendary* child of life. Whatever. I just had a very long adolescence. It was really fun: I could go from San Francisco to New York to Chicago to LA to Miami—and I did—and find all the right boys and bars. One of my gay fathers, Gary Gerard Robinson, said that when he got to an airport, he told the taxi driver, "Take me to the nearest gay bar." And in a pretty intimate way, you're like, "Oh, where are the places that I can go to be safe, and where are the places that I can go to get dirty?" We have to go to where knowledge is produced. He was right on that: The point of production matters.

Ponce de León: *Yep. OK, going back to what you were talking about earlier regarding the relationship between homosexuality and vice: In your talk at Stanford ["It Is the Libido"] you talked about the consolidation of what you refer to as a "gay and lesbian neoliberal norm." I wanted to ask you more about how your work stands in relationship to that. We talked a bit about* Sweetest Hangover, *but I also wanted to talk about that in relation to* El Santo Joto. *On one hand, you're using the form of* altares, *and it's a story of remembrance and of a death and a funeral, but it also has this capacious, perhaps utopian call for what Juan Rodríguez Day should be. So I* *want to ask you both about the form you use and about writing that kind of play in the context of the predominant gay and lesbian politics that you critique.*

Bracho: Well, I was talking about our condition as ephemera and also about the way we've been technologized. That play is about my friend Juan Rodríguez. Juan Rodríguez did the very first national media campaign for HIV awareness by, for, and about Latino gay men. The very first. And you can find maybe three to five things online that attest to that. So, I guess the whole of that text figures as an altar for that very sad fact. Juan took a class at Proyecto [ContraSIDA]; he worked there as well, but he took a class that Celia [Herrera] Rodriguez taught called "Retablos del retrovirus." He made a retablo about his family's migration from Mexico to San Diego, and it was dedicated to El Santo Niño de Atocha. I love that piece he did so much. I just wanted to invoke that—and then also to trouble that. So in *Santo Joto* you have his character with the gourd and all the other accoutrements of Santo Niño, and then you have a leather queen getting ready at his vanity to go to the bar, and a dyke smoking a doobie on her porch in a rocking chair, who is all about the 49ers. All those things can live together, 'cause they actually do in the Althusserian Real we're trying to get to, I guess. I didn't really think through the aesthetic; it just presented itself that way.

Ponce de León: *I love that the day for commemorating Juan [in the play] is about reclaiming the glory holes and free healthcare and all of that as a gesture of remembrance. It's this very powerful and forward-looking way of thinking about what a remembrance could be.*

Bracho: I kind of don't like the memorial mode or the candlelight vigil. Vigilance can be fun, and a wake is celebratory for a good reason. We should not just stay in our stillness in the social fabric if it doesn't accommodate both the politics we want to have and how we want to do right by our ancestors, I think. It's not a one-size-fits-all ideology.

Ponce de León: *Now I want to talk about* Ni Madre. *I see in it a critique of the romanticized ideology of mestizaje and the accompanying mythification of conquest. Why did you make this commentary on Mexican nationalist ideology and Chicano discourses of mestizaje and the mythology these entail?*

Bracho: Well, I remember all those driver's license frames that celebrated the quincentennial-whatever for cars in California. I guess it was the moment I was doing something online, researching Malinche, and it was around her five hundredth birthday, and I was like: "Nobody did anything for her! We didn't even bake her a cake." So then Diane Rodriguez commissioned a group of Latino play-wrights to do an anthology show based on this book called *Amor Eterno* by Pa-tricia Preciado Martin, and we all got assigned a certain kind of love. Now, I'd already known I was going to write this play, and I figured it fits either love of na-tion or love of mother, which, as our compatriot Fran Ilich notes, particularly in PRIista Mexico,[9] are figured around the Virgin. But I am *never* going to write a play about Catholicism, and I work in negation. Therefore, the loveliness of our language formed *Ni Madre*.[10] So I wanted to think through the Malinche mythos, and then the actual thing: from [her] being a slave to having slaves. That, to me, is far more interesting than the rest of the discourse that we produce around her. And if that's what's up, what would that be like? And then the play readily formed around the intersubjective struggle between the different class and caste of In-dian women and girls.

Ponce de León: *I also really like that about it. When we talk about Malinche, we of-ten talk about the "hijos [children] of Malinche" in reference to this biological idea of mestizaje that flattens history and, in many ways, denigrates and dismisses Indige-nous Mexicans.[11] Whereas your play focuses on the Indigenous subjects —*

Bracho: —and the Nana spits it out when she hears the catechism story! Yeah. I was working on the history of the California Mission system. You would go get baptized because then you would have a feast. And this is during the Mexican-Indian war in California and people were starving. The missions were all built so that they have a tower lookout to the tallest tree so in the distance they could see, "Oh, they're doing a ceremony out there," or "Oh, look, they're fucking," because both things were true. We can and do reject that. And that is as true of Cathol-icism as it is of mestizaje. I don't know why I chose that moment to take it on, 'cause that kind of resentment is part of my every day.

The play came into being because Eduardo Machado, at a table read of it in New York, suggested that Cherríe [Moraga] be the dramaturg of the whole play since her piece, which was called "Waiting for da God" at the time, was the most substantive work. She did that, but the show never got produced, and then she kept on with her play and kept my little play with revisions in it. She saw my Ma-linche character as a provocation, which I didn't really mean it to be. 'Cause I don't think Cortés raped her. In the moment where the nineteen girls are given to them, and they're quickly baptized and given Christian names so that they can go off and be screwed by these men, that's fucked up. But it seems like whatever produced their offspring, El Bastardo, Martín Cortés: I felt like there's a little moment of choice. And I don't think that's a bad thing. We shouldn't be so presentist, as our ideas of agency and consent and will can't time travel, actually, nor should they. I remember I said that at UC San Diego and I got someone really upset. (Later this same woman played Malinche during grad school at Stanford!) But I don't know why we want so much to be the children of violation. That tendency in Chicano studies is the fault of the bad education that we've gotten, and because so little work in Spanish is translated into English, and Octavio Paz is one of the few Mexican writers that was being read when Chicano studies was founded.[12] Going to him is like going to William Buckley [Jr.] to understand the US. There are other things to read and places to go rather than getting caught in that conservative and racist trap. We just accepted it too readily, some of his readings, and I think there are other ways to go. Both these short plays, these threes, these Hegelian tripartite formations I'm making (which I didn't even know until I said it) function like that: as the various ways that we are placed by the state and we comment on our placing. And if Malinche was doing so from . . . you know, she had a nice place on that lake by the end of her life. She did. We are uncomfortable with that, and I like being uncomfortable. We don't have a way to talk about servant/served relations unless they are inter- rather than intraracialized. And that's also true of the criollo mestizos of the Latin American left and their Indian servants right here, right now.

Ponce de León: *I was thinking about what you said about why are we so stuck on this idea of being children of the raped. It's a kind of irony of being so willing to accept that as an originary myth, but also in lieu of recognizing the ongoing colonial violence that the whole mestizaje mythos contributes to. That is, it's displaced onto this originary myth. Perhaps that makes it more palatable or circumscribed.*

Bracho: We do have this bewildering idea that they came, they conquered, they raped, and thus we were born as a people, which is so—it's biblical, it's apocalyptic. Not Genesis, I guess. It's pretty New Testament of us Chicanos. I don't have the Bible as a frame of reference. I never get some of the things we do, like the way people glorify freaking silence (and particularly I'm thinking about some Indigenous-identified artists and activists in LA). I think we need to break through that. And sometimes the breaking through of that is revealing. Like that the woman wrapped in that huipil: It was carried in Louis Vuitton luggage, and it was not carried by her. We don't really want to talk about that. I do, though. And also, it's fun. People were like, "Where did you get this idea of Malinche?" and really, Britney Spears was my inspiration.

Ponce de León: *What?*

Bracho: Because Britney Spears—pre-decay, pre–Kevin Federline—was a young woman from the South of minimal means and education when she started out, and she took over the nation. And she presented with a certain amount of unknowingness, and it was readily figured around her sexuality. And then, once she came to terms with it, dancing with snakes on stage, then we belittled her for it. She's like, "Oops, I did it again," like, "I didn't have control over this thing I call a vagina." Then when she *did* claim it, we're like, "Silly girl, get offstage." You really can't say to a group of young people trained in Chicana feminism that Britney Spears was your model for Malinche. But she was.

Ponce de León: *I would never have known.*

Bracho: I bourgeois her up, definitely. But even if you read through the *crónica* [by Bernal Díaz del Castillo],[13] she had fame. And also, you're talking about societies where people did not travel. And from Veracruz, which I've gone to on an overnight train from Mexico City to Veracruz: You're talking about people walking or by burro. People don't wanna do that, and particularly highborn people or concubine, which she had become. And she went to what is now Belize. So from the Gulf Coast to the isthmus. And she went in warfare and on the side of the mighty, but she saw all of that. That's incredible. And she became known and feared. There's a moment in *la crónica* where she is reunited with her mother and brother, and they cry, and it's kind of left at that. But you can't tell if it's a moment of reunion or fear of retribution, and I wanted to look at that. I guess that's why the whipping happened. My brother Beto told me the story of the passion fruit flower. He's a geographer and at the time he was working at a swamp conservatory in, I think, Torrance. He came with the passion fruit—I love them. You've seen those crazy-looking things, right? They look like sea anemones—and he told my niece Fiona that story, all of its meaning, and I was like, "That is some fucked-up shit." I had read a slave catechism in one of Frederick Douglass's autobiographies. I knew what that kind of colonial theology was made to produce. And also, because that was the Passion play, or that was the mode of theater. There's also one at the end of John Reed's *Insurgent Mexico* on the Mexican Revolution: They show up in some town and they go see a play. It also keeps getting interrupted by life happening, like someone coming in to go get their brother. That's the kind of theater world I would love to do work in. So let's have a revolution and I'll stage it.

Ponce de León: *So now I want to ask you about* Mexican Psychotic, *which I really love.*

Bracho: You are part of a handful of people who have seen it.

Ponce de León: *Yeah, I know, and I want to see it produced again. Weren't you talking about doing a video of it?*

Bracho: Well, I was talking with Ela Troyano about it, because I love working with her, as doing it kind of both as a kind of gallery installation and as a . . . You know that Puerto Rican playwright John Jesurun? He does this thing he calls "live film." So his shows include both filming the actor in the space they're in and then another actor who's being filmed off-site at the precise same moment are then in dialogue onstage. But *Mexican Psychotic*, since it's silent, you could just shoot it, what they call MOS, without sound. But also, people could watch that process as well. I thought that would be really interesting. I'm always into transparency around the apparatus. That play came together when I was living in New York and I wanted to apply for the Mabou Mines residency and I was like, "Oh, I don't know what project I should have." I was reading the *Village Voice* when people still touched paper and there was a review of, I think Adolf Wölfli, one of the other "outsider artists" or such-termed folks. And there was one in there and then one in the *New Yorker*, and both mentioned Martín Ramírez, and I think both referenced him as the "Mexican Psychotic," and I was like, "That is the best title ever. So whatever it is I'm going to write, it's going to be called that." And then I was like, "Oh, who is this Martín Ramírez?" and I just started to do research. I did a first run of the first part of that play in the Mabou Mines studio at the end of that six-month residency, which was great, which was my version of getting an MFA. They were incredible people. It was so much fun. But another thing we can lay at the feet of Octavio Paz: Much of the information that I had to work with was false and manipulated and just outrageous lies. And that became revealed by new researchers and growing interest in Ramírez's works. And that's the second half of the play. So that's the remix, I guess. The thing around psychosis and asylums, which is where Martín Ramírez produced all of those insanely great drawings, is that they were carceral institutions. It was the Depression. There were full-to-bursting insane asylums at the time in the same way that in the Inquisition people were becoming monks and nuns 'cause there was no grain in the bodega. So people were being institutionalized, and a lot of what asylums did for programming is show films. But also, since he'd been born at the same time as cinema, I just thought, "Oh, I'll just keep those things tightly combined through the play." And I wanted to work with silence. As our friend Keith Harris points out, although it's called "silent cinema," it's not a cinema that doesn't speak. There's the fact that they were performed with musical accompaniment. So that's why I have use of the onstage/offstage done away with through the play. The actors who aren't in the scene are making the sounds, whether it's a laugh or dropping pennies at the end or whatever it is. You can see them do that; there's no magic trick. But I still want to play with this frame of silent movie also because I love its exaggeration. I'm a fan of melodrama. I don't know why we gave it up. But we didn't: We just watch the Kardashians now.

Ponce de León: *I think you mentioned—maybe in your talk "Forming Content"— that at the same time you were writing* Mexican Psychotic *you returned to the appendices on colonial disorders in* Wretched of the Earth *[by Frantz Fanon].*[14]

Bracho: Yeah. They're incredible. They're talking about sessions, and these are his notes. So, from the French colonial daughter of a general who she knows to be a brutal murderer. How do you go to Sunday dinner with that? Or the couple who the woman was raped in front of him by French officers, and that's the bed they have to sleep in every night still. *Those* are the postcolonial conditions, not, I don't know, Homi Bhabha. Also, because he's literally talking about people or groupings of people, they remind me of playlets and of [Bertolt] Brecht's *Fear and Misery of the Third Reich*. Those are these great, disparaged little plays. It'll be a scene where a woman is making dinner and setting the table and then Nazis come in and take her away, and that's the end of it. I think that's just as it should be, although it defies plot and motivation because those things defy that.

Ponce de León: *In* Mexican Psychotic *you're dealing with Mexicans' neocolonial condition and the life of Martín Ramírez that it produces. Given that you made a play that's as much about the lies told about him, it's also about the silencing of him, which is juxtaposed with the promotion of a totally fabricated and exoticized personage.*

Bracho: Yeah, in some ways he's [Jean-Michel] Basquiat. Also, what physically broke him was modernity, was building infrastructure. Working on the rails was brutal labor, and his work is filled with tunnels and train tracks and trains. We really want to mythologize that intellectual rural idyll, but empire-building is a lot of work, and literally that is what the man was tasked to do, as rails connected the US across the continent. We're probably talking about sixty years or whatever when he was born after California had become part of the US. So getting across the continent was an incredible amount of labor and mostly done by Mexican and Chinese laborers and—as I'm reading in the book I'm currently editing, written by Sarah Haley—Black chain gang labor, including women and girls in Georgia.[15] That's why we have roads and train tracks. Yeah, and it's as much a part of the fact that he was emerging from Mexico's messy revolutionary process and was a Catholic conservative. But somehow, we have made him a model Indian, and we can do that if we accept the myths and the muteness. We can project a lot of things onto that and make him our subaltern, but there is something far more wily at work in his drawings and the fact that he worked so hard to preserve and contain them.

Ponce de León: *What is it about theater, particularly, that has the most interest to you?*

Bracho: This year [2015] marks my twenty-fifth year of working professionally in theater. I marked that because I was Cherríe [Moraga]'s assistant director to her program DramaDIVAS at Brava [Theater Center] and they paid me to do that, and above minimum wage.[16] That's a good thing, it's like, "Oh good, I got a god-damn job." The things that I used to do are now unpaid internships, and there are a lot more duties and labor than I did. So that's twenty-five years, and I think I might be done with theater. I wanted to do it because I already had a public persona as a political person and I am an intellectual, and I'm always going to resist the move to mark those of us who aren't within the academy (and Chicanos and other people of color) as being removed from community or movement because we're artists. I was like, "No. All those places need them and us." And I thought, "Oh, well, theater is literally a forum." Not only do I not want to be the only one—I know I'm not always right, even if I pose otherwise. I need to be checked about my bullshit; I need to be put in my place. I'm fine with that; discipline is good. And also, theater is a collaboration. Although it's hierarchized, you're not the only one, and I like that. And I don't have a novel in me. I read short stories, novels, and theory books, and I write none of that, nor plan to. But I do like the social, so I thought, "Oh, I can be a socially engaged intellectual and use the stage as my medium." But I didn't quite think through the provinciality of American theater. They're just getting to diversity, and we're still having arguments, and people are still doing yellowface productions of *The Mikado* [by Gilbert and Sullivan] in New York City. The discussion we do need to have about that is: "No." But that is the theater world. I've never really lived in it in a true way. It's not like it isn't easy to be gay in, but it is hard to have sexual politics in and to stage them. I think that is one of the things that people fight about *Puto*; it's what people really resist. *Sissy* is the second play that I wrote, 'cause I wrote it during *Sweetest Hangover*'s rehearsal process in the workshop with Cherríe, and people were completely frightened of that play.

Ponce de León: *Of* Sissy?

Bracho: Because the child had sexual thoughts, the sister smokes weed. It really took the fact of an articulated queer youth movement in the US nearly a decade later for those parts of that show's politics to not frighten people away from producing it. So I feel like both *Puto* and *Mexican Psychotic* are the best things that I have done. I think *Mexican Psychotic* to be high tone about it on formal terms, and I am particularly invested in the politics that *Puto* brings to its audiences. But theater institutions don't want it, so they don't want me. And I'm fine 'cause I didn't wanna live there anyway. But I'm glad that we're doing this also 'cause you and I get to laugh about things, but also what you wanted, to get this project going, and there will now be a book of me, and I won't have to chase down universities to pay me for reader's fees anymore. Just go buy the book. And then I'm interested in what other kind of writer I may become to be, to be Guattarian about it.

Ponce de León: *What would you like to change about the way theater is produced, if you could change it completely?*

Bracho: There was just this big brouhaha in LA because the Actors' Equity union wants to change some of the rules around these ninety-nine-seat-or-less theaters that allow union actors to do shows for no or just shit wages. And everyone's like, "No, this is not the time to do it." The actor Tim Robbins, who runs a theater in LA, is all opposed to it. I was like, "Motherfucker, you're a multimillionaire. Everybody better be getting paid at least fifteen dollars minimum wage in your space at all times, out of your own goddamn pocket." So, yes. So, that would be a good change: Write a check. But first of all, we haven't done the kind of standard practice of organizing: We have not asked people what they need or want. I remember when Jesse Johnson was starting up Proyecto ContraSIDA in San Francisco: He just went around and had coffee with various community people and asked them what did they want or need. We don't ask people that. I think those are the kinds of things that need to happen. I guess what I think about everything is: People need to take it over. It's like what Walter Benjamin says in "Program for a Proletarian Children's Theater."[17] He was just talking about watching a bunch of Soviet children at a preschool, and they were basically playing revolution, and the tendency for children to do that sort of creative destructive work. I think that we never ask people what they want; we just give them things we think they need. I don't want to be government cheese or butter. And that is what nonprofit theater kind of ends up being, like, 'cause they'll have a free day and bus in all the children, and I'm uncomfortable with that. I do know people whose idea of becoming a playwright was Broadway, and I never want to do that. If you look at where my shows have been done, it's feminist, queer, Latino, and community-based spaces, 'cause that's where I'm at. I don't feel diminished by that in any way. I just don't want to do the work anymore of maintaining institutions, 'cause I'm viejo [old] and I have to sit home and watch TV, and there's got to be a boy to talk to.

Ponce de León: *Do you feel like too much of that work is put on artists?*

Bracho: Yeah, as Hans Abbing says (I'm always tooting his horn 'cause I want to grow up to be him: the artist, the Marxist, the economist), it's our third job, usually, and we have the other two to pay for it and our rent.[18] On the new Joanna Newsom album, *Divers*, she has a line, "As life goes on, the only thing that happens is rent keeps going up." That is true. So, just finding ways to be in that and to make work that engages people, but not in easy ways. I don't like celebrations, and it's weird because I like a party. But I don't like a parade, I guess, the kind of sit-by-the-sidelines and "Yay, the float is passing me by." I don't want it.

Ponce de León: *Do you think a lot of the theater is like that?*

Bracho: I think there's a tendency to want that, and particularly when you are trying to get what they always call "nontraditional audiences." I always do plays and work on plays where people have never been to the theater before. And they know what to do, and then what you really realize is that all of our conventions about it are stupid. We have this idea that audiences need the "well-made play." Well, they don't know it.

Ponce de León: *Yeah. Why would they?*

Bracho: When I produced Vicki [Grise]'s play *blu*, a lot of people came who had never seen a show. And it was directed in that jazz aesthetic mode, and it's a collective poem that is really invested in rhythm and repetition. And none of those avant-garde modes put people off, because it was a story about prison and their uncle went to one. Just flat out, that was why. They did not care that it was two women raising these children; it did not get in their way. And they didn't need anything explained to them, because they already know. So, since people do already have that knowledge, I don't like this idea . . . I kind of hate the way Theater of the Oppressed is used in the US because, first of all, those workshops have oppressive fees. They're fucking expensive. But I've always felt like the picking up of [Paulo] Freire in the Global North never spoke to the conditions in which he was working. And my parents taught a lot of people to read. My mom taught every gangster. That's how come I came out alive! 'Cause I was Mrs. Bracho's son. I might've been her gay, sissy, faggot son, but yet, I was Mrs. Bracho's son. And I remember my dad, I was watching him teach this man to read and he's like, "Oh, take out what's in your pockets." I thought you were supposed to use a book to teach somebody and he had a pack of Marlboros. So, if the man was a smoker, that was something already in his everyday life, so they read that. It was fascinating.

It was in my kitchen and I remember being so stilled by it because it wasn't this imposition of the alphabet. He started with the idea that the man had it already in him because he knows enough to get his brand, so then let's work from that. I would like to see theater go where its audiences are already going, and I don't mean their Pasadena and Palm Springs vacation home–owning, retired bourgeois patrons. I mean the folks on the bus.

NOTES

Note: Title by Ricardo A. Bracho from a conversation with Randall Williams, November 2023.

1. Genet quote is from an interview with Madeleine Gobeil that is reprinted in Genet, *The Declared Enemy*, 14.

2. Moraga's talk comprises the beginning of her essay "Queer Aztlán."

3. Bracho and Cortiñas, "Towards Translocalism," 69–70.

4. Bracho, "A Proclamation on, of, and by Negation."

5. *El Norte* is a 1983 film by Gregory Nava.

6. Bracho refers to interpellation as it was theorized by the French Marxist philosopher Louis Althusser. It refers to a social process of address, inscribed in material practices, through which individuals are enjoined to identify with a subject in ideology. In his "Ideology and Ideological State Apparatuses (Notes Towards an Investigation)," Althusser analyzed interpellation though an allegorical scene, which he described as a "theoretical theater," in which an individual is addressed by a cop and turns to meet his call. See Althusser, *On the Reproduction of Capitalism*, 261–64.

7. "El nuevo hombre" (the new man) refers to a member of a socialist society who has developed a socialist political consciousness. The concept is used to acknowledge that struggles to transition from capitalism to socialism and then communism necessarily entail the struggle to transform humans' consciousness and create new forms of subjectivity. Chilean writer and performance artist Pedro Lemebel's "Manifiesto (Hablo por mi diferencia)" is perhaps his best-known comradely critique of Chile's communist left.

8. Bracho is referring to José Esteban Muñoz's essay "Feeling Brown."

9. PRIista refers to the Partido Revolucionario Institucional (Institutional Revolutionary Party), known by the shorthand PRI, which dominated institutional politics in Mexico from its founding in 1929 until the late twentieth century.

10. *Ni madre* is a variation of the Mexican slang phrase *ni madres*, which refers to "mothers" if translated literally (i.e., "not even mothers"), and is used as an expression of emphatic refusal akin to the expression "no way in hell!"

11. Mestizaje refers to the supposedly "racial" intermixing of European peoples and Indigenous Americans that has occurred in Latin America. See the introduction, n9.

12. Bracho is referring to Octavio Paz's canonical essay on Mexican identity "The Labyrinth of Solitude" and the section "The Sons of La Malinche," in particular.

13. Díaz del Castillo, *The True History of the Conquest of New Spain*.

14. Fanon, *The Wretched of the Earth*, 181–219.

15. Haley, *No Mercy Here*.

16. DramaDIVAS was a writing and performance group for queer and trans youth of color based out of the Mission District in San Francisco. Cherríe Moraga founded and directed DramaDIVAS, and Ricardo A. Bracho acted as their assistant director for six years.

17. Benjamin, *Selected Writings*.

18. Abbing, *Why Are Artists Poor?*

AFTERWORD

Juana María Rodríguez

Bracho was never an easy love. Known as the kind of friend that would read you to filth, finish the last bit of whatever high you still had, and then act like it was you that left the mess. I have just enough history with their erudite, raunchy, tenderly wistful self to claim eternal affection with none of the burn. If you know him well, or think you do, you might know the whirlwind of stories that follow her up and down one coast to another, even now after having aged into kaftan-era loungewear. But if you are still mad at her for whatever homosexual melodrama happened the last time you shared space, you and everyone else must admit that the work always slaps. With stop-you-in-your-gag dialogue capable of reminding you of every delicious demon you ever let into your pants, your heart, or your collective, Bracho is simply that bitch. And if you have been in the presence of their voice or their visions, you know that you have been touched by genius.

I first met Ricardo through our shared work at Proyecto ContraSIDA por Vida, a Latinx HIV prevention agency in the 1990s of San Francisco in a moment throbbing with the heartbreak and urgency of the AIDS pandemic. Proyecto gave Bracho a platform to both archive the sizzling scraps of multilingual wordplay that were always bubbling in the air, and a thousand different ways to activate that language for justice, love, and survival. As both a utopian vision and a state-funded organizational reality, Proyecto allowed Bracho to translate his Chicano punk aesthetics, revolutionary imagination, and well-earned Berkeley degree into public performances of mourning and care—classes, readings, events, dialogues, and parties that brought a grieving community together to document the courage of that moment, to archive our lost loves, and to fabulate our own sexual futures. That space and that job, because it was also a job, also offered him a community of creatives to imagine with—Jaime Cortez, Marcia Ochoa, Pato Hebert, Ana Ruíz, Wuru-Natasha Ogunji, Jorge Cortiñas (to name just a few), an audience hungry to see their sexual cultures and communities represented, and an endless number of surfaces onto which he could slap bits of textual virtuosity. And while Proyecto was always an exercise in collective empowerment and world-making, a unified effort to use meager resources to feed a community hungry to live, so often it was the piercing octave of Bracho's poetic voice, his flair for wordplay and his commitment to intellectual promiscuity that radiated most forcefully from the countless flyers, posters, and events that Proyecto produced. In fact, Proyecto's mission statement, and a deeply felt understanding of their true mission, grew out of a collective writing exercise that Bracho developed for his coworkers: "to form a community dedicated to living, to fighting the spread of HIV disease and the other unnatural disasters of racism, sexism, homophobia, xenophobia and poverty."

The hallucinogenic high of that moment, captured first in *The Sweetest Hangover (and Other STDs)*, is felt throughout the body of Bracho's work. Like that early production, his plays create sensory worlds, wildly familiar and wholly fantastic, that fold into palimpsests of time. Chronicler of queer of color triggers and traumas, Bracho's language is always close to the bone. Ever ready to rip through the fatty layers of multicultural caca and neoliberal commodification, his dialogue is poised to carve gang signs on your liver and serve up your tripas for lunch. These are politics that bite. In these radical queer mappings of the world, diasporas of all kinds scrape together to reveal the places rubbed raw when difference comes home. Always ready to live with all the contradictions—revolutionary-Marxist-feminist-puto who pays the bills with Benjamins that Daddy Franklin himself helped found—the work refuses innocence, censure, and hypocrisy. Instead Bracho presents the kinds of relational confrontations on stage that demand that you own your shit—your Grindr preferences and your class status, your consumer habits and your taste in porn.

In Bracho's work, these intimate encounters with all the ways that racial and sexual politics mark our flesh are cast against a world on fire. Melting icepacks soak a ground already seeped with the sweat and blood of those who have long lived closer to catastrophe, a never-ending Nakba of Indigenous dispossession, emptying into oceans of dead Africans rising as vengeful ghosts to demand reparations. But Bracho also knows when to deliver rhapsodic salves, honeyed elixirs blessed by the Orishas that remind us of the ancient spells we used to fell our enemies and the radical visions of our lost prophets—Essex, Lolita, Malintzin, Tupac. In Bracho's hands, all of history is made queer, blessed by the ancestors of the global majority, thrown into a vortex of memory and dreams, and activated as resources for pleasure and politics. Bracho crawls into the places where queer Brown pain lives, and his plays circle around the holes those hurts create, pulling fragments of speech and action, tone and intention, into that vortex of violation. Through the power of theater and imagination, he shapes our collective wounds into something new, reworked they are delivered back to us, made available for Brown jouissance, revolutionary escapades, and play parties for the future.

That both theater and political action demand the work of a collective, a group of people willing to claim their private hurts, attachments, and wildest fantasies in public seems core to Bracho's creative practice. Like Walter Benjamin's Angel of History, Bracho "would like to stay, awaken the dead, and make whole what has been smashed." The theatrical worlds he builds are designed to transport us to these other planes of consciousness, "to make whole all that has been smashed," to return us back to ourselves when all seems lost and broken. The plays collected here are fever dreams for a future that Bracho makes us all responsible for creating. And the message that he sends is clear: Stay searching for one another, keep forming balls, clusters, cadres, orgies, cells, familias, troupes, and worlds. Stay finding places and people to make life more livable and more meaningful, especially when it hurts. Keep making the survival of the planet and those that live on it a daily practice of art and care, of imagination and concerted action. Let it be so.

.

BIBLIOGRAPHY

Abbing, Hans. *Why Are Artists Poor?* Amsterdam: Amsterdam University Press, 2008.

Ahmad, Aijaz. *In Theory: Classes, Nations, Literatures*. New York: Verso, 2000.

Althusser, Louis. *On the Reproduction of Capitalism: Ideology and Ideological State Appa-ratuses*. Translated by G. M. Goshgarian. New York: Verso, 2014.

August 29th Movement. *Fan the Flames: A Revolutionary Position on the Chicano Na-tional Question*. Self-published, 1974.

Barthes, Roland. *A Lover's Discourse: Fragments*. Translated by Richard Howard. New York: Hill and Wang, 1978.

Barthes, Roland. *Mythologies*. Translated and edited by Annette Lavers. New York: Far-rar, Straus and Giroux, 1972.

Benjamin, Walter. *Selected Writings*, vol. 2: *Part 1, 1927–1930*. Edited by Michael W. Jen-nings, Howard Eiland, and Gary Smith. Cambridge, MA: Belknap Press of Harvard University Press, 1999.

Bersani, Leo. "Is the Rectum a Grave?" In *Is the Rectum a Grave and Other Essays*. Chi-cago: University of Chicago Press, 2009.

Bonfil Batalla, Guillermo. *Mexico Profundo: Reclaiming a Civilization*. Austin: University of Texas Press, 1996.

Bracho, Ricardo A. "Anger and Love." Talk at Human Resources, Los Angeles, Novem-ber 24, 2014.

Bracho, Ricardo A. "It Is the Libido." Talk at Stanford University, May 7, 2008.

Bracho, Ricardo A. "A Proclamation on, of, and by Negation." Presented in "5-Minute Manifestos" at The Fun and the Fury, annual meeting of the American Studies Associ-ation, Los Angeles, California, November 2014.

Bracho, Ricardo A. Skype interview with Jennifer Ponce de León. December 4, 2015.

Bracho, Ricardo A. Talk at the University of Pennsylvania, February 18, 2020.

Bracho, Ricardo A., and Jorge Ignacio Cortiñas in conversation with José Esteban Muñoz. "Towards Translocalism: Latino Theatre in the New United States." In *Trans-Global Readings: Crossing Theatrical Boundaries*, edited by Caridad Svich. Manchester: Manchester University Press, 2004.

Brecht, Bertolt. *Brecht on Theater: The Development of an Aesthetic.* Edited and translated by John Willett. New York: Hill and Wang, 1964.

Brecht, Bertolt. *Fear and Misery of the Third Reich.* Edited and translated by John Willett and Tom Kuhn. London: Bloomsbury, 2015.

Brecht, Bertolt. "Letter to Mr. X, 2 June 1927." In *Brecht on Theater: The Development of an Aesthetic*, translated and edited by John Willett. New York: Hill and Wang, 1992.

Brecht, Bertolt. *The Messingkauf Dialogues.* Translated and edited by John Willett. London: Bloomsbury, 2012.

Butler, Octavia. *Parable of the Sower.* New York: Grand Central, 2000.

Díaz del Castillo, Bernal. *The True History of the Conquest of New Spain.* Vols. 2 and 3. Edited by Genaro García, translated by Alfred Percival Maudslay. Cambridge: Cambridge University Press, 2010.

Duggan, Lisa. *The Twilight of Equality? Neoliberalism, Cultural Politics, and the Attack on Democracy.* Boston: Beacon, 2004.

Dyer, Richard. "In Defence of Disco." *Gay Left* 8 (Summer 1979).

Fanon, Frantz. *The Wretched of the Earth.* Translated by Richard Philcox. 1961. New York: Grove, 2004.

Fregoso, Rosa Linda. *MeXicana Encounters: The Making of Social Identities on the Borderlands.* Berkeley: University of California Press, 2003.

Freud, Sigmund. "Thoughts for the Times on War and Death." In *The Standard Edition of the Complete Psychological Works of Sigmund Freud*, vol. 14, translated and edited by James Strachey. 1915. London: Hogarth, 1957.

Genet, Jean. *The Declared Enemy: Texts and Interviews.* Edited by Albert Dichy, translated by Jeff Fort. Palo Alto, CA: Stanford University Press, 2003.

Gilmore, Ruth Wilson. *Abolition Geography: Essays Towards Liberation.* New York: Verso, 2022.

Gilmore, Ruth Wilson. *Golden Gulag: Prisons, Surplus, Crisis, and Opposition in Globalizing California.* Berkeley: University of California Press, 2007.

Gómez, Alan Eladio. *The Revolutionary Imaginations of Greater Mexico: Chicana/o Radicalism, Solidarity Politics, and Latin American Social Movements.* Austin: University of Texas Press, 2016.

Grise, Virginia. *Blu.* New Haven, CT: Yale University Press, 2011.

Guevara, Ernesto "Che." "Socialism and Man in Cuba" (March 1965). Marxists.org, accessed May 27, 2025. https://www.marxists.org/archive/guevara/1965/03/man-socialism.htm.

Haley, Sarah. *No Mercy Here: Gender, Punishment, and the Making of Jim Crow Modernity.* Chapel Hill: University of North Carolina Press, 2019.

League of Revolutionary Struggle. "The Struggle for Chicano Liberation." *Forward*, no. 2 (August 1979).

Lemebel, Pedro. "Manifiesto (Hablo por mi diferencia)" [Manifesto (I Speak for My Difference)]. In *A corazón abierto: Geografía literaria de la homosexualidad en Chile*, compiled by Juan Pabo Sutherland. Santiago, Chile: Editorial Sudamericana, 2001.

Liu, Petrus. *Queer Marxism in Two Chinas.* Durham, NC: Duke University Press, 2015.

Mariscal, George. *Brown-Eyed Children of the Sun: Lessons from the Chicano Movement, 1965–1975*. Albuquerque: University of New Mexico Press, 2005.

Moraga, Cherríe. "Queer Aztlán: The Re-Formation of Chicano Tribe." In *The Last Generation: Prose and Poetry*. Boston: South End, 1999.

Muñoz, José Esteban. "Feeling Brown: Ethnicity and Affect in Ricardo Bracho's *The Sweetest Hangover (and Other STDs)*." *Theatre Journal* 52, no. 1 (2000): 67–79.

Nair, Yasmin. "American Gay: Pete Buttigieg and the Politics of Forgetting." Yasminnair .com, June 18, 2019. https://www.yasminnair.com/american-gay-pete-buttigieg-and -the-politics-of-forgetting.

Newsom, Joanna. *Divers*. Produced by Joanna Newsom and Noah Georgeson. Drag City (US). Released October 23, 2015.

Olguín, Ben, and Edward Giardello. "The Forgotten Foundations of Chicana/o/x and Latina/o/x Studies: El Plan de Santa Barbara and Damián García's Revolutionary Communist Synthesis, 1967–1980." *Aztlán: A Journal of Chicano Studies* 48, no. 2 (2023): 213–45.

Paz, Octavio. *The Labyrinth of Solitude and Other Writings*. Translated by Lysander Kemp, Yara Milos, and Rachel Phillips Belash. New York: Grove Press, 1961.

Ponce de León, Jennifer S. "After the Border Is Closed: Fascism, Immigration, and Internationalism in Ricardo A. Bracho's *Puto*." *American Quarterly* 73, no. 4 (December 2021): 743–66.

Puar, Jasbir. *Terrorist Assemblages: Homonationalism in Queer Times*. Durham, NC: Duke University Press, 2007.

The Red Army Faction. "The Urban Guerrilla Concept." In *The Red Army Faction, a Documentary History*, vol. 1: *Projectiles for the People*, edited by J. Smith and André Moncourt. Binghamton, NY: PM Press, 2009.

Reddy, Chandan. *Freedom with Violence: Race, Sexuality, and the US State*. Durham, NC: Duke University Press, 2011.

Reed, Adolph, Jr. *Class Notes: On Posing as Politics and Other Thoughts on the American Scene*. New York: New Press, 2000.

Reed, John. *Insurgent Mexico*. New York: International Publishers, 2001.

Rodríguez, Richard T. *Next of Kin: The Family in Chicano/a Cultural Politics*. Durham, NC: Duke University Press, 2009.

Saldaña-Portillo, María Josefina. *The Revolutionary Imagination in the Age of Development*. Durham, NC: Duke University Press, 2003.

Schwarz, Roberto. "Brecht's Relevance: Highs and Lows." *New Left Review*, no. 57 (May/ June 2009): 85–104.

Spade, Dean. "Under the Cover of Gay Rights." *NYU Review of Law and Social Change* 37, no. 79 (2013): 79–100.

Spivak, Gayatri Chakravorty. "Can the Subaltern Speak?" In *Marxism and the Interpretation of Culture*, edited by Cary Nelson and Lawrence Grossberg. Basingstoke, UK: Macmillan Education, 1988.

Tenayuca, Emma, and Homer Brooks. "The Mexican Question in the Southwest." *The Communist* 18, no. 3 (1939): 257–69.

Third World Gay Revolution. "What We Want, What We Believe." In *Out of the Closets: Voices of Gay Liberation*, edited by Karla Jay and Allen Young. New York: Jove/HBJ, 1977.

CONTRIBUTORS

Ricardo A. Bracho is Abrams Artist in Residence at the University of Pennsylvania's Center for Research in Feminist, Queer, and Transgender Studies and the Penn Program in Gender, Sexuality, and Women's Studies. Bracho is a writer, editor, and teacher who has worked in community and university, theater and video/film, politics and aesthetics for the past three decades. His other academic appointments include Visiting Multicultural Faculty at the Theatre School at DePaul University in Chicago and Artist-Scholar in Residence at the Center for Chicano Studies at the University of California at Santa Barbara. His award-winning plays have been produced in Los Angeles, New York, and San Francisco, as well as workshopped and stage read nationwide. He is at work on a manuscript of poems, "The Salt of Him."

Cherríe Moraga is the coeditor of the seminal feminist text *This Bridge Called My Back: Writings by Radical Women of Color*. Her many works include *A Xicana Codex of Changing Consciousness*; *Loving in the War Years and Other Writings* (2023); and the memoir *Native Country of the Heart*. She is the recipient of the United States Artists Rockefeller Fellowship for Literature, the American Studies Lifetime Achievement Award, two Fund for New American Plays Awards, and, most recently, the Dramatists Guild Foundation's 2024 Legacy Playwrights Award. Moraga is a Distinguished Professor Emerita of English at the University of California, Santa Barbara, where she cofounded Las Maestras Center for Xicana[x] Indigenous Thought, Art, and Social Praxis.

Jennifer S. Ponce de León is associate professor of English at the University of Pennsylvania, where she is also faculty in Latin American and Latinx Studies and Comparative Literature. She is associate director of the Critical Theory Workshop / Atelier de Théorie Critique and author of *Another Aesthetics Is Possible: Arts of Rebellion in the Fourth World War* (Duke University Press, 2021). As a selected member of the School of Social Science at the Institute for Advanced Study (2025–26), Dr. Ponce de León is currently writing a monograph that critiques culturalist tendencies in contemporary critical theory and compares these to Marxist accounts of imperialism, fascism, and racism. She is also coediting an anthology on US Latinx Marxism.

Juana María Rodríguez is a professor of ethnic studies and performance studies at UC Berkeley. She is the author of *Puta Life: Seeing Latinas, Working Sex* (Duke University Press, 2023), *Sexual Futures, Queer Gestures, and Other Latina Longings* (2014), and *Queer Latinidad: Identity Practices, Discursive Spaces* (2003) and served as a coeditor of the special issue of *TSQ: Transgender Studies Quarterly* on "Trans Studies en las Américas." In 2023 Dr. Rodríguez was honored by the Center for Gay and Lesbian Studies with the prestigious Kessler Award in recognition of her lifelong contributions to the field of LGBT studies.

Richard T. Rodríguez is professor of English at the University of California, Riverside. He is the author of *A Kiss Across the Ocean: Transatlantic Intimacies of British Post-Punk and US Latinidad* (2022) and *Next of Kin: The Family in Chicano/a Cultural Politics* (2009), both published by Duke University Press. He is currently finishing a collection of poems about his time living in Chicago, and a book on labor and cinematic representations of Latino male sexuality.

Randall Williams is a writer, developmental editor, and independent labor researcher. He is the author of *The Divided World: Human Rights and Its Violence* (2010). Most recently he served as developmental editor on Felipe Luciano's memoir, *Flesh and Spirit: Confessions of a Young Lord* (2024). Earlier, Williams worked as a labor researcher for the International Transport Workers' Federation (ITF), based in London. He trained as a researcher and strategic campaigner with the Hotel Employees and Restaurant Employees International Union (HERE-IU), and he cut his teeth as a socialist activist in the late 1980s and early 1990s with the AIDS activist group ACT-UP in San Francisco.

Andrés González-Bonillas, *Bracho and Gang,* 2024.
"A History of Hands: queer and trans Philly."

www.ingramcontent.com/pod-product-compliance
Lightning Source LLC
Chambersburg PA
CBHW032348280326
41935CB00008B/493